Basic Music Knowledge

By the same author
Read, Sing and Play
Additional Sightsinging Exercises
A Graded Music Course
Score Reading, Form and History (Book 4 of *A Graded Music Course*)
Harmony
Melody Writing and Analysis
Analyses of Musical Classics Book 1
Analyses of Musical Classics Book 2
Analyses of Musical Classics Book 3
Graded Aural Tests for All Purposes

Basic Music Knowledge

A text book which can be flexibly adapted to meet the requirements of various examinations

ANNIE O. WARBURTON

LONGMAN

LONGMAN GROUP LIMITED
London

Associated companies, branches and representatives throughout the world

First published 1967
Sixth impression 1974

ISBN 0 582 32592 7

Printed in Hong Kong by
Yu Luen Offset Printing Factory Ltd

Preface

THIS book is a kind of vade-mecum for those students who start serious music study rather late, for whatever reason, and then want to take an examination such as music in the Certificate of Secondary Education (C.S.E.), O Level in the General Certificate of Education (G.C.E.), or grade V theory, without a great deal of time to do it in. The aim is to cover all essentials in such a way that anything not required for a particular examination can be left out.

Teachers are advised to look carefully at all the material and all the exercises before giving them to their pupils, so that they only give them what they require and do not confuse them with unnecessary material. This book is unique in that, although it covers all elementary essentials, it is possible to leave out large sections of it without causing any difficulty in the later sections. For example, much of the theoretical work which is required for grade V theory can easily be omitted for the C.S.E. examination candidate, while the later parts of the book will be useful for the C.S.E., though not required for grade V theory. The book is signposted in such a way that, given a little care on the part of the teacher, there should be no confusion. The very detailed 'Analysis of Contents' should be helpful in this connection.

But the book is not only for examination candidates. It can equally well be used by students of any age who want to fill in the gaps in their musical knowledge for their own greater understanding of music.

C.S.E. There are many examining boards for this certificate and all their requirements are different. Also the syllabuses will probably undergo frequent changes as the teachers who run them survey their effectiveness. But, in addition to the most valuable practical side of the examination, all require some knowledge of notation, of training in listening, and of information leading to the intelligent and musical understanding of prepared or unprepared works. An adaptable text book, such as this, to which students can refer, and from which they can pick out just the amount of knowledge they need, should prove helpful.

G.C.E. O Level. Again there is a good deal of variation between the requirements of the different boards. But if the examination requires little or no harmonic or contrapuntal writing, or if the candidates take a practical test as an alternative to a harmony paper, then this book may provide sufficient information, particularly for those candidates who have little time for preparation. In other cases the book might be used as a preliminary or revision text book before starting the G.C.E. course itself. And if further harmony study is necessary, students may find the author's *Harmony* a useful continuation book.

Grade V Theory, or a similar theoretical examination, or theoretical questions in a practical examination. Students who are mainly performers often have a rather sketchy theoretical background, and may wish to cover the ground quickly for what is perhaps their first theoretical examination. Again, they can pick out just what they require from this book.

In all these cases, study of this book should be followed by working papers previously set for the particular examination concerned.

This book, then, is not meant to be worked steadily through as a ' course ', nor is it a beginners' book. It assumes that most students are familiar with music but may be rather vague about many of its facts; and it attempts to compensate for the lack of a course in earlier stages by giving all the facts, from which the student or the teacher can select what is required.

The book is divided into sections, each dealing with a particular aspect of music. But within each section the information is arranged in order of difficulty or complexity, so that any part of a section can be omitted at will, without affecting later stages. The student may, for example, learn how to read, write or compose melodies in simple time but not in compound, in major keys but not in minor; to recognise intervals by number without learning about their quality; to use and recognise primary triads in isolation without learning how to connect them. Such things as the barring of melodies, correcting faulty rhythmic grouping, the C clef, the notation of the chromatic scale, melody writing, transposition, modulation and the use of ornaments can be omitted or included at will. There are plenty of exercises at each stage.

Short sections are included on musical instruments, score reading, musical form and history so that, if necessary, students can manage with one text book. Those with little time to give to music may find this is sufficient, at any rate, for C.S.E. examinations. But candidates for C.S.E. or G.C.E. would be well advised to read other books, perhaps from the school library, which give more information about any set composers or set works. And G.C.E. candidates should really have a text book which gives more information on this side of their work, such as the author's *Score Reading, Form and History*.

Ideally everyone should have been given a graded course of music listening, linked up with notation and general musical knowledge, which should have started in the infant school and continued to school-leaving age. But, as far as one can see ahead, there will always be students who have missed this and then discover their need for it later, when perhaps they respond to a growing love of music, and wish to acquire knowledge and skills that have so far been denied them. For such people I have written this book.

Analysis of Contents

This detailed analysis of contents is intended to help the teacher and student to find out which sections and exercises he needs and which he can omit.

1 Time

1 *The pulse or beat. Varied rhythmic patterns heard over the beat*

Everyone is aware of the varied rhythmic patterns they hear in music, and most people can reproduce them, if they know them well enough. But not everyone is *consciously* aware that there is always an underlying pulse which can be felt as a steady beat of constant length throughout a section of music, at the same time as the rhythmic pattern. (Pulse and beat are two words which mean the same thing.)

Exercise 1
Mark a steady pulse while listening to music containing varied rhythmic patterns. Do not be tempted to change to the rhythmic pattern by mistake, or to pause when a long note occurs at the end of a phrase.

2 *Simple time: note values and rests when the crotchet is the beat*

There are many kinds of notes used to indicate the length of a sound, and any one of them can be used for the beat. The crotchet is the most common. Here are the signs for all the notes and rests, with their length in relation to the crotchet as the beat.

NAME	NOTE	REST	LENGTH IN RELATION TO THE CROTCHET BEAT
Breve	𝅜	𝄺	8
Semibreve	𝅝	𝄻	4
Minim	𝅗𝅥	𝄼	2
Crotchet	♩	𝄽 or 𝄾 (reversed)	1
Quaver	♪	𝄾	$\frac{1}{2}$
Semiquaver	𝅘𝅥𝅯	𝄿	$\frac{1}{4}$
Demisemiquaver	𝅘𝅥𝅰	𝅀	$\frac{1}{8}$
Semidemisemiquaver	𝅘𝅥𝅱	𝅁	$\frac{1}{16}$

Notice the following points:
(a) HOOKS When notes shorter than a crotchet belong to the same beat their hooks are usually fastened together, thus:

♫; 𝅘𝅥𝅯𝅘𝅥𝅯𝅘𝅥𝅯𝅘𝅥𝅯; ♪♪𝅘𝅥𝅯𝅘𝅥𝅯𝅘𝅥𝅯𝅘𝅥𝅯.

Two Exceptions: 1 In old, printed vocal music the hooks are separated if notes belong to different syllables thus:

danc - ing a - long.

2 Stems are sometimes separated if the notes belong to different phrases, thus:

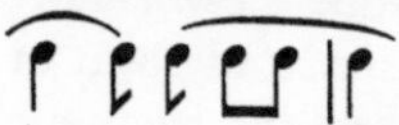

Notice that stems which turn up are placed after the note, and those which turn down go before it. But hooks are always placed to the right of the stem.

(b) STEMS The stems of the notes normally turn up if they are below the middle line of the stave or if, in the case of a group of notes, they are mostly below the middle line. Correspondingly they turn down if the notes lie above the middle line. This is to keep the signs as much as possible within the stave, thus:

Exception: when two melodic lines or two different rhythms share the same stave the upper part has its stems up and the lower its stems down, thus:

(c) RESTS Rests normally start in the third space, and any extra hooks go on the spaces below, thus:

Exception: If two parts share a stave the rests may be higher or lower to indicate which part they refer to, thus:

(d) BAR'S REST A semibreve rest is always used for a whole bar's rest, whatever the bar's actual length may be.

(e) REST OF SEVERAL BARS When a rest of more than one bar's duration occurs the number of bars is indicated thus: 5 or thus: 5

(f) THE TIE When two notes of the same pitch are tied together they make one sound. Thus, 𝅗𝅥 ⁀ ♩ lasts for three beats.

(g) THE DOT A dot placed after a note or a rest makes it half as long again. A second dot is half as long as the first dot. Thus:

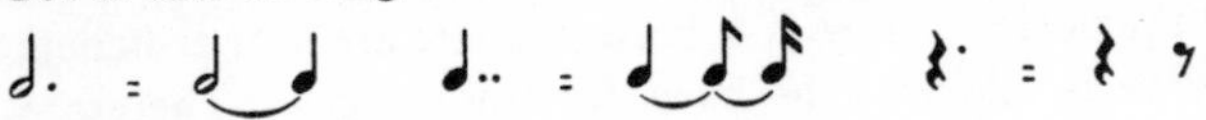

Exercise 2

Write (1) one note, (2) one rest, plain or dotted, to equal each of the following rhythmic patterns:

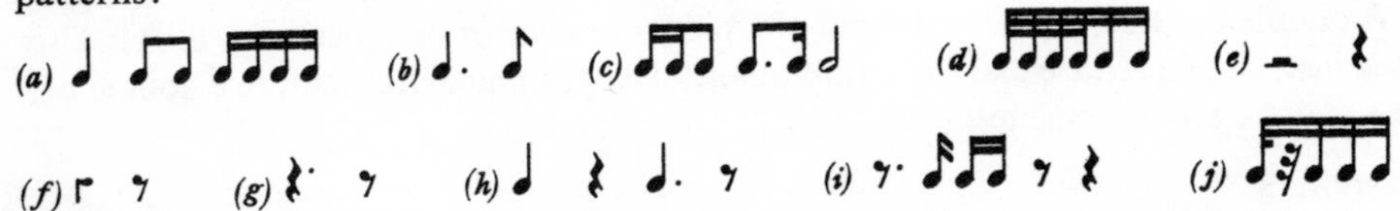

Exercise 3

Write a rhythmic pattern consisting of a series of notes and rests which together add up to (a) one semibreve; (b) one dotted crotchet; (c) one dotted minim. Complete one crotchet beat at a time, joining together the hooks of notes which belong to the same beat.

Exercise 4

Correct the following notational errors by rewriting each example correctly. The beat is the crotchet.

3 *The bar line. Simple time signatures when the crotchet is the beat: music starting on the first beat of the bar*

Music is divided into bars by means of bar lines.
The first note *after* the bar line carries the strongest accent.
Duple time has two beats in a bar.
Triple time has three beats in a bar.
Quadruple time has four beats in a bar.
Music with five or seven beats in a bar is very occasionally found.

Music in which a simple, ordinary note (i.e. not a dotted note) is written as the beat is said to be in *simple* time.
Music in which a dotted note is written as the beat is said to be in *compound* time.

Each bar in a piece of music normally contains the same number of beats, and this is indicated by a *time signature* at the beginning. This consists of two figures, thus: $\begin{smallmatrix}2\\4\end{smallmatrix}$ (A time signature is *not* a fraction and there is no line between the figures).

In simple time the top figure in a time signature indicates *how many* beats there are in a bar.

When the crotchet is the beat the bottom figure is 4, because there are four crotchets in a semibreve, and the semibreve is taken as the basis for this purpose. Therefore 4 *represents* a crotchet.

So the simple time signatures most usually found are $\frac{2}{4}$, $\frac{3}{4}$ and $\frac{4}{4}$. $\frac{4}{4}$ is also called *common time*, and C is sometimes written, in place of a time signature.

A double bar line, ||, marks the end of a piece of music or of a section of it. It is also used instead of a phrase mark in hymn tunes. The bar immediately before a double bar line may be an incomplete one.

Exercise 5

Listen to music which is played or sung to you, and state its time signature, assuming that the beat is to be written as a crotchet. Alternatively, you can think of music you know and, by singing it to yourself, decide its time signature.

Exercise 6

Add time signatures to the following phrases. The beat is the crotchet.

Exercise 7

Add bar lines to these phrases. They all start on the first beat of the bar, and are exactly four bars long. Add the time signature if it is not given. (As each phrase is four bars long, divide the total number of beats by four in (d) (e) and (f) to discover the number of beats in each bar.

4 *Anacrusic rhythm*

When a musical phrase starts with an incomplete bar, instead of on the first beat of a bar, its rhythm is said to be *anacrusic*.

A phrase is usually exactly two or four bars long, so if it starts with an incomplete bar it will end with one. This is particularly the case with dance rhythms. Each phrase of a gavotte begins on the third crotchet in $\frac{4}{4}$ time and ends on the second; whereas a bourrée, also in $\frac{4}{4}$ time, begins on the last crotchet and ends on the third. This is the essential difference between the two dances.

Exercise 8

Add bar lines to these anacrusic phrases. They are all exactly four bars long. Sing or play them, in order to feel where the accent naturally occurs. Add the time signature if it is not given. The phrase marks do not necessarily coincide with the bar lines.

5 *The sound of note lengths when the crotchet is the beat: their rhythm names and shorthand*

Learn the following table:

LENGTH	NOTE	RHYTHM NAME	SHORTHAND
4	𝅝	taa - aa - aa - aa	hm
3	𝅗𝅥.	taa - aa - aa	m
2	𝅗𝅥	taa - aa	h
1	♩	taa	l
Halves	♫	ta te	V
Quarters	♬♬	ta fa te fe	W

Exercise 9

Sing the following rhythmic phrases. It helps to mark the pulse in some way and to sing the rhythm names.

Exercise 10

Write down the rhythm of phrases dictated by your teacher. It helps to sing the rhythm names to yourself, while you mark the pulse, and to write the rhythm in shorthand at the same time. (The note lengths should be confined to those given in the table above at this stage. Unless required for a particular examination, it is recommended that rests should not be given in ear tests.)

Exercise 11

Make up a four-bar rhythmic phrase (rhythm only) for (a) a minuet; (b) a gavotte; (c) a bourrée.

6 *The most common rhythmic patterns using varied note lengths when the crotchet is the beat: their rhythm names and shorthand. Syncopation*

Study the following table:

NOTE VALUES AND RHYTHM NAMES SHORTHAND

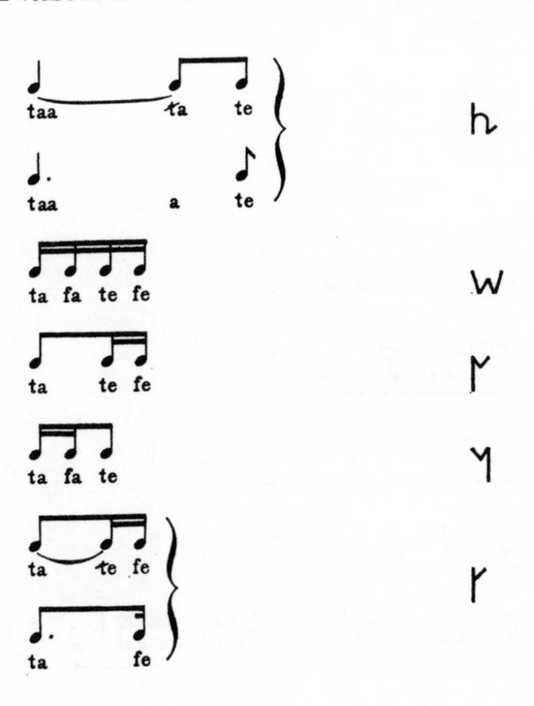

♩. ♪ and ♪.♬ are two commonly-used rhythmic patterns which are often confused. Realise that you can hear a second beat in the middle of ♩. ♪, taa *a* te; while ♪.♬ occurs inside one beat.

Syncopation occurs when the usual rhythmic accent is disturbed, and a normally unaccented note carries an accent. This may be caused by (a) a long note on an unaccented part of the bar, e.g.

or (b) a tie or its equivalent, e.g.

ta te ta te ta te ta te a te a te

or (c) rests, e.g.

Exercise 12

Sing the following rhythmic phrases:

(a)

(b)

(c)

(d)

(e)

(f)

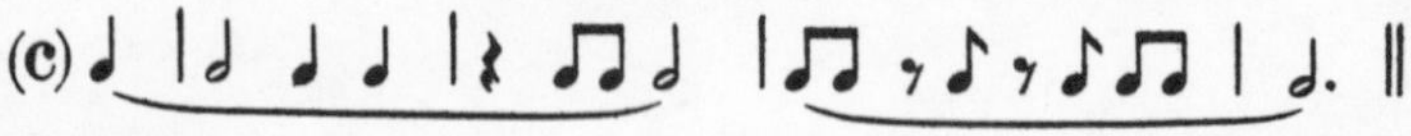

Exercise 13

Write down the rhythm of phrases dictated by your teacher. (These should be carefully graded. Syncopation and the more difficult rhythmic patterns should be avoided unless required by a particular examination.)

Exercise 14

Make up a four-bar rhythmic phrase (rhythm only) for (a) a march; (b) a waltz; (c) a polka; (d) any modern dance, of your own choice.

Exercise 15

Add bar lines and time signatures to these phrases. They are all exactly four bars long

7 *Grouping of notes and rests when the crotchet is the beat*

Notes are usually grouped together if they belong to the same beat, but are separated if they belong to different beats.

It is common, however, to group together a number of notes of the same length (a) for a whole bar: 3/4 ♪♪♪♪♪♪ |, or (b) for the first half or the last half of a bar in quadruple time: 4/4 ♩ ♪♪♪♪ | ♪♪♪♪ ♩ . It is not considered so good to group together such notes if they occur on the second and third beats of the bar: 4/4 ♩ ♪♪♪♪ ♩ because they cut across the accent which usually occurs on the third beat.

Exercise 16

Group the following notes into beats. Rhythm names are a help.

(a) 2/4

(b) 3/4

Exercise 17

Correct the grouping in the following rhythmic patterns:

(a) 3/4 (b) 4/4

(c) 2/4

Similarly, rests show the beat by separating one beat from the next. But the following are exceptions:

(a) A rest for a whole bar, in any kind of time, is always a semibreve: 3/4

(b) One rest can be used for the first half or the last half of a bar in quadruple time: 4/4 ‖ but not: 4/4 ‖.

Exercise 18

Correct the rests in the following rhythmic patterns, without altering any of the notes.

Exercise 19

Complete the following bars with rests. Then work the exercise again, completing the bars with notes.

(a) (b) (c) (d)

8 *Compound time: note values and rests when the dotted crotchet is the beat*

Our system of note values is based on division by two: semibreves, minims, crotchets, quavers, semiquavers, etc., are all half the length of the next note of greater value.

But beats frequently divide into three, and this means there is no note to show this division. One method adopted to show thirds is that 3 is put over or under any three notes of equal value. This turns them into thirds, instead of halves, of the next note of greater value: etc. These three notes make a *triplet*.

When the crotchet is the beat the rhythm name of is ta te ti, and a possible shorthand for it is . Sing the following, using the rhythm names:

An *occasional* division of a beat into three is shown by this method. But if music is written in which the beats *regularly* divide into three instead of two, this method is cumbersome. It is easier, in this case, to make the beat a dotted note, so that, for example, can be divided into without the need for the triplet sign.

When the beats regularly divide into three, music is said to be in *compound* time. Its beats are always written as dotted notes.

The dotted crotchet is the most common kind, though other dotted notes are occasionally written as the beat.

Here are the lengths of all the signs for notes and rests, in relation to the dotted crotchet as the beat:

NOTE	REST	LENGTH IN RELATION TO THE DOTTED CROTCHET BEAT
𝅝.	𝄻.	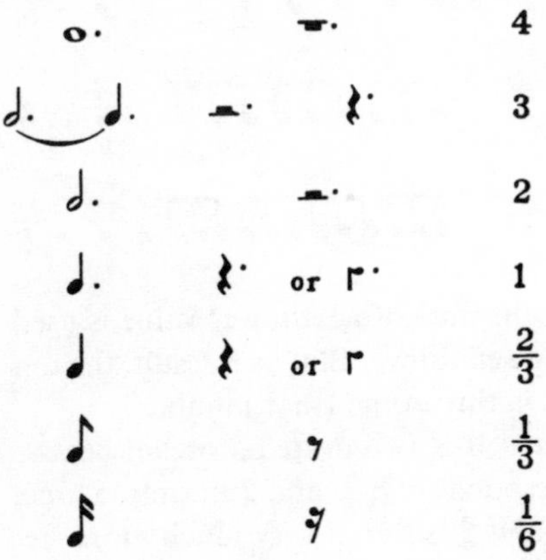 4
𝅗𝅥. ‿ 𝅘𝅥.	𝄼. 𝄽.	3
𝅗𝅥.	𝄼.	2
𝅘𝅥.	𝄽. or 𝄾.	1
𝅘𝅥	𝄽 or 𝄾	$\frac{2}{3}$
𝅘𝅥𝅮	𝄾	$\frac{1}{3}$
𝅘𝅥𝅯	𝄿	$\frac{1}{6}$

Exercise 20

Write (a) a dotted note or two tied dotted notes, (b) a dotted rest or rests to equal each of the following rhythmic patterns in compound time.

(i) *(ii)* *(iii)*

(iv) *(v)*

Exercise 21

Write a rhythmic pattern consisting of a series of notes and rests which together add up to (a) two beats; (b) three beats; (c) four beats in compound time, when the beat is a dotted crotchet. Complete one beat at a time, joining together the hooks of the notes which belong to the same beat.

9 *Compound time signatures when the dotted crotchet is the beat*

In compound time signatures the bottom figure cannot indicate its proportion of a semibreve, because dotted notes do not divide an equal number of times into a semibreve.

Study the following table, to see how notes are turned into figures:

	SIMPLE	COMPOUND
Duple	♩ ♩ = 2/♩ = 2/4	♩. ♩. = 2/♩. = ♪♪♪ ♪♪♪ = 6/♪ = 6/8
Triple	♩ ♩ ♩ = 3/♩ = 3/4	♩. ♩. ♩. = 3/♩. = ♪♪♪ ♪♪♪ ♪♪♪ = 9/♪ = 9/8
Quadruple	♩ ♩ ♩ ♩ = 4/♩ = 4/4	♩. ♩. ♩. ♩. = 4/♩. = ♪♪♪ ♪♪♪ ♪♪♪ ♪♪♪ = 12/♪ = 12/8

From this you will see that, in compound time, the note of next lower value is used for the bottom figure, because this *can* divide into a semibreve. But, as a result, the top figure no longer tells you the number of beats: it is three times that number.

6/8 represents six quavers, but *not* six quaver *beats:* it is two dotted crotchet beats.

Learn that 6/8, 9/8, and 12/8 in compound time correspond to 2/4, 3/4, and 4/4 in simple time.

In simple time 2/4, 3/4 and 4/4 are equally common. But 6/8 is found very much more frequently than 9/8 and 12/8 in compound time; and compound duple time, with the beat as the dotted crotchet, i.e. 6/8 time, may be the only compound time you will need to use or know about.

Exercise 22

Listen to music which is played or sung to you, and state its time signature, assuming that the beat is to be written as a crotchet or dotted crotchet. You have to listen for two things: (a) the number of beats in the bar; (b) whether the beats, themselves, divide into twos or threes.

Exercise 23

Add time signatures to the following phrases. The beat is the crotchet or the dotted crotchet.

Exercise 24

Add bar lines and time signatures to these phrases. They may be in simple or compound time and may begin at any part of a bar. But all are exactly four bars long.

10 *The sound of note lengths and of some of the most common rhythmic patterns, with their rhythm names, when the dotted crotchet is the beat*

Study the following table:

NOTES LASTING A BEAT OR LONGER			DIVISIONS OF THE BEAT	
4	o.	taa - aa - aa - aa	ta te ti	ta te fe ti
3	d. d.	taa - aa - aa	ta e ti	ta e fe ti
2	d.	taa - aa	ta te i	ta 2 te (a duplet)
1	♩.	taa	ta fa te fe ti fi	

Exercise 25

Sing the following rhythmic phrases:

Exercise 26

Write down the rhythm of phrases dictated by your teacher. (It is suggested that dictation is confined to 6/8 time, with [dotted quaver–semiquaver–quaver figure] as the only pattern using semiquavers.)

Exercise 27

Make up four-bar rhythmic phrase (rhythm only) in 6/8 time for (a) a lullaby; (b) a hunting song; (c) a gigue.

11 *Grouping of notes and rests when the dotted crotchet is the beat*

The rules for grouping notes and rests are exactly the same as for simple time. Re-read them, before working the next exercises.

Exercise 28

Group the following notes into beats:

(a) 6/8

(b) 6/8

(c) 9/8

Exercise 29
Correct the grouping in the following rhythmic patterns:

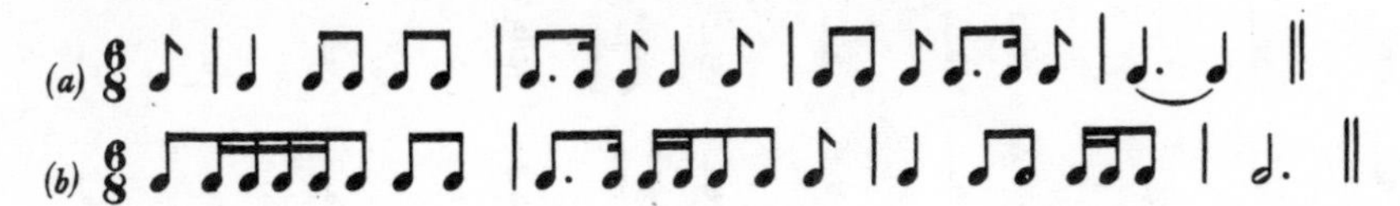

Exercise 30
Correct the rests in the following rhythmic patterns, without altering any of the notes:

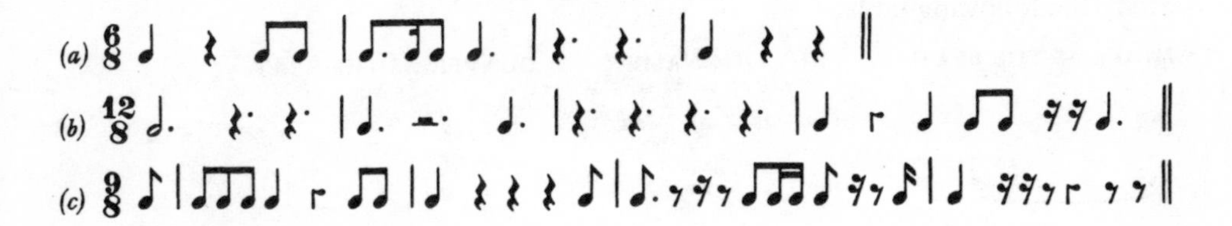

Exercise 31
Complete the following bars with rests. Then work the exercise again, completing the bars with notes.

(a) (b) (c) (d)

12 *Other note lengths as the beat in simple time. Rhythmic patterns with their corresponding rhythm names*

Other notes, such as the minim or the quaver, are sometimes written as the beat in simple time. Beethoven, for example, sometimes uses a minim beat for his quick movements and a quaver beat for his slow ones. And most old hymn tunes have a minim for the beat.

You will probably prefer to keep the usual crotchet beat for any melodies or dictation tests you write in simple time. But you need to be able to read music with other notes as the beat.

Here is a table of simple time signatures:

The beat always sounds the same, however it is written. So always think of it as taa. Study the following table:

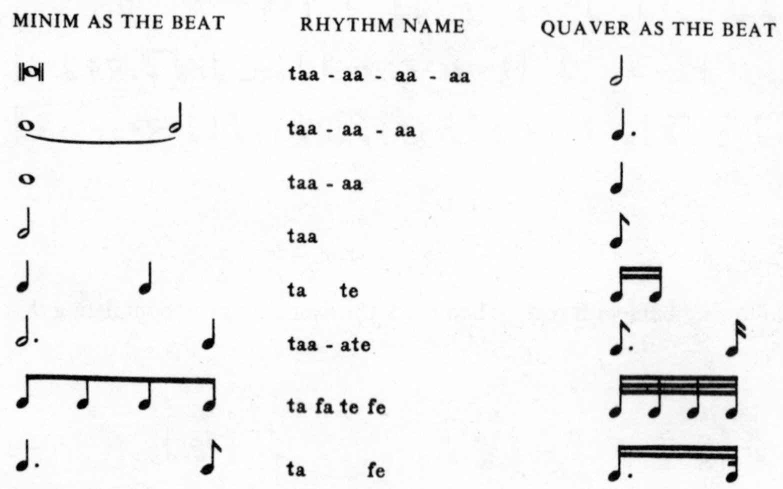

Exercise 32

Sing the following rhythmic phrases. Notice the time signature in each case.

Exercise 33

Add time signatures to the following melodies. Then rewrite them all with the crotchet as the beat:

Exercise 34

Add bar lines to the following melodies:

13 *Other note lengths as the beat in compound time. Rhythmic patterns with their corresponding rhythm names*

A dotted minim or a dotted quaver is occasionally found as a beat in compound time. You need to be able to read the rhythm of such music correctly, though you are advised to keep to the dotted crotchet for any music you write in compound time.

Here is a table of compound time signatures:

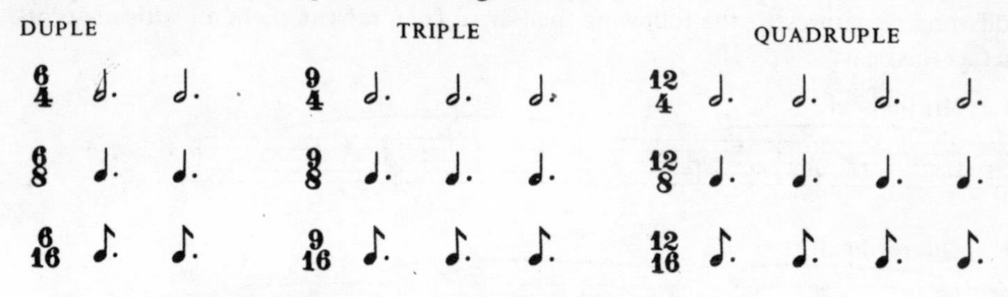

Study the following table:

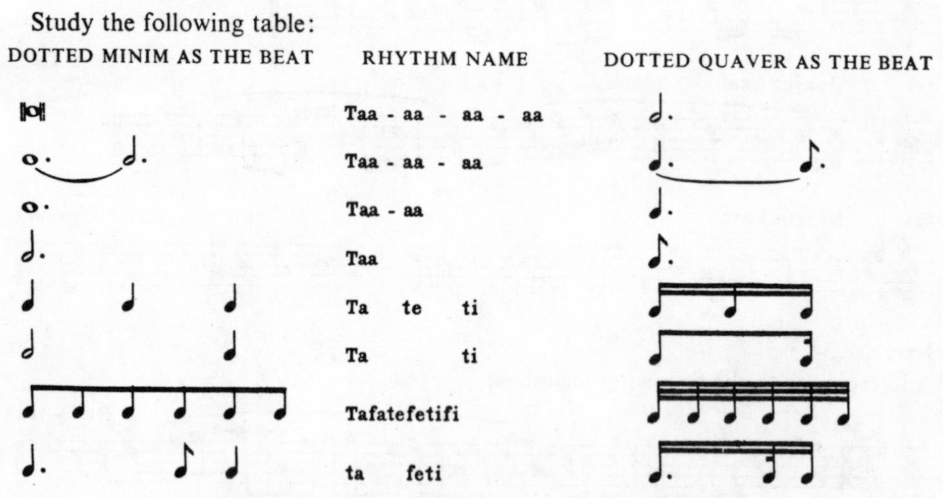

Exercise 35

Sing the following rhythmic phrases. Notice the time signature in each case.

Exercise 36

Add time signatures to the following melodies. Then rewrite them, with the dotted crotchet as the beat.

Exercise 37

Add bar lines to the following melodies:

2 Fixed Pitch

1 *The use of letter names to indicate fixed pitch*

The word ' pitch ' in music refers to the height or depth of sounds. A woman's voice is of higher pitch than a man's; a violin is of higher pitch than a 'cello.

The first seven letters of the alphabet, A–G, are used to fix the pitch of sounds. The eighth sound (the octave) is so much like the first that it is given the same letter name.

The A which violins use for tuning makes the air vibrate at 439 times a second. The A an octave higher (A') produces vibrations twice as fast. This applies whatever voice or instrument makes the sound. It is scientifically fixed, as is the pitch of all the other sounds.

2 *The great stave*

The monks of the Middle Ages were the first people to think of using lines to represent the pitch of notes. They realised that eleven lines were sufficient to represent the pitch of all the different kinds of human voice.

They fixed the middle line of the eleven as middle C, and put a C *clef* on this line. It is a sound of middle pitch, which both men and women can sing.

All the other lines and spaces of the great stave were therefore fixed in relation to this.

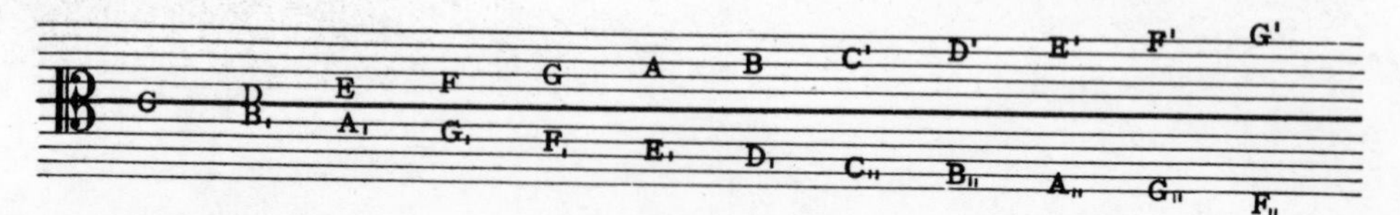

But it is too complicated to read notes on an eleven line stave, and a set of five lines has normally been used, as this is enough for any one kind of human voice. Any set of adjacent five lines can be taken, to suit the voice or instrument required.

3 *The treble stave*

The top five lines of the great stave fit the range of the treble voice, so they are called the *treble stave*. But as middle C is the sixth line it cannot be used to fix the pitch. So a G clef 𝄞 is put on the G two lines above middle C, thus:

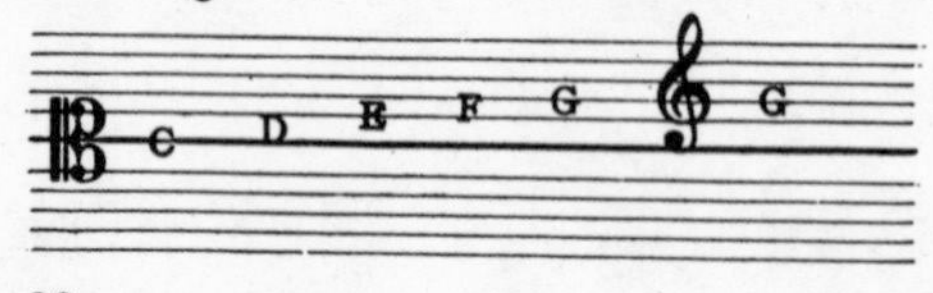

The treble stave is also used for the notes normally played by the right hand on the piano, for the violin, the flute, and all other instruments of high pitch.

Most people learn to read from the treble stave before learning any other. So they tend to think it is the easiest, though of course, in reality, all staves are equally easy to learn. However, because of this, it has become quite common to write for men's voices and for low brass instruments on the treble stave, an octave higher than they sound.

If lines above or below the stave are required extra short lines (leger lines) are used for the purpose.

Here is the range of notes on the treble stave. (It could be extended higher or lower, by means of more leger lines.)

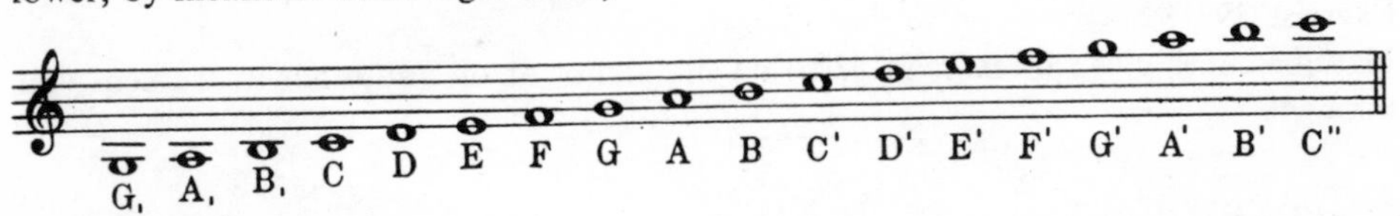

Realise that no note on a stave has a *fixed* pitch until a clef has been put on the stave. So, if you mean to fix the pitch, always put in the clef at the beginning of each line.

It is helpful to realise the order of the lines and spaces on the treble stave:

Learn these, if you are not sure of them. Higher and lower notes can be calculated from them.

Exercise 38

(a) Copy and name the following notes:

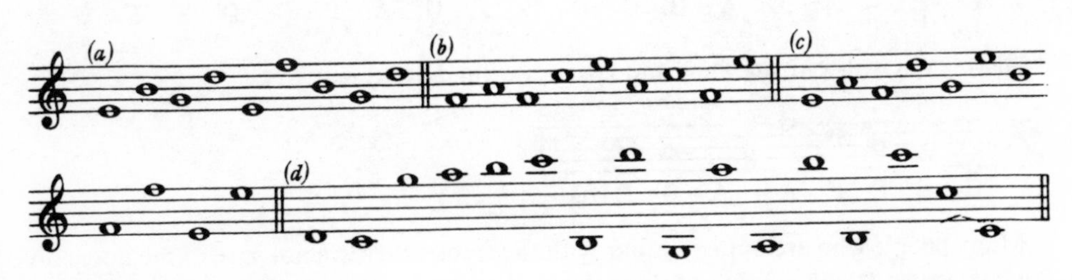

(b) Copy the following tunes, and write the letter names above each note. Name the tunes, if you know them:

Exercise 39

Play the tunes given in exercise 38(b) on the piano, or on any other instrument you know.

4 *The bass stave*

The bottom five lines of the great stave fit the range of the bass voice, so they are called the *bass stave*. But, again, middle C is not one of the lines. So an F clef (𝄢 or 𝄢) is put on the F two lines below middle C, thus:

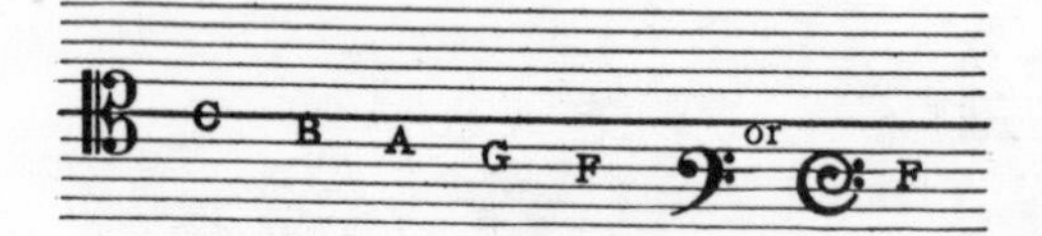

The bass stave is also used for the notes normally played by the left hand on the piano, for the 'cello, the bassoon, and other instruments of low pitch.

Leger lines are again used for notes above and below the bass stave.

Here is the range of the bass stave:

Here is the order of the lines and spaces on the bass stave:

Many people who are quite familiar with the treble stave are not sure of the notes on the bass stave. If you are one of these, learn the bass stave notes now. It will save you much trouble later on.

Exercise 40

(a) Copy and name the following notes:

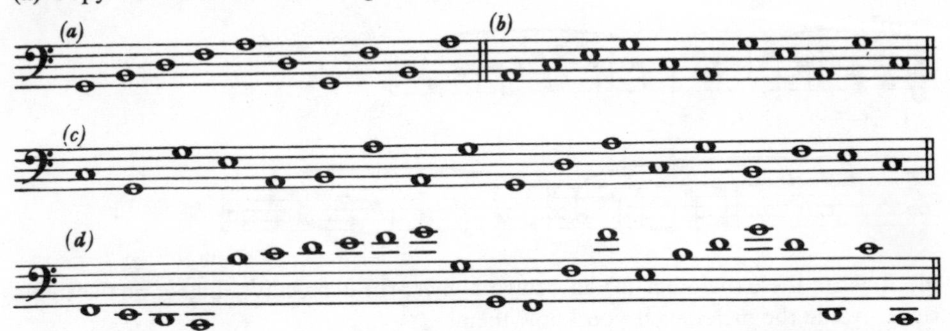

(b) Copy the following tunes, and write the letter names above each note. Name the tunes if you know them:

Exercise 41

Play the tunes given in exercise 40(b) on the piano, or any other instrument of low pitch that you know.

Exercise 42

(a) Rewrite these melodies at the same pitch on the bass stave:

(b) Rewrite these melodies at the same pitch on the treble stave:

(c) Rewrite these melodies (a) an octave lower; (b) two octaves lower on the bass stave. Try to hear them as you write, and name the melodies if you know them.

(d) Rewrite these melodies (a) an octave higher; (b) two octaves higher on the treble stave. Name the melodies if you know them.

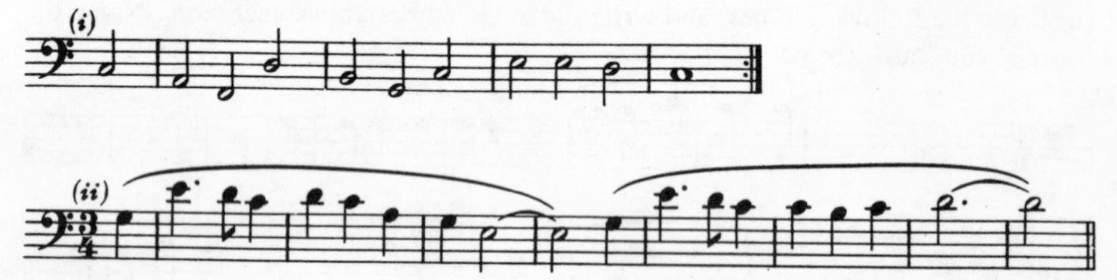

5 *Alto and tenor staves*

The C clef is used for any set of five lines from the great stave on which it is present, i.e. for all except the top five and the bottom five lines.

At one time the C clef was in much more general use than it is now. But the alto stave is still used by the viola; and the tenor stave is used for the upper notes of the 'cello and the bassoon. Also, in older scores, the alto trombone uses the alto stave and the tenor trombone the tenor. So if you play any of these instruments, or if you want to follow an orchestral score, you must be able to read from these staves.

Exercise 43

Name the following notes and play them on the piano, as a proof that you are sure of their exact pitch.

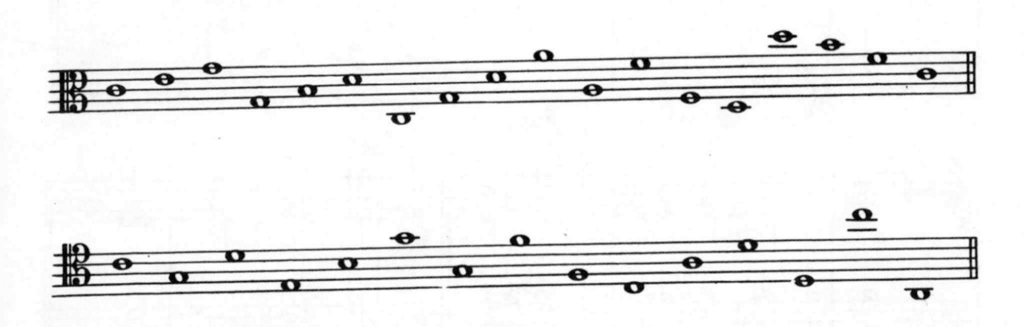

Exercise 44

(a) Rewrite the following melodies at the same pitch, using (1) the alto stave; (2) the tenor stave. Name the melodies, if you know them.

(b) Rewrite the following hymn tune in open score, using treble, alto tenor and bass clefs:

(c) Rewrite the above hymn tune on four staves for a string quartet.

6 *Tones and semitones. The piano keyboard*

The usual step from one note to the next in a scale is called a *tone*.

A *semitone* is half this size. It is the smallest interval that most people can sing and the smallest distance from one note to the next on a keyed instrument. A violinist can play less than a semitone, but then we say he is playing ' out of tune '. Similarly, we say a singer is ' sharp ' or ' flat ' if he sings a little higher or lower than the correct note.

The letter names A–G are not the same distance apart in pitch. Most of them are a tone apart, but B–C and E–F make semitones. If you look at the diagram of a piano keyboard, shown below, you will notice that, although the white notes are all equally wide and adjacent to one another, there is no black note between B and C, and E and F. If you try to sing a sound between each pair you cannot do so, whereas you can easily sing a sound between C and D.

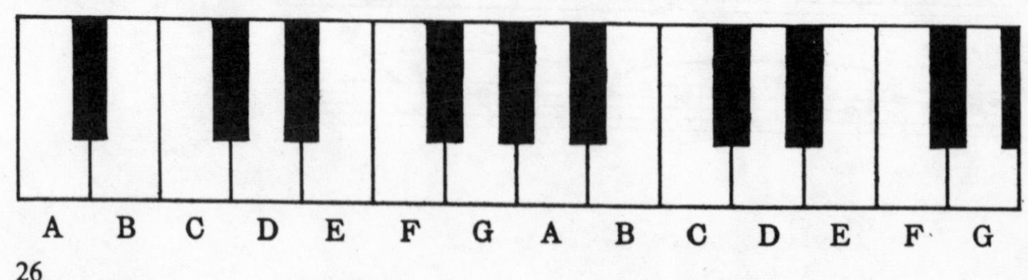

If you are a string player it is obviously important that you should be able to distinguish between the sound of a tone and a semitone. But, in reality, it is equally important for all musicians to be able to tell the difference; and it has been said that this ability is at the root of all musicianship.

Exercise 45
Listen to your teacher playing tones and semitones and say which is which.

Exercise 46
Sing (a) a tone; (b) a semitone above or below any sound given to you by your teacher.

7 *Accidentals*

When any of the sounds A–G is raised a semitone it is said to be sharpened, and ♯ is written *after* its name, thus: A♯, but *before* its note on the stave, thus:

If you look at the diagram of the piano keyboard above you will see that a sharp is not always a black note. A♯ is the black note between A and B, but B♯ is the same sound as C.

Similarly, when any letter-name sound is lowered a semitone it is said to be flattened. It is written thus: A♭, . Again a flat is not always a black note. C♭ is the same sound as B.

If a note which has been sharpened or flattened returns to its original letter name, a *natural* is used, thus: A♮,

Notice, therefore, that a natural is always a white note on the piano, because the plain letter names are all white notes.

A letter-name sound can also be raised a whole tone. This is called a *double sharp*, and is written thus A𝄪, . It is the same sound as B.

A letter-name sound which is lowered a whole tone is called a *double flat*, and is written thus: A𝄫, . It is the same sound as G.

All these signs are called *accidentals*.

An accidental affects all the notes of the same pitch throughout one bar, unless contradicted. And if it occurs on the last note of a bar it can also carry over to the first note of the next bar.

If you study the piano diagram you will realise that A♯, B♭ and C♭♭ are the same sound. All the sounds can have three names except one. By working it out on the piano diagram discover which sound has only two names.

A change of name but not of sound is called an *enharmonic change.*

Exercise 47

By means of enharmonic changes another name for each of these sounds: (1) A♯; (2) C♭; (3) F𝄪; (4) E♯; (5) B♭♭; (6) D♭; (7) B𝄪; (8) F♭♭; (9) D♯; (10) D𝄪.

3 Relative Pitch

1 *Tonality*

Section 2 told you that every sound has a scientifically fixed pitch. But one sound, in isolation, does not make music. As soon as you get two or more sounds of different pitch they have a relationship to each other and this relationship is called *tonality.*

The relationships between the time of notes (rhythm) and the pitch of notes (tonality) are fundamentals of music; and the appreciation of them is what makes a person musical. Though most people have a certain amount of this appreciation instinctively, it can be trained and developed, and thus lead to ever greater enjoyment.

Most of the music you hear today bases its tonality on the sound of the major and minor scales.

2 *The major scale. Its technical names. Its sol-fa names*

The major scale is a mixture of tones and semitones. The semitones occur between the third and fourth, and the seventh and eighth degrees. If you start with C (the *scale* of C) the notes are therefore:

Notice that, in this scale, the semitones coincide with the letter names that makes semitones, i.e. E–F and B–C. The scale of C is the only major scale that can be built entirely on the white notes of the piano.

Two sets of names, the *technical names* and the *sol-fa names*, are used to express the relationship between the sounds of the scale.

DEGREE	TECHNICAL NAME	SOL-FA NAME
1	Tonic	Doh
2	Supertonic	Ray
3	Mediant	Me
4	Subdominant	Fah
5	Dominant	Soh
6	Submediant	Lah
7	Leading note	Te
8	Tonic	Doh'

A very small minority of people have such a good memory for the fixed pitch of sounds that if, for example, they hear G or C, they know what note it is, without having to think about it. We say they have a sense of *absolute pitch.*

Notice that this has nothing to do with the appreciation of relationships: a person with absolute pitch may or may not be musical.

What makes a person musical is the recognition, for example, of the particular effect of dominant moving to tonic, soh doh. This may be G C if doh is C, but it sounds very similar whatever note is doh, and quite unlike the effect of submediant tonic, lah doh.

It is this faculty, developed so that one can appreciate all the other relationships of one sound to another, one chord to another, one key to another, that makes a person sing or play with sensitive understanding, or able to recognise the shape of a tune and to write it down on paper.

You need to learn the technical names because many text books and examination papers refer to the relative pitch of sounds by their means. But the sol-fa names are easier to think of quickly and to sing, so they are really the more useful set of names.

If, for any reason, you are not thoroughly familiar with sol-fa names it will pay you to become so now. It is invaluable to have a set of names to express such a fundamental element in music, one which is quite different from fixed pitch.

If you are required to sing at sight, to work ear tests, or study harmony you will find that you are able to hear relationships better if you are familiar with sol-fa, that you are no longer just guessing, and that your aural ability continually improves. And, as a result, your own playing or singing, as well as your appreciation of all kinds of music, will also improve.

Exercise 48

Think of simple tunes in the major mode that you know well and sing them to yourself to sol-fa names. You can do this at odd moments during the day, perhaps when you are out walking by yourself. You will be surprised to discover how much your ear improves by constant mental singing to sol-fa in this way.

3 *Major keys and key signatures*

A moment's thought or a glance at the keyboard diagram will tell you that there are twelve sounds of different pitch in every octave. A major scale can be built on every one of these.

It is customary to start with the scale of C (which is used for music in the *key* of C) because this is the scale without any sharps or flats.

It consists of two sets of four notes (two tetrachords) which are exactly the same shape—tone, tone, semitone.

SECTION 3 PART 3

Compare the scales of C and G:

You will see that the top tetrachord of the scale of C is the same as the bottom tetrachord of the scale of G, and that F♯ is required to produce the semitone between te and doh' in the key of G.

You can continue in this way, making a new scale by starting with the top tetrachord of the previous scale, i.e. five notes higher, until you have a scale all sharps:

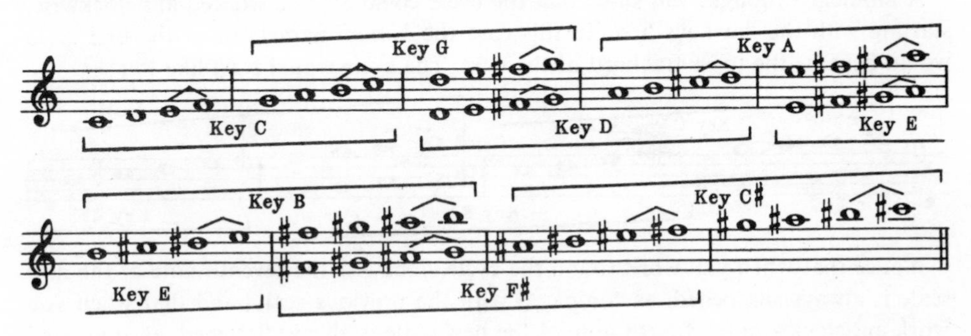

This series could be continued by starting a scale on G♯, but now you would require F𝄪. Rather than do this, it would be preferable to make an enharmonic change and start thinking in flats.

Here is the continuation, repeating C♯ but writing it as D♭, and continuing until we get back to C.

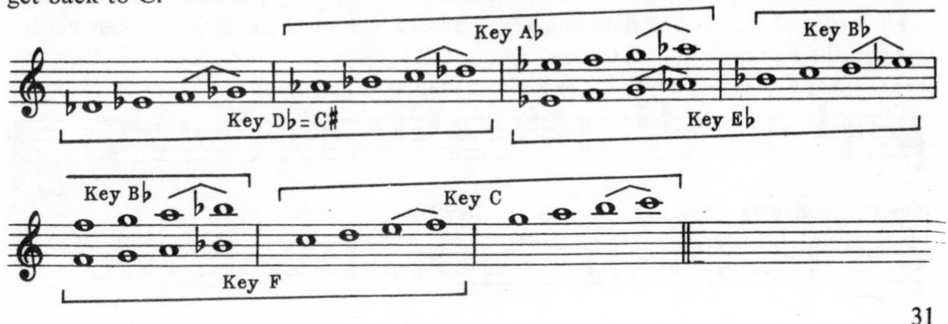

This makes a complete cycle of major scales, using all the twelve notes of different pitch. Here it is, in the form of a clock:

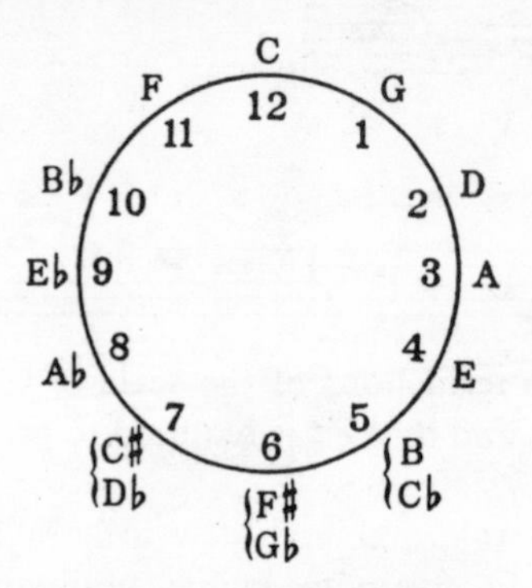

A moment's thought will show that the cycle could also be worked anticlockwise, starting with the flat keys first. In this case the *bottom* tetrachord of the first scale would become the top tetrachord of the next. The cycle would start like this:

Notice that when you work round the cycle clockwise the seventh note of the new scale is always sharpened, as compared with the previous scale; and that when you work anticlockwise the fourth note of the new scale is always flattened, as compared with the previous scale. In each case there is just *one* different sound. We say these keys are *closely related.*

Instead of inserting all the sharps or flats required for a particular key every time they occur, it is customary to place them together, in a *key signature*, at the beginning of the music. This key signature must be repeated at the beginning of every line of music to which it applies, unlike a time signature which is only placed at the beginning.

The order of sharps and flats in a key signature is that of the order of their occurrence in the key cycle shown above.

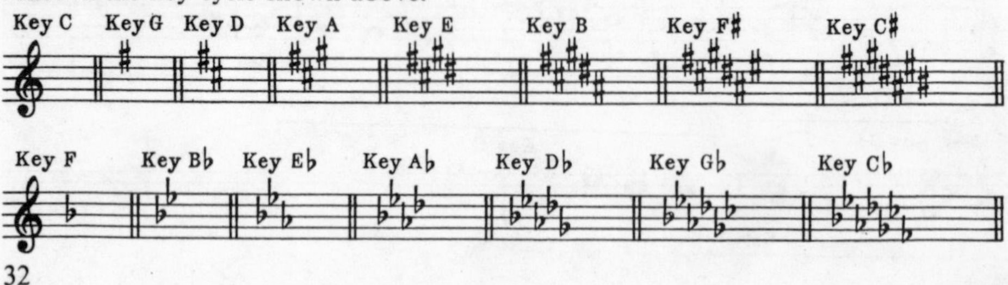

This is the position of the sharps and flats on the stave when other clefs are used:

How to name a key signature:
Sharps Doh is a semitone above the last sharp.
Flats Doh is the last flat but one.
How to write a key signature:
Sharps Write sharps a fifth above each other, starting with F♯ until you come to te.
Flats Write flats a fourth above each other, starting with B♭, until you come to doh. Then write one more.

Exercise 49

Work any of the following questions which are appropriate to your needs.

1 Write out the complete cycle of major scales, without key signatures. Mark the semitones.

2 Write out the complete cycle of major scales, with key signatures. Mark the semitones.

3 Write the following major scales, without key signatures: (a) A; (b) E♭; (c) B; (d) C♯; (e) D♭; (f) B♭; (g) F♯; (h) G♭; (i) E; (j) C♭.

4 Write the major scales given in question 3, with key signatures.

5 Name the following major keys:

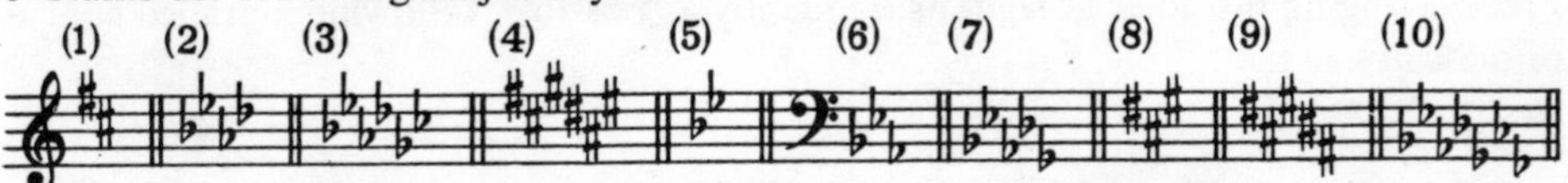

6 Write the following key signatures, on both treble and bass staves: (a) E♭; (b) G♭; (c) C♭; (d) C♯; (e) F♯.

7 Write the key signatures given in question 6 on the alto and tenor staves.

8 Name the following key signatures:

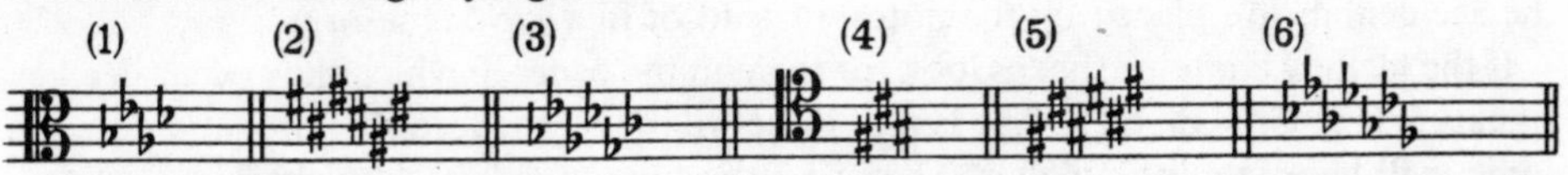

9 Name the following notes, in major keys: (a) dominants of D and E♭; (b) leading notes of C♯ and G♭; (c) submediants of E and F♯; (d) mediants of D and D♭; (e) subdominants of B and A♭.

10 Write (a) the major scale of G♭, ascending in crotchets, starting on the mediant, on the treble stave, with key signature; (b) the major scale of B, descending in minims, starting on the subdominant, on the bass stave, without key signature; (c) the major scale of C♭, descending in semibreves, starting on the submediant, on the bass stave, without key signature.

11 Write (a) the major scale of F♯, descending in crotchets, starting on the leading note, on the alto stave, without key signature; (b) the major scale of D♭, ascending in quavers, starting on the dominant, on the tenor stave, with key signature; (c) the major scale of C♯, descending in minims, starting on the supertonic, on the alto stave, with key signature.

4 *Singing melodies in major keys*

There is no room in this book to include melodies for singing at sight, grading them according to difficulty, with examples in every key and in various kinds of time. But singing a melody is the only proof you can give that you have really heard what the printed music should sound like—you can play it on an instrument without having heard it mentally. So there is no better way of developing your musicianship than regularly singing melodies at sight.

Make use of sol-fa names, developing your aural memory of the mental effects of the various sounds of the scale by linking them with sol-fa, so that eventually you *know* what the next note should sound like, instead of just guessing.

Exercise 50

Practise singing melodies at sight as frequently as possible, following a graded course of difficulty.

5 *Recognition of the key of a written melody* (*major*)

Some examinations require the candidate to recognise the key of a passage in which the accidentals are placed by the notes, instead of in a key signature.

If the melody contains sharps look for them in the order in which they occur in a key signature (F♯, C♯, G♯, etc.). The last of these will be te, the leading note; and doh, the tonic, will be a semitone higher. Then sing the tune to sol-fa, as a check.

Similarly, in a tune containing flats, the last flat will be fah, the subdominant; and doh, the tonic, will be the last but one.

Exercise 51

Write the correct key signature for the following tunes, and name the key. Then sing the melody to sol-fa, and name it, if you know it.

6 *Writing down a melody from dictation* (*major*)

Here is a good method of writing down a melody from dictation:

(a) Get the pitch of the first note. If you start on the wrong note the whole tune will probably be wrong. So sing the tonic to yourself as soon as you hear it, and continue to sing it until you hear the first note. Then write down the sol-fa name of the first note at once.

Suppose the tune you are to write down is this:

You will write down soh, thus:

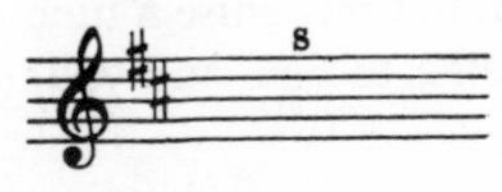

(b) The next stage is to memorise the melody. Sing as much of it as you can immediately after it is played *each time*. This is better than attending to one bit of it and not listening to the rest. Memorising comes before analysis—apart from the essential first note.

(c) Having memorised at least a part of the melody, now proceed to analysis. Attend to the pitch of the notes before the rhythm, as you will probably find it harder. Relate each note you hear to the one before it, singing up or down to it by step, using sol-fa names. Write the sol-fa names over the top of the staff, checking each note by singing it mentally, as you write it. Your tune will now look like this:

(d) Now put tiny dots on the right lines and spaces, thus:

(e) Put in the bar lines next. A bar line is a thing you *hear*, if you listen for it. Faulty rhythm is often caused by thinking about the note values before the bar lines, and then putting in the bar lines arithmetically to fit, instead of listening for the accent. For example, you may have confused ♫. and ♩. ♪, a common mistake; and if you work out your bar lines arithmetically they will obviously be wrong, too. You are more likely to notice your mistake if you have to make your rhythmic pattern fit your bar lines. Your tune will now look like this:

(f) Now sing the tune to rhythm names and turn the little dots into notes. A dot can be part of the edge of a semibreve or minim, but should be enlarged for a black note, such as a crotchet or quaver.

(g) Finally, add the time signature.

Memorising plays an important part in all dictation tests. It is a faculty that needs training, as it is essential to the enjoyment of any music lasting more than a few bars. Repetition is frequently used in all kinds of music, and if you cannot recognise a tune when it recurs later in the piece, the music will seem quite shapeless to you, and your enjoyment of it will be very much less.

Exercise 52

Write down melodies in the major key which are dictated to you by your teacher.

7 *Self Dictation*

It is not always possible to find people to give you as much dictation as you think you need. If you want to help yourself, try to write down the first phrase of any major key tune you know. Then play what you have written, or find a copy of the melody for checking purposes. It does not matter if you have written it in a different key.

Exercise 53
Write down or play the first phrase of any tunes you know which are in a major key.

8 *The minor scale, harmonic and melodic. Its technical names. Alternative versions of sol-fa names*

The minor scale owes its name to the fact that it has a smaller, *minor*, third from the tonic, as compared to the major, which has a larger, *major*, third.

There are two forms of minor scale in use today; harmonic and melodic.

The *harmonic* minor scale is used most of the time, but perhaps more particularly for harmonies, hence its name.

As compared with a major scale on the same tonic, its third and sixth notes are flattened, i.e. they are a semitone lower, which does not necessarily make them flats. (If the note was a sharp, for example, it would become a natural when flattened.)

Compare C major and C minor:

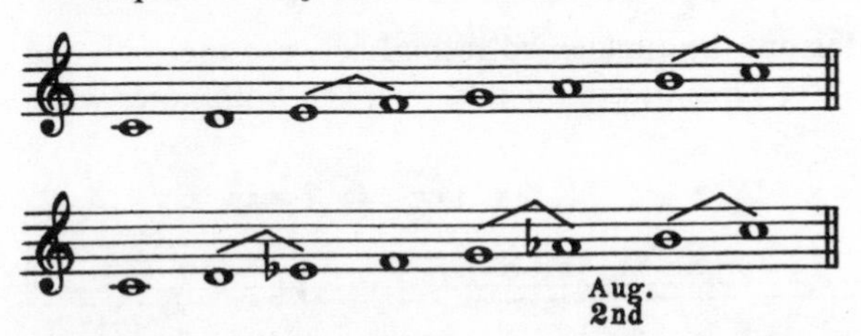

This results in three pairs of semitones: between the second and third, the fifth and sixth, and the seventh and eighth notes. There is a tone and a half, called an *augmented* second, between the sixth and seventh degrees.

There are conflicting opinions about what set of sol-fa names to use for the minor scale.

One school of thought thinks that the same name should be used for the same sound as in a major key, arguing that, for example, the movement of the leading note to the tonic has the same effect in each mode, and should therefore be called te doh' in both.

The other school of thought thinks more about the notation than the sound (you will understand the point of this better when key signatures are discussed later in this section). It thinks of C minor as an appendage of E♭ major, and therefore calls the tonic of the minor key lah. E♭ major is called the relative major of C minor, and C minor the relative minor of E♭ major, because the relationship of the two keys is so close—just as C major is closely related to G major.

Here are the alternative sets of sol-fa names, in relation to the technical names:

	DOH MINOR	TECHNICAL NAME	LAH MINOR
1	doh	tonic	lah,
2	ray	supertonic	te,
3	maw	mediant	doh
4	fah	subdominant	ray
5	soh	dominant	me
6	law	submediant	fah
7	te	leading note	se
8	doh'	tonic	lah

N.B. When any sol-fa name is flattened, its ending changes to ' aw ': me becomes maw. When a sol-fa name is sharpened, its ending becomes ' e ': soh becomes se.

Here is the scale of C minor, showing both sets of sol-fa names:

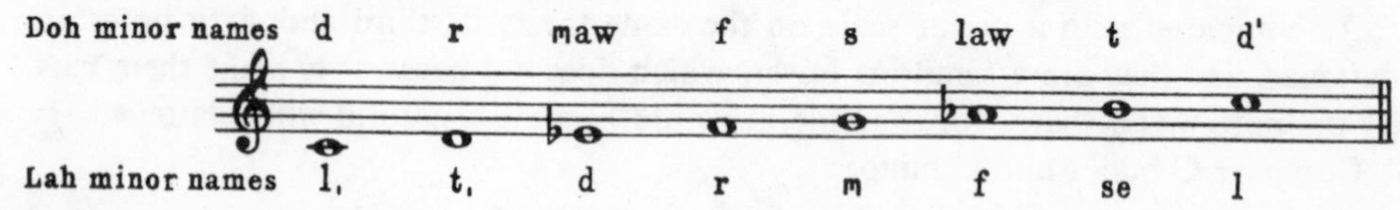

The *melodic* minor scale smooths out the augmented second between the sixth and seventh degrees by raising both notes when ascending and lowering both notes when descending, thus:

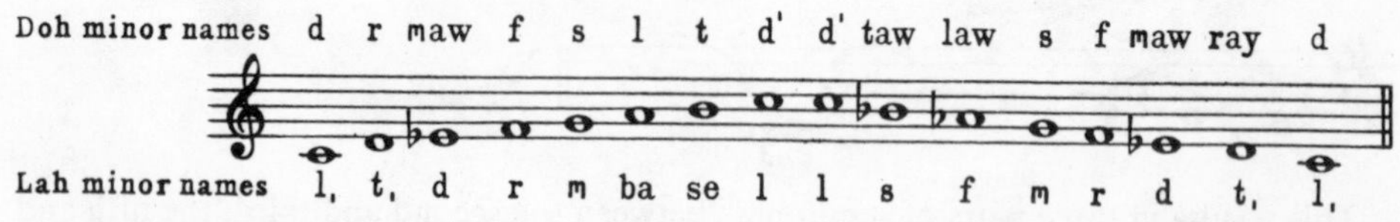

Notice that, in both harmonic and melodic forms of the scale, the first five notes are the same, that is, they have a flattened third, in relation to the major scale on the same tonic (the tonic major). The top half of the melodic minor scale, in its ascending and descending forms, is used in melodies to avoid the augmented second of the harmonic form, hence its name ' melodic '.

It may help you to realise that the top tetrachord of the melodic minor ascends like its tonic major (C minor like C major), and descends like its relative major (C minor like E♭ major).

Most people learn about one kind of minor scale before the other. But, whichever you learn first, it is helpful to realise that the *essential* difference between music in a major key and a minor key consists of the position of the third of the scale. The tonic chord (the most important chord, which establishes the key) is doh me soh, C E G, in C major, and doh maw soh (or lah doh me), C E♭ G, in C minor. This is what you should listen for in deciding whether music you hear is in a major or minor key.

Music in a minor key is quite often (but not always) sadder than that in a major key, largely owing to the presence of this lowered third degree. If your teacher were to play the national anthem in G major and then in G minor, you would at once feel this difference. But 'Charlie is my darling' is a cheerful, jolly tune in a minor key. However, it would sound even more cheerful if it were sung or played in C major instead of C minor.

Exercise 54
Listen to music played by your teacher, or on a record, and decide whether it is in a major or minor key.

Exercise 55
Think of simple, minor key tunes that you know well, and sing them to yourself to sol-fa names.

9 *Minor keys and minor key signatures*

The easiest way to sing, play or write a harmonic minor scale is to think of the major scale and flatten the third and sixth notes, thus:

The melodic minor scale is not quite so simple. For the first tetrachord, think of the tonic major scale, as before, and flatten the third note. The top half of the scale, the second tetrachord, is the same as the tonic major ascending, and uses the same notes as the relative major descending. This means that you must know what is the relative major of any minor scale before you start. It is always the key three letter names and three semitones higher. E.gs.: C minor, E♭ major; D minor, F major; C♯ minor, E major; E♭ minor, G♭ major (not F♯ major).

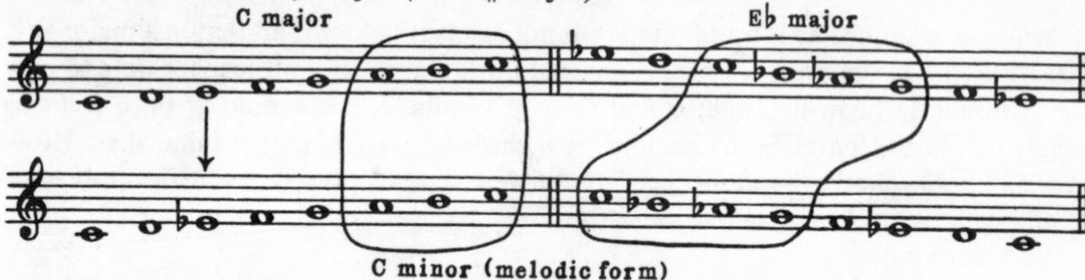

You can play round the cycle of minor keys—C, G, D, etc.—as you did the major. And, if you are not very sure of the notes, it is as well to practise this.

One would expect the key signature of C minor to consist of E♭ and A♭, as this would correspond with the harmonic minor form, the most common form of the minor scale, thus:

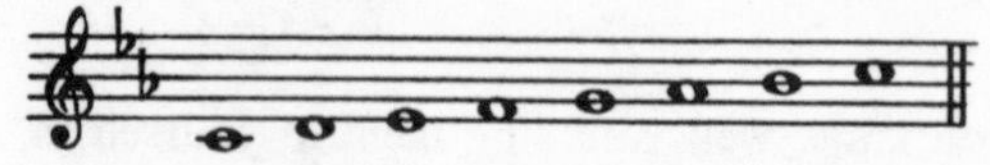

This would have the double advantage of showing at once that the music was minor (as no major key has this key signature) and also of accounting for all the black notes of the scale (as in the major) so that no accidentals were necessary in the music, except when the occasional use of the melodic minor occurred.

But unfortunately minor scales do not have a key signature of their own. They borrow that of their relative major, and so accidentals are required for the notes that are different from the major key. People very often forget to put them in, and this is particularly true of the leading note, te (se). They ' think ' the right sound, but forget it is not in the key signature.

Here is E♭ major, followed by the harmonic and melodic forms of C minor, using the key signature of E♭ major.

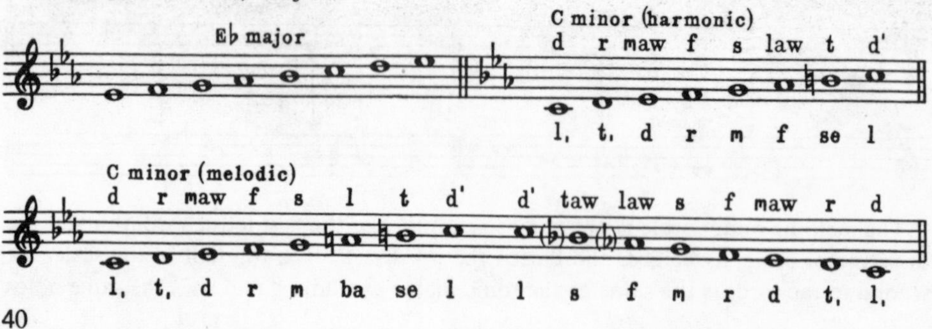

Here are the key signatures of the minor keys, borrowed from their relative majors. The leading note is shown in brackets, in every case.

The ' lah minorist ' uses the same sol-fa names for the same notes in C major and A minor, keys which have the same key signature, even though the effect is quite different. It is slightly easier; and it has been said that it is possible to sing a tune without knowing if it is in a major or a minor key—though whether this is a musical thing to do is a matter of opinion.

Realise that a key signature can represent two keys, a major and its relative minor. You must look at the actual music, in order to decide which it is. Given the key signature of one sharp, for example, you will probably find the tonic chord of G major (G B D) at the end, if the key is major; and you will probably find a number of D♯s and possibly some C♯s too, if the key is E minor, with the tonic chord of E minor (E G B) at the end.

Exercise 56

Work any of the following questions which are appropriate to your needs. In questions 1–4 you can use the harmonic or the melodic minor, or both.

1 Write out the complete cycle of minor keys, without key signatures. Mark the semitones.

2 Write out the complete cycle of minor scales, with key signatures. Mark the semitones.

3 Write the following minor scales, without key signatures: (a) C; (b) B; (c) A; (d) C♯; (e) B♭; (f) A♭; (g) E; (h) E♭; (i) F; (j) F♯.

4 Write the minor scales given in question 3 with key signatures.

5 Name the major and minor keys which have the following key signatures:

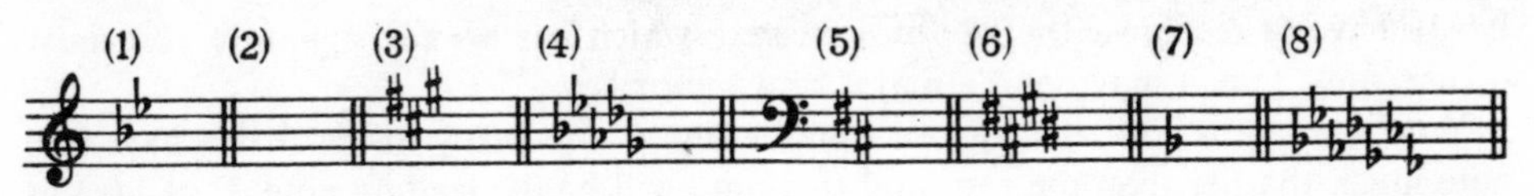

6 Write the key signatures of the following minor keys, on both treble and bass staves; (a) G; (b) G♯; (c) A♭; (d) E♭; (e) D♯. Indicate the leading note on the stave in each case.

7 Write the key signatures given in question 6 on the alto and tenor staves, indicating the leading note, as before.

8 Name the minor keys which have the following key signatures:

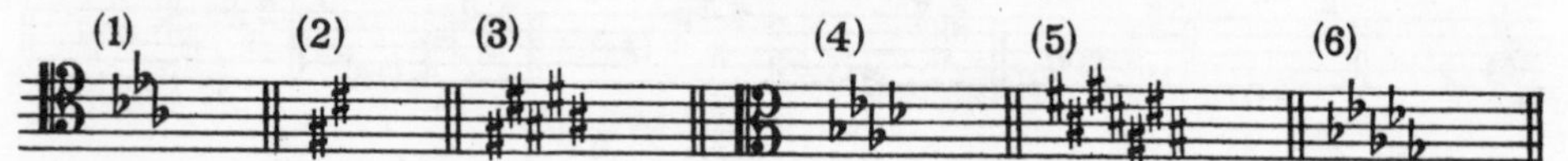

9 Name the following notes, in minor keys: (a) mediant of E and E♭; (b) dominant of A and B♭; (c) supertonic of F♯ and D♭; (d) leading note of C and C♯; (e) subdominant of F and G♯.

10 Write (a) the harmonic minor scale of C♯, ascending in minims, starting on the submediant, without key signature, on the bass stave; (b) the melodic minor scale of G, in crotchets, starting on the dominant, without key signature, on the treble stave; (c) the melodic minor scale of F♯, in semibreves, starting on the subdominant, with key signature, on the bass stave; (d) the harmonic minor scale of B♭, descending in quavers, starting on the leading note, with key signature, on the treble stave.

11 Write (a) the melodic minor scale of C, without key signature, so as to make four bars of $\frac{4}{4}$ time, on the alto stave; (b) the harmonic minor scale of F♯, with key signature so as to make two bars of $\frac{6}{8}$ time, on the tenor stave; (c) the melodic minor scale of B♭, with key signature, so as to make four bars of $\frac{3}{4}$ time, on the alto stave; (d) the major scale of C♭, followed by its relative minor in its harmonic form, without key signature, on the tenor stave.

10 *Singing melodies in minor keys*

Everyone finds it harder to sing a melody in a minor key than in a major. Persevere with sol-fa names, whatever method you adopt, until you can automatically link the sol-fa names with the sounds, and apply them to every key.

Exercise 57
Follow a graded course of singing melodies at sight in minor keys.

11 *Recognition of key (major or minor) in a written melody*

If you have to recognise the key of a passage which has no key signature you must realise, now, that it may be in a major or a minor key.

You have learnt how to recognise a major key. A minor key will probably have one note much sharper than the rest, and this note will be the leading note, E.gs.: (a) in E minor there will be a D♯, but also a G♮: in a major key a passage with a D♯ would also contain a G♯; (b) in B♭ minor there will be an A♮ but also a D♭; A♮ is a ‘ sharper ’ note than A♭, which comes before D♭ in a key signature, so A♮ is the leading note;

(c) in G minor there will be B♭, E♭ and F♯: F♯ is the leading note.

Unfortunately the use of the melodic minor may cause a little confusion, because a passage in G minor may contain both F♮ and F♯. But the general impression of the key of G minor should leave you in no doubt.

You should increasingly be able to tell the key of a passage by hearing it in your head and feeling the tonality. Sometimes a passage may include a note which does not belong to the key. (This is called a chromatic note, and a particularly common note to be included in this way is fe.) At other times there may be a key signature, but extra accidentals in the passage or your feeling for tonality should tell you that the music is in a different key.

Exercise 58

Work any of the following questions which are appropriate to your needs. In every case sing the tune to sol-fa, and name it, if you know it.

1 Are the following passages in a major or a minor key? Name the key.

2 Insert the correct key signature for the following tunes and name the key. Then rewrite the tune with the correct accidentals, given the key signature. Name the tune, if you know it.

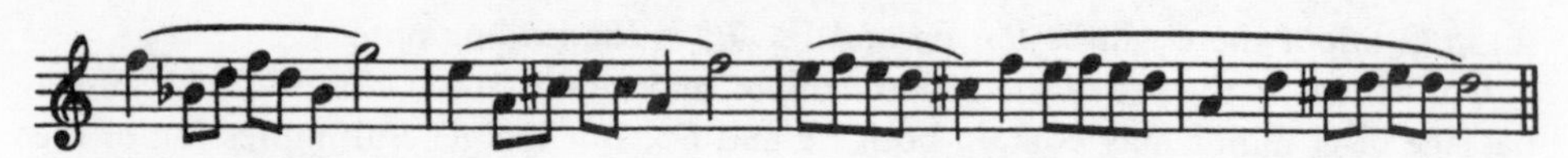

3 Name the key of the following. Give the title of the piece, if you know it.

Allegretto grazioso

Allegro moderato

Andante con moto

12 *Writing down a melody from dictation (minor)*

Work in the same way as suggested for dictation in a major key. But always check that you have remembered to put in the accidental for the leading note. And if notes occur in the top half of the scale listen carefully to hear if they use the melodic minor, thinking of their sol-fa names, and inserting or contradicting any accidentals as necessary.

Exercise 59
Write down melodies in the minor key which are dictated by your teacher.

13 *Self dictation*

Continue to make use of this method of improving your ear.

Exercise 60
Write down or play the first phrase of any tunes you know which are in a minor key.

14 *The chromatic scale. Harmonic and melodic forms. Their sol-fa names*

The *chromatic* scale consists entirely of semitones, and therefore has twelve sounds to the octave.

Those notes in a piece of music which belong to the key of the piece, whether it is major or minor, are called *diatonic*. The others are the chromatic notes, and they can be used, in both major and minor keys, to add 'colour' to the music (chrome=colour). As the chromatic scale includes every sound, it contains both diatonic and chromatic notes.

Two forms of the *notation* of the chromatic scale exist, though both, of course, contain the same sounds. These are: (a) the *harmonic* chromatic, which is used for any chromatic harmonies wanted in the particular key; and (b) the *melodic* chromatic, which is used for adding chromatic decorations to a melody.

The harmonic chromatic scale (like the harmonic minor scale) is the same ascending and descending. It contains one note on the first and fifth degrees of the scale and two on every other degree, thus:

The melodic chromatic scale is different ascending and descending (like the melodic minor scale). It contains one note on the third and seventh degrees ascending, and is the same as the harmonic chromatic scale descending, thus:

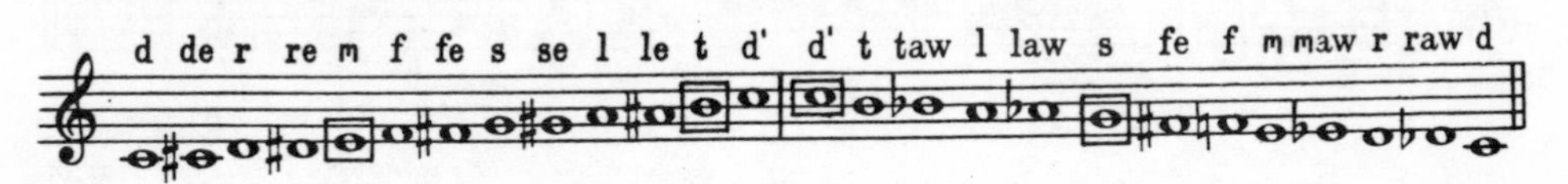

The notation of both chromatic scales differs according to whether they are written with or without a key signature. Here is the melodic chromatic scale of D written (a) without a key signature, and (b) with one:

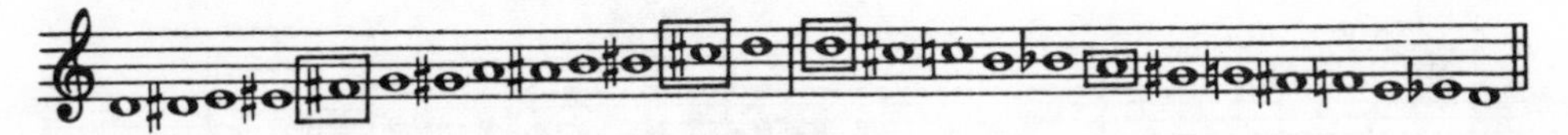

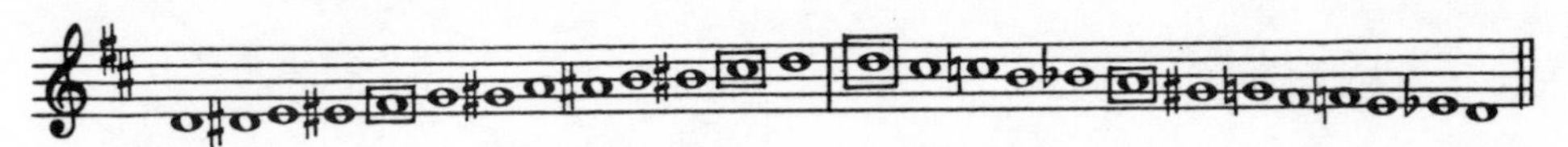

In an actual piece of music the use of accidentals may be further affected by the need to contradict accidentals which have been used in the same bar. Compare (a) and (b) below, which are the same except for the position of the bar line.

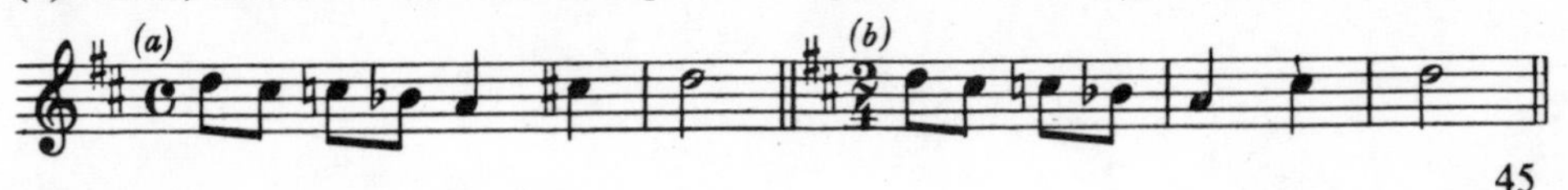

Exercise 61

Work any of the following exercises which are appropriate to your needs.

1 Write out the harmonic chromatic scales of E and A♭, without key signatures.

2 Write out the harmonic chromatic scales of F and B, with key signatures.

3 Write out the melodic chromatic scales of G and C♯, without key signatures.

4 Write out the melodic chromatic scales of A and D♭, with key signatures.

5 Write (a) the harmonic chromatic scale of D, descending in crotchets, on the bass stave, using a key signature; (b) the melodic chromatic scale of F♯, in minims, on the bass stave, without a key signature.

6 Write (a) the melodic chromatic scale of C♯ on the alto stave, with a key signature; (b) the harmonic chromatic scale of B♭ on the tenor stave, without a key signature.

7 Copy the melodies given below, and write the sol-fa names above each note. Try to hear them as you write.

4 Intervals

1 *Intervals by number*

An interval is the difference in pitch between two sounds.

In numbering intervals we count both ends: C to G is a 5th. Notice that *any* kind of C to G is a 5th—C to G♯, C♯ to G, C♭ to G♭, etc. Similarly any kind of C to F is a 4th. So [C–G♭] is a 5th, and [C–F♯] is a 4th, even though they produce the same sounds. In a piece of music they would have a different effect, because they would occur in different keys:

If the two notes of the interval occur within the same octave it is helpful to realise that 3rds, 5ths, and 7ths are both lines or both spaces, whereas 2nds, 4ths, 6ths and 8ves are opposites. It is particularly helpful to a pianist to realise that octaves are opposites, as they occur so often at the top and bottom of the keyboard: the octave is read by general impression rather than by counting leger lines. See below:

Intervals larger than an octave are sometimes called *compound.* For example, a tenth is a compound third. But it is usual to call C to E a 3rd, no matter how many octaves intervene.

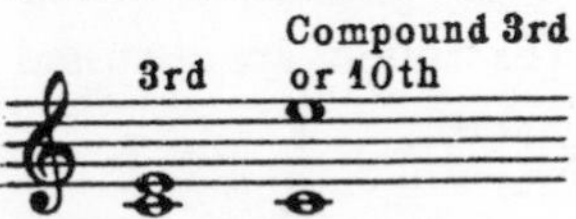

Intervals can be *melodic*—the sounds occurring after one another in a melody, or *harmonic*, the notes being heard at the same time, as harmony.

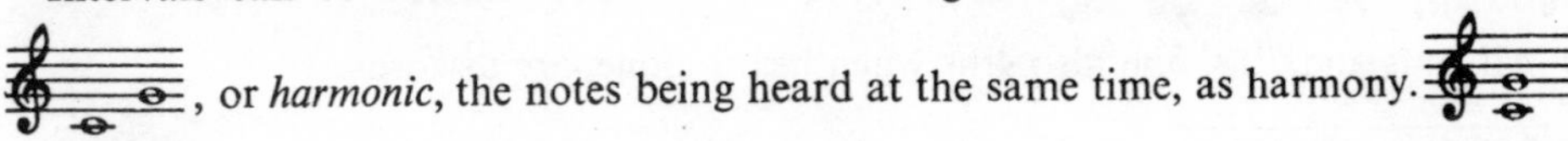

Exercise 62

Give the number of each of the following intervals:

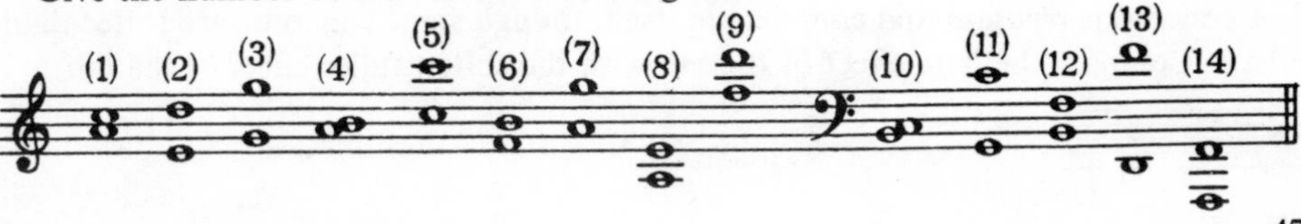

Exercise 63

1 On the treble stave write: (1) E and a 5th above it; (2) B and a 6th below it; (3) A and a 10th above it; (4) F and a 9th below it.

2 On the bass stave write: (1) D and a 3rd below it; (2) C and a 4th above it; (3) G and a 2nd below it; (4) F and a 6th below it.

3 Complete the following passage in the key of C by writing the stated intervals above and below the given notes. The two notes which make each interval must be on a different stave. Then name the tune you have produced on the treble stave, if you know it.

2 *The sound of intervals* (*number only*)

Intervals are divided into *concords* and *discords*.

Unisons, 3rd, 5ths, 6ths and octaves are usually concords. (Exceptions are discussed later.)

All 2nds and 7ths, and also 4ths when heard alone, are discords.

A concord is pleasant and complete in itself, though some concords are softer than others. Compare the bare effect of the 5th with the softer, fuller effect of the 6th:

Discords have varying degrees of harshness, but they always sound incomplete and require a *resolution*. Listen to the discordant effect of the 4th and the 2nd in these progressions, and compare them with the concordant 6th and 3rd on which they resolve.

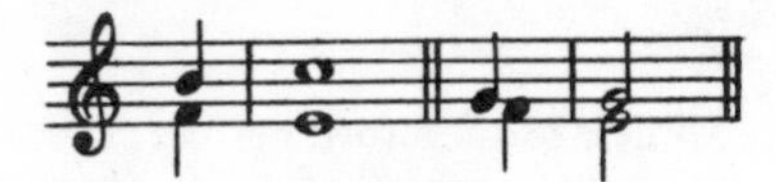

Many examinations require the candidate to recognise the number of an interval by ear, the two notes usually being within the octave.

Here is a method of working:

(a) Listen intently to the two sounds, as they are played together, until the bottom sound ' comes through ', and you are able to sing it to yourself. It is rather like going outside on a dark night: at first you can see nothing, then the trees begin to loom up out of the darkness. In the same way the bottom sound will begin to ' loom up ', to differentiate itself from the one above. Wait until it does so.

(b) When you are sure you have really *heard* the bottom note and are not just imagining a sound that blends with it, sing by step from the bottom note to the top one, counting as you go.

(c) Now check. Is the interval small, medium or large? If small, it is either a discordant 2nd or a concordant 3rd, and the difference is obvious: . If large, it is either a concordant 6th or a discordant 7th, and again the difference is obvious:

A medium sized interval will be a 4th or a 5th. Both are bare, but the 4th is a discord and wants to move, whereas the 5th may remind you of the tuning interval used by the strings:

Exercise 64

State the number of an interval after it is played to you by your teacher.

3 *Quality of intervals*

If two people play or sing the same sound (a unison) they make a *perfect* concord.

The next most perfect interval is the octave, the upper note having twice as many vibrations a second as the lower.

The 5th and 4th from the tonic, as they occur in a major or minor scale (doh soh and doh fah) are also closely related in the number of their vibrations, and so they, too, are called perfect intervals.

All other intervals are called *imperfect*.

In a major scale the 1st, 4th, 5th and 8ve from the tonic are therefore perfect; the 2nd, 3rd, 6th and 7th from the tonic are a particular kind of imperfect interval called *major*.

So C–G is a perfect 5th. But C–G♯ and C–G♭ are also 5ths, though no longer perfect intervals, and no longer concords.

When a perfect interval is made a semitone larger it is called *augmented;* when it is made a semitone smaller it is called *diminished.*

So C–G♯ is augmented, as is C♭–G. C–G♭ is diminished, as is C♯–G. C♯–G♯, being the same size as C–G, is still perfect.

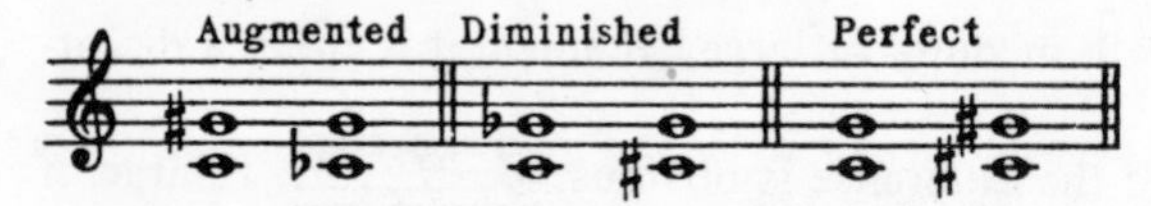

When a major interval is made a semitone larger it, also, is called augmented. C–D is major; C–D♯ is augmented. But when it is made a semitone smaller it is called *minor*, not diminished. C–E is a major 3rd; C–E♭ is a minor 3rd. It has to be made a semitone smaller again to be called diminished.

So intervals are modified thus:

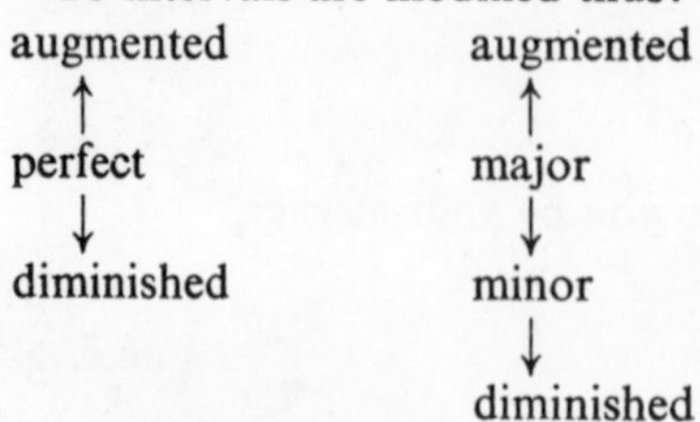

Notice that a perfect interval can never become major or minor, and a major or minor interval can never become perfect. There is no such thing as a perfect 3rd or a major 4th. So learn: *1sts, 4ths, 5ths and 8ves can be perfect but never major or minor; 2nds, 3rds, 6ths and 7ths can be major or minor but never perfect.*

If you are asked to write an interval think of the bottom note as the tonic of a major scale and work up from there. (This assumes you know the major scales.) C–G is a perfect 5th in whatever key it occurs, and C–G♯ is an augmented 5th in any key.

If the interval you are to write is a 1st, 4th, 5th or 8ve think of the perfect interval first, i.e. the note that occurs in the scale on that tonic. Then augment or diminish it, as necessary.

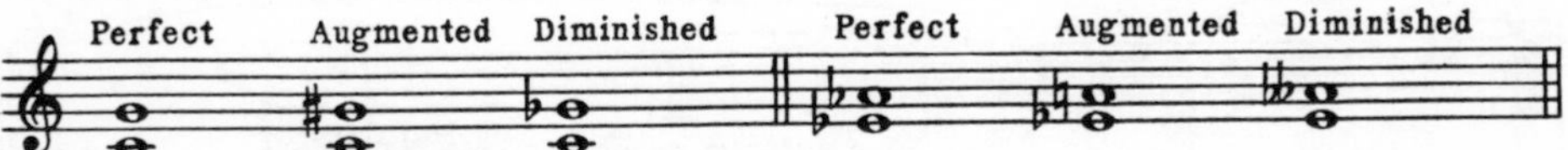

Similarly, if the interval is a 2nd, 3rd, 6th or 7th think of the major interval, i.e. the note that occurs in the major scale on that tonic. Then enlarge it to augmented, or decrease it to minor or diminished, as necessary.

Major Augmented Minor Diminished Major Minor Augmented

Exercise 65

Work any of the following questions which are appropriate to your needs:

1 Write the following intervals: (a) perfect 5ths on G and G♭; (b) augmented 4ths on D and A♭; (c) diminished 5ths on F♯ and E♭; (d) major 3rds on A and A♭; (e) minor 6ths on E and B♭; (f) augmented 2nds on A♭ and F; (g) diminished 7ths on C♯ and B.

2 Write the following intervals: (a) a perfect 4th on F on the treble stave; (b) a diminished 8ve on B on the bass stave; (c) a diminished 7th on A♯ on the bass stave (think of it on A and then move the whole interval a semitone up); (d) a major 6th on C♯ on the treble stave; (e) a minor 2nd on F♭ on the bass stave.

3 Write the following intervals: (a) a major 7th on A♭ on the tenor stave; (b) a minor 10th on D♭♭ on the alto stave; (c) a diminished 5th on C𝄪 on the alto stave; (d) an augmented 6th on B on the tenor stave.

4 Write the following intervals below the given note. (Find the letter name of the lower note first and then think upwards from it as the tonic, making any necessary modifications to the bottom and not the top note): (a) a minor 3rd below E; (b) a major 6th below C♯; (c) an augmented 4th below B; (d) a diminished 7th below B♭; (e) a perfect 5th below A♭.

5 Complete the following two-part passage by writing the stated intervals above and below the given notes. The two notes which make each interval must be on a different stave. Then add the key signature, name the key, and name the tune in the bass, if you know it.

If you are asked to name an interval, again think of the bottom note as the tonic. If the upper note is not part of the major scale on that tonic decide how much it is higher or lower, and name it accordingly, starting from major or perfect.

Exercise 66

Work any of the following questions which are appropriate to your needs:

1 Name the following intervals:

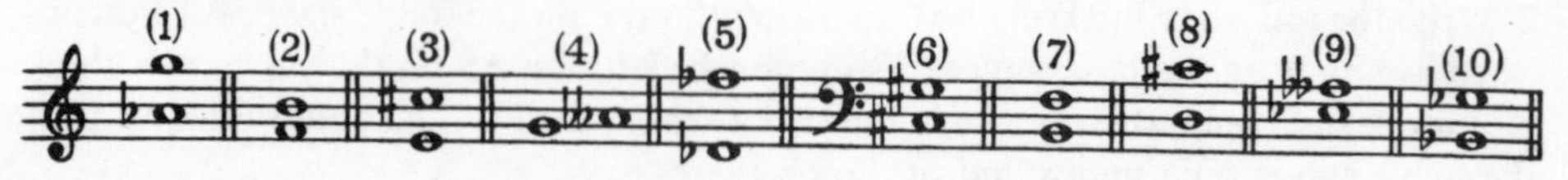

2 Name the following intervals:

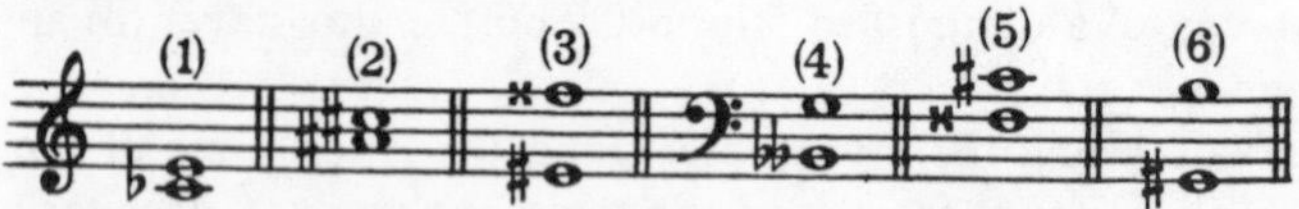

3 Name the following intervals:

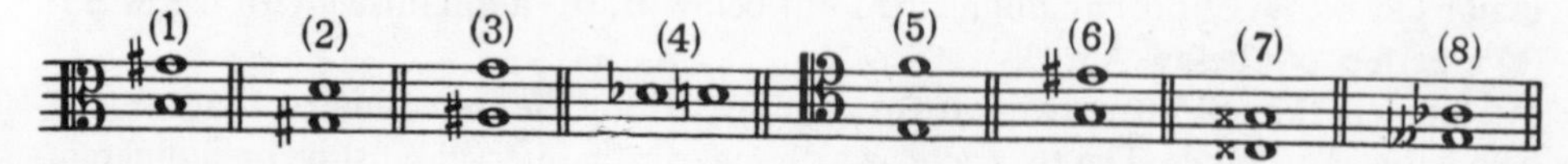

4 Enharmonically change one note of the intervals given in question 1, and rename the interval.

4 *Inversion of intervals*

When the top and bottom notes of an interval change their relative positions the interval is said to be *inverted.* In the following example (b) and (c) are both inversions of (a):

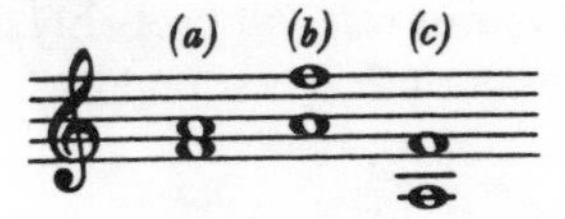

From this you will see that a 3rd inverted becomes a 6th. A 3rd and a 6th add up to 9, not 8, because one note, the A in the above example, is counted twice.

So an easy way to find the inversion of an interval is to subtract it from 9: a 5th becomes a 4th, a 2nd becomes a 7th, etc.

The following shows what happens to the *quality* of an interval when it is inverted:

Perfect remains perfect
major becomes minor
minor becomes major
diminished becomes augmented
augmented becomes diminished.

If you are asked to name the inversion of an interval you can work it out from the information given above. But then check it by naming the interval in the normal way.

Exercise 67

Invert and rename the intervals given in exercise 6, question 1.

5 *The sound of intervals, number and quality*

When you are asked to name an interval by ear in isolation (i.e. not as part of a musical passage) two ways of giving the test are possible: (a) the interval is heard without relation to a tonic; (b) the tonic chord is played before the interval is heard. The following are suggested methods of working in each case:

(a) *If the interval is to be named without the previous sounding of the tonic.* Begin by deciding its number, using the method suggested earlier in this section. Then think about its quality.

A minor 2nd and a major 7th are more discordant than a major 2nd and a minor 7th, because the two notes are only a semitone apart:

A major 3rd gives the impression of the tonic chord of a major key, whereas a minor 3rd suggests a minor key. Most people can hear this difference:

But realise that the inversion of a major 3rd is a minor 6th. A minor 6th will probably sound to you like me doh', part of a major chord. Similarly a major 6th will sound like part of a minor tonic chord:

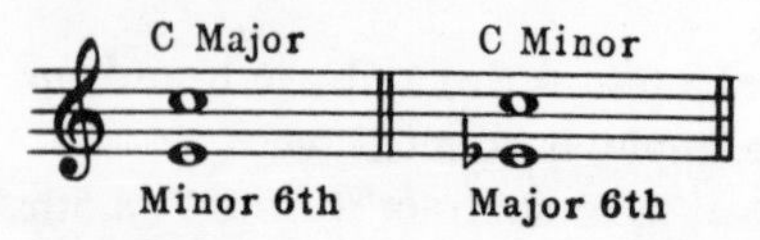

A perfect 4th sounds like doh fah, and a perfect 5th like doh soh:

The following interval may sound to you like an augmented 4th or a diminished 5th: ; and if you have not been given a tonic both answers are equally correct. Another possible answer is the 'tritone', because the two notes are three tones apart:

These are the only intervals you can name if you have not been given the sound of the tonic. For example, C–D♯ and C–E♭ sound exactly the same, if no tonic is given, so you cannot be asked to recognise an augmented 2nd; you will naturally hear it as a minor 3rd.

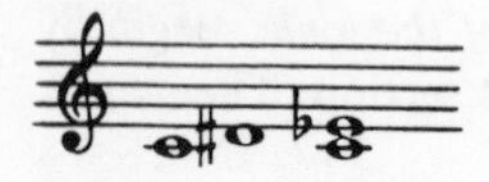

(b) *If the tonic chord is played first.* In this case the most musical method of working is to hear each note separately, in relation to the tonic, using sol-fa names and listening for the lower note in the way suggested before. Then write the notes down on the stave, and name the interval you have written, using the reasoning suggested earlier in this section. Finally, check your reasoning by aural analysis of the sound of the interval the two notes make.

You will need to know on what parts of the scale diminished and augmented intervals may occur. These are (a) in the major key:

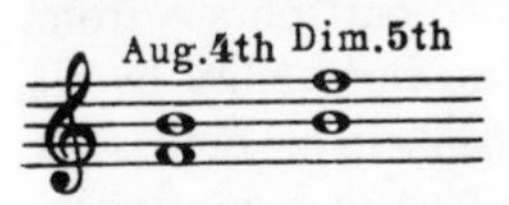

(b) in the minor key (harmonic form of the scale):

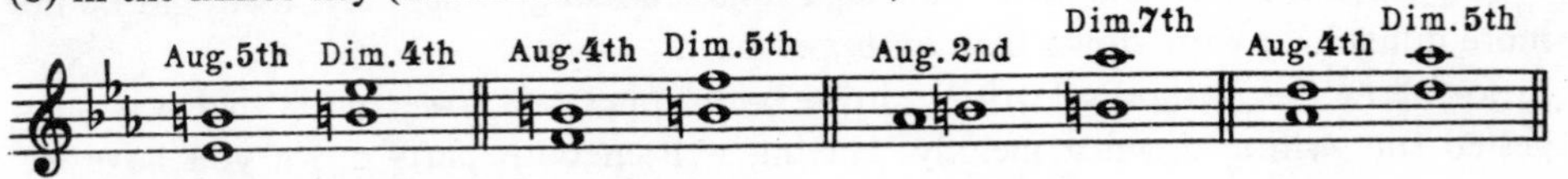

Learn where these occur, using sol-fa names.

An augmented interval wants to resolve outwards:

A diminished interval wants to resolve inwards:

There is one interval which can only occur in a chromatic scale. This is the augmented 6th, and its inversion, the diminished 3rd:

This interval would only be given in an advanced kind of ear test, as it is obviously chromatic in both C major and C minor.

Exercise 68

State the number and quality of an interval which is played to you by your teacher (a) without a tonic chord given; (b) given a tonic chord.

6 *Two-part singing at sight*

Practise singing in two parts as often as possible. Develop the ability to see and hear the other part besides your own, so that you are aware of how the parts should fit.

Exercise 69

Practise singing in two parts, following a graded course of difficulty.

7 *Writing a short two-part phrase from dictation*

The chief difference between writing a melody and writing a two-part phrase from dictation lies in the ability to hear an underneath part. Develop this ability by all means in your power. Listen to tunes played by lower instruments in an orchestral work, or to the lower part of a two-part song, or to the bass part of hymn tunes. When you can follow the lower part as a tune, and sing it mentally, it should be no more difficult to write down than an upper part.

So follow the method of writing down both upper and lower parts that was suggested for writing down a melody. Having written both parts down you have an additional method of checking. Look at the intervals made by the two parts, and see if they sound like what you have written: that a 6th or 7th sounds like a 6th or 7th, an augmented interval sounds like one, and so on.

Exercise 70
Write down two-part phrases dictated by your teacher.

5 Musical Terms, Signs and Abbreviations

1 *The use of musical terms*

The Italians were the first musicians to think of stating how they wanted their music to be performed. Composers of other countries soon began to use these same Italian terms, and now they are nearly universal.

Sometimes composers of other countries—English, French and German, for example—have used their own language. But it is an obvious advantage to use one language rather than to expect many to be known; and Italian is the universal language, as far as music is concerned. Only Italian terms are listed in this book, and only those most frequently used are included.

2 *Italian terms for speed*

Grave, very solemn, grave
Lento, very slow
Largo, slow and broad
Adagio, leisurely
Moderato, at a moderate speed
Andante, at a walking pace
Andantino, not as slow as *andante*
Mosso, moved (used with *piu* or *meno*, see below)
Allegretto, not as fast as *allegro*
Allegro, fast
Vivace, with vivacity
Presto, very quick
Prestissimo, as quickly as possible

All the above terms can be modified by the addition of (a) *molto*, very: *allegro molto*, very quick; (b) *assai*, extremely: *Allegro assai*, extremely quick; (c) *piu mosso*, more moved, quicker; (d) *meno*, less: *meno mosso*, less moved, slower.

3 *Italian terms for modifications of speed*

Getting quicker:
Accelerando, get quicker
Stringendo, hurrying

Getting slower:
Rallentando, slow down
Allargando, broadening
Ritardando, holding back
Ritenuto, held back

A tempo, *Tempo primo*, back to the original speed
Tempo rubato, literally, ' robbed time ', in a free, expressive rhythm

4 *Italian terms for intensity*

Pianissimo, *pp* and *ppp*, as soft as possible
Piano, *p*, soft
Mezzo piano, *mp*, rather soft
Mezzo forte, *mf*, rather loud

Forte, *f*, loud
Fortissimo, *ff* and *fff*, as loud as possible
diminuendo, *dim*
decrescendo, *decresc* } > getting softer
Crescendo, *cresc*, < getting louder
Piu and *meno* may be added to these terms
sforzando, *sf*, > or ∧ over or under one note, forcing the tone, accenting the note

5 *Italian terms of expression*

Agitato, agitatedly
Animato, animatedly
Appassionata, passionately
arco, bowed (string instrument)
Brillante, brilliantly
Cantabile, in a smooth, singing style
Capriccioso, capriciously
con, with:
- *Con brio*, with vigour
- *Con fuoco*, with fire
- *Con forza*, with force
- *Con moto*, with movement
- *Con sordini*, with mutes
- *Con spirito*, with spirit

Divisi, divided
Dolce, sweetly
Energico, with energy
Espressivo, with expression
Furioso, furiously
Giocoso, gaily
Giusto, exact (*Tempo giusto*, exact speed)
Grandioso, grandly
Grazioso, gracefully
Leggiero, light
Maestoso, majestically
Marcato, marked
Mesto, sadly
Ped (*pedale*) or *con ped*, use the sustaining pedal on the piano
pesante, heavily
pizzicato, plucked (strings)
poco a poco, little by little, gradually
Risoluto, resolutely
Scherzando, playfully
Sempre, always
Serioso, seriously
Simile, in the same manner
Sordino, mute. *Con sordini*, with mutes
Senza sordini, without mutes
Sostenuto, sustained
Sotto voce, under the voice, softly
Subito, suddenly
Tacet, be silent
Tanto, so much
Tenuto, held
Tranquillo, tranquil
Tre corde, literally, three strings: cease to use the soft pedal on the piano
Troppo, too much; *allegro ma non troppo*, quick, but not too quick
Tutti, everyone plays or sings
una corda, literally, one string: use the soft pedal of the piano
Vigoroso, vigorously
Vivo, lively
Volti subito, *V.S.*, turn over quickly

6 *Musical signs*

Music can be performed *legato*, smoothly, one note joined to the next, or *staccato*, detached, each note being separated from the next.

Legato playing is sometimes shown by the word *legato*, but more often by means of a slur ⌒ over or under the notes to be joined. *Staccato* playing is sometimes shown by the word *staccato*, but more often by small dots placed over or under the notes:

The last note of a slur is frequently shortened, i.e. it is played *staccato*. This particularly applies when the slur is only over two or three notes. It may occur at a cadence in a feminine ending (a phrase ending on a weak beat), and then the last note should be played both shorter and softer.

Notes which are to be played *very* short are shown thus:

whereas notes which are nearly their full length are shown thus:

This last sign is also shown over repeated notes to indicate, in effect, that they are to be played as long as possible, just allowing time to make a fresh start to the next note:

These marks of *legato* and *staccato*, indicating how the music is to be performed, are sometimes called *phrasing marks*, and they are a feature of piano music. Do not confuse them with *phrase marks*, which are used to indicate the structure of the music, and are not concerned with methods of performance. E.g.:

Also, do not confuse them with bowing marks, which are used for string music. The sign ⁀ over two or more notes indicates that they are to be played with the same bow. But, of course, this means that they are also *legato;* and bowing marks are, in effect, phrasing marks, too.

Signs for *legato* and *staccato* are also found in vocal music.

Other signs found in music:

(a) 8va ┄┄┄┐ over notes indicates that they are to be played an octave higher, thus avoiding leger lines:

(b) 8*va bassa* under bass notes indicates that they are to be played an octave lower, thus again avoiding leger lines:

(c) *Con* 8 under notes indicates that the octave below the written note is to be played as *well;*

(d) A pause 𝄐, over or under a note or chord indicates that it can be held for an indefinite length.

(e) G.P., general pause, means that all the instruments or singers pause. It is often placed over a rest.

(f) *Arpeggio* chords are found in piano music. They imitate the harp by playing one note after another, starting with the lowest note, and are indicated thus:

(g) A metronome mark placed at the beginning of a piece of music, or wherever there is a change of speed, indicates how many pulse notes there are to be to the minute. This is measured by a metronome, an invention of Maelziel, a friend of Beethoven. So the speed is indicated thus: M.M. (Maelziel's metronome) 𝅗𝅥 = 92.

(h) Op. 65 is short for *opus* 65, and indicates that the music is the sixty-fifth work that the composer wrote and had published.

7 *Musical abbreviations*

Musical abbreviations save the time of the composer and of the printer, and they also save paper. The most common ones are:

(a) Repeat marks at the beginning and end of the section to be repeated:

(b) *D.C., da capo*, go back to the beginning.

(c) *D.S., dal segno*, go back to the sign, 𝄋 .

(d) 1 and 2 or ima volta and 2do volta or 1st time and 2nd time indicate a varied ending to a repeated section.

(e) If, as a result of a repetition, a piece of music ends in the middle of the music copy, the word *fine* (Italian for finish) is used to indicate the ending.

(f) Abbreviations found in orchestral music are:

(i) repeated notes or groups of notes. The number of strokes over or under the notes or through the stems indicate the length of the repetitions, one stroke meaning quavers, two strokes semiquavers, etc.

If the repetitions are very rapid and are played by string instruments the effect is called *tremolo* and it is highly exciting.

(ii) If a figure is to be repeated several times it is shown thus:

(iii) If an entire bar is to be repeated it is shown thus:

Exercise 71

Listen to any melody in Section 6 of this book, as it is played to you by your teacher, and insert expression marks according to the method of performance.

6 Phrase Lengths and Plans Melody Analysis

1 *Phrase lengths*

Phrases are usually two or four bars long.

It is usual, particularly in simple tunes and in dance forms, for every phrase to begin in the same part of the bar.

It is quite common for the end of one phrase and the beginning of the next to occur in the same bar, as in the gavotte above. Do not confuse the function of a phrase mark with that of a bar line.

The last few notes of a phrase make a *cadence*. There are different kinds of cadences, and some sound more finished than others, according to the chords with which the cadence is harmonised. (See Section 12, part 22.) If a melody is heard without harmony the chords are implied by the melody notes.

Compare the cadences at the end of each phrase of the following tune. The first phrase is unfinished and has an imperfect cadence; the second phrase is finished and has a perfect cadence.

A strong cadence (a *masculine ending*) ends upon a strong beat. A weaker, more graceful cadence (a *feminine ending*) ends upon a weak beat. Compare the following cadences:

2 *Phrase plans*

Most music contains a great deal of repetition. If a song consists of four phrases it is very unlikely that each phrase will be completely different, i.e. A B C D.

Here are some examples of very common phrase plans:

Exercise 72

Add phrase marks and letter the phrases (A B, etc.) in order to show the shape of the following tunes:

Exercise 73

State the phrase plans of melodies which are played by your teacher. (Suggestions: The Bonnie Briar Bush; Golden Slumbers; Drink to me only; Awake my Soul (tune Warrington); The Lincolnshire Poacher; All Things Bright and Beautiful (to tune of same name).

3 *Varied repetition*

The desire for repetition in music is very strong, because repetition gives shape to it, and makes it more easily understood and remembered. But there are many ways of varying the repetition, thus making the music more interesting. Here are some methods:

Decoration The repeated phrase is varied or decorated in some way.

Where the Bee Sucks. Arne

Sequence A phrase is repeated immediately at a higher or lower pitch.

Lillibulero

Rhythmic development A phrase often splits up into smaller sections, and then the same rhythm is often repeated with variations of pitch. In the following example there are no exact sequences, as the intervals are different at each repetition. But the whole eight bars is rhythmically developed from the first bar.

Minuet in F. Mozart

Inversion, augmentation and diminution Sometimes a phrase returns with the intervals falling where they rose before, and vice versa (*inversion*). Or it is contracted rhythmically by playing the notes more quickly (*diminution*), or expanded by making the notes longer (*augmentation*). These kind of devices occur frequently in contrapuntal music by composers such as Bach. But they occur surprisingly often in more modern music, or even in simple tunes.

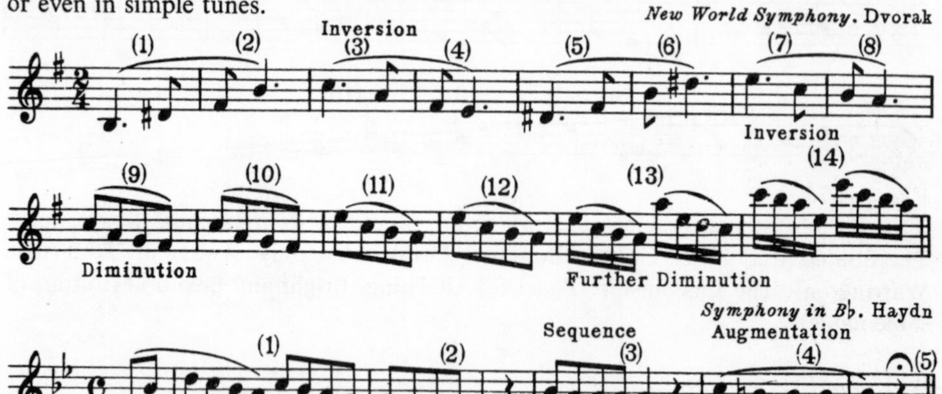

Phrase extension and contraction Sometimes a phrase is made longer or shorter than the rest of the phrases in a tune by extending or contracting it in some way. It is particularly common for the final phrase of a tune to be extended, perhaps by repeating or prolonging the cadence.

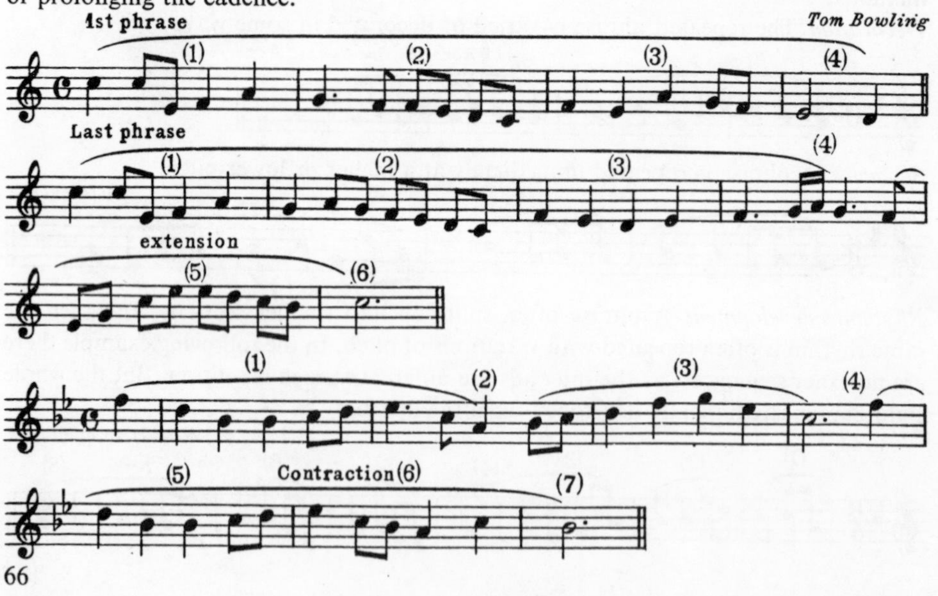

Exercise 74

Label the phrases of these melodies to show where the repetitions occur. Then point out any examples of varied repetition, explaining what the composer has done; and comment upon any unusual phrase lengths.

Violin Concerto. Mendelssohn
(d)
(1) (2) (3) (4) (5) (6)
(7) (8) (9) (10) (11) (12)
(13) (14) (15) (16) (17) (18)
(e)
(1) (2) (3) (4) (5)
(6) (7) (8) (9) (10) (11)
(12) (13) (14) (15) (16) (17) (18)
5th Symphony. Beethoven
(f)
(1) (2) (3) (4)
(5) (6) (7) (8) (9) (10) (11)
(12) (13) (14) (15) (16) (17)
(18) (19) (20) (21) (22)

Hark! hark the lark. Schubert

7 Melody Writing

1 *Writing an answer to a two-bar phrase*

(Study Section 6, part 1 beforehand.)

The simplest sort of a tune consists of two two-bar phrases, in the form of a question and answer. The following hints should help you in your first attempts to write tunes:

(a) *Hearing* Even though you find it difficult, try very hard to *hear* what you write.

(b) *The Phrase* Conceive a phrase as a musical thought. Do not think of one note at a time, any more than you think of one word at a time. The only way to do this is to sing the complete phrase, either aloud or mentally, memorise it, and then write it down as if it were a dictation test.

(c) *Leaps* Even small leaps can sometimes sound ungainly. You can write any leap if you are sure you have heard it, like it, and can write it correctly. But if in doubt it is perhaps wise, in the early stages, to avoid leaps larger than a third unless they are part of the tonic or dominant chords. In any case, many beautiful tunes move largely by step. Augmented intervals (see Section 4, parts 3 and 5) usually sound ungainly, though you may occasionally want them for a particular tune.

(d) *Phrase endings* Your tune is more likely to sound satisfactory if you keep to masculine endings (see Section 6, part 1) when you first start to write tunes. Most tunes end on the tonic.

(e) *Rhythm* The rhythmic style does not usually change in a short tune. If the first phrase starts anacrusically on the third beat of a bar the second phrase will probably do the same. (See Section 6, part 1.)

Exercise 75

Write answers to the following phrases, working as many questions as are appropriate to your needs:

2 *An eight-bar melody, using repetition*

(Study Section 6, part 2 beforehand.)
The simplest kind of eight-bar tune consists of A B A B, with the first B sounding unfinished and the second B slightly changed at the cadence so as to end on the tonic.

A B A C is also a very natural scheme. (See ' London Bridge ', Section 6, part 2.)
A B C A is quite common, provided that the ending of the second A is modified so to make it sound finished.

A B C B is another possiblity, but again the endings of B must be different each time.

When the plan A A B A is used (as in ' All through the Night ') A usually ends on the tonic each time it occurs. This brings the perfect cadences too close together to be suitable for a melody of less than sixteen bars. But the plan can be used for an eight-bar melody if the ending of A is modified each time it occurs—though it is less suitable than the other plans just mentioned.

Exercise 76
Take the beginnings given in exercise 75 and write eight-bar melodies on the plans A B A B, A B A C, A B C A, or A B C B. Some of these beginnings will also work on the plan A A B A , if you modify the endings of A each time.

3 *An eight-bar melody, using varied repetition*

(Study Section 6, part 3 beforehand.)
One of the best ways of learning how to write melodies is to study the tunes written by the great composers. Analyse the melodies in Section 6, part 3; and take the opportunity to study any other tunes which you play or sing yourself. Then practice the devices referred to in Section 6, part 3 by taking one of the beginnings given in exercise 75 and using whatever devices seem appropriate to the tune. It is helpful to take the same beginning over and over again, and see in how many ways it can be treated.

Here are three melodies beginning with exercise 75(a), illustrating some of these devices:

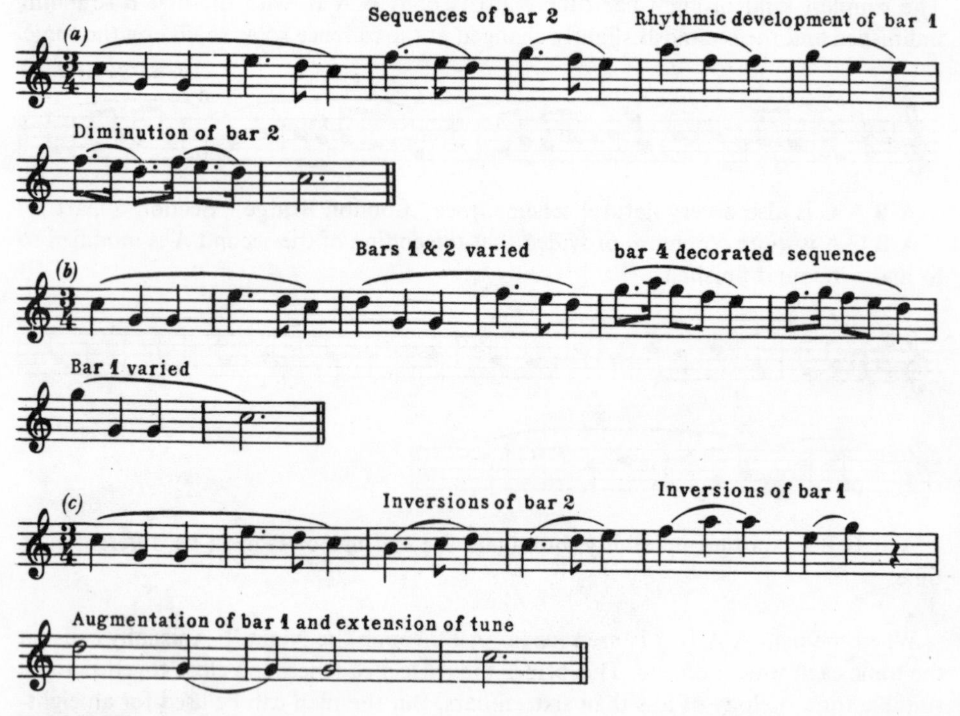

Exercise 77
Take some of the beginnings given in exercise 75 and write eight-bar melodies using some of the devices mentioned above. They can be a bar longer or shorter if you can manage to use extension or contraction convincingly.

Melodies of twelve or sixteen bars usually contain at least one modulation. Advice on how to write such melodies is given in section 10, parts 3 and 4.

8 Melody Writing to Words

1 *Word spacing Syllabic division Note grouping*

Word Spacing When writing a tune to words the notes have to be written further apart than usual, in order to allow room for the syllables, which should be placed *exactly* under the notes to which they belong.

Write the words in a straight line, not too close to the stave, so as to allow room for any low notes below the stave, and for expression marks.

Syllabic division Every syllable makes a fresh sound, so it requires at least one note. Listen to the way you say words, in order to decide how many syllables come in each word. Here are some examples of syllabic division: wel-come; si-lent; sil-ly; wan-dered; lone-ly; re-turned; un-twist-ed (compare the use of the 'ed' ending in the latter two); strength-ened; fier-y (2, not 3); ev-ery (2 not 3); vio-let (2, not 3); us-ual 2, not 3); beau-ti-ful; con-so-la-tion; do-min-ion (3, not 4).

Notice that a hyphen is always used between the syllables of the same word.

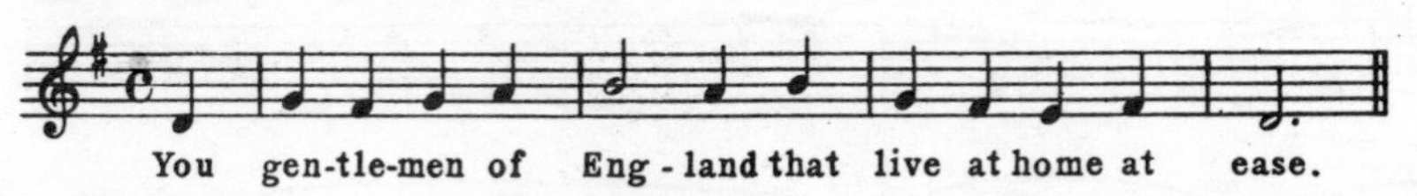

If you want to write more than one note to the same syllable, put the whole syllable under the first note, dashes under the following notes, and a slur over the top, thus:

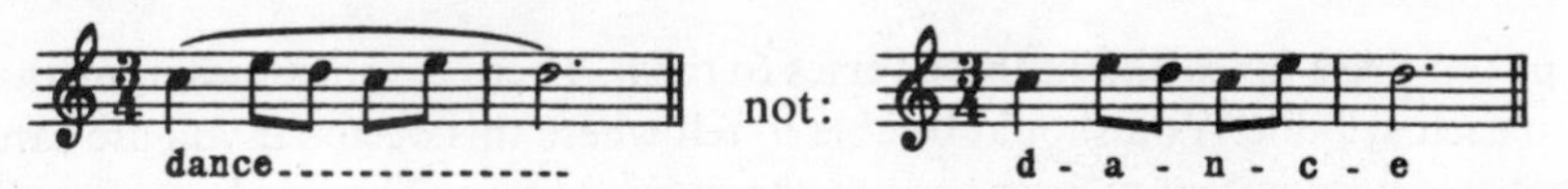

Note grouping It used to be the custom to separate stems if they were to be sung to separate syllables, even though they belonged to the same beat, thus:

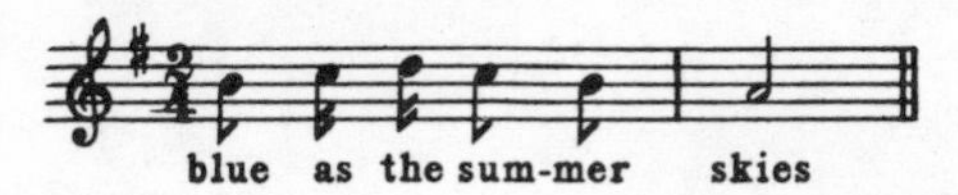

You may still come across older copies of music which do this. But more recently it has become the custom to follow the ordinary rules of note grouping, thus:

This has the advantage of showing clearly which notes belong to the same beat; and providing that the notes are spaced well apart and that the syllables are written exactly under their own notes, the result is quite clear.

Exercise 78

1 Copy out these tunes and fit these verses to them, putting each syllable exactly under its own note. There is one note to each syllable:

(a) Tomorrow at the garden gate
I will wait for you.

(b) Amongst the princely paragons,
Bedecked with dainty diamonds,
Within mine eyes, none doth come nigh
The sweet red rose of England.

T. Deloney

2 Copy out these tunes and fit these verses to them. There is sometimes more than one note to each syllable. You should be able to tell where this occurs if you are careful to see that the word accent corresponds to the music accent. The bar lines come before the words that are marked with an accent.

(a) Spríng the sweet spríng
Is the yéar's pleasant kíng;
Then bloóms each thíng,
Then maíds dance in a ríng.

T. Nashe

(b) In the hóur of mý distréss,
When temptátions mé oppréss,
And when Í my síns conféss,
Sweet spírit, cómfort mé.

Herrick

2 *Writing a rhythm to a verse of poetry*

(Study Section 6, part 1 and Section 7, part 1 beforehand.)

Words carry a natural accent of their own, just as rhythmic patterns do in music. You will have realised this in working exercise 78.

When you read either prose or poetry aloud you probably accentuate the words quite correctly. So all you have to do, in setting a verse to a rhythm, is to be aware of what you say and translate it into musical rhythm.

Read the following lines aloud. Then write them out, dividing the words into syllables, and marking the accents, thus, , over the strong syllables.

The sun doth arise
And make happy the skies.
The merry bells ring
To welcome the spring.

W. Blake

If you have read them correctly you will have put the accent on the second syllable on ' arise ' and on the first on ' happy ', ' merry ' and ' welcome '. And you will not have an accent on the first syllable of any line.

You will also discover that you have got two accents in every line, so it will be quite natural to have two bars of musical rhythm to every line, and therefore to write two-bar phrases. Write a rhythm to these words.

Here are three rhythmic settings to these words. Two of them are good, one is bad. Say them aloud to the given musical rhythm, in order to decide which is the poor one. Then compare the good ones with your version. There are usually many rhythmic versions possible to any set of words. But if a version produces false accents it is obviously wrong.

In the kinds of verse you are likely to be asked to set you will find that there are usually two or four main accents in many, if not most, of the lines, so each line will naturally make a two-bar or four-bar phrase. If you find there are three main accents it will still be wise to spread the rhythm over two or four bars, probably by having a long note or a rest at the end of each line, as in exercise 78, 2(b). Three-bar phrases usually sound unnatural.

Be careful about the subordinate accents, too, so as to be sure that the words can be said or sung in a natural speech rhythm.

For example: $\frac{3}{4}$ How do you like to go up in a swing is good;

while $\frac{2}{4}$ How do you like to go up in a swing is poor, though the main accents, and therefore the bar lines, occur in the same places in each version.

Exercise 79

Write a rhythm to each of the following verses:

(a) March brings breezes loud and shrill,
Stirs the dancing daffodil,

Sara Coleridge

(b) He who shall hunt the little wren
Shall never be beloved by men.

Blake

(c) The rain had fallen, the poet arose,
He passed by the town and out of the street,
A light wind blew from the gates of the sun,
And waves of shadow went over the wheat.

Tennyson

(d) We'll plant a cornflower on his grave,
And a grain of the bearded barley,
And a little bluebell to ring his knell,
And daisies, crimson and pearly.

T. Westwood

(e) The honeysuckle waits
For summer and for heat,
But violets in the chilly spring
Make the turf so sweet.

C. Rossetti

3 *Writing a melody to a verse of poetry*

(Some study of Sections 6 and 7 should have been made beforehand.)
Here are some points to note in setting a verse of poetry to a melody:
(a) *Range* Keep the singer in mind, and write within his or her range, avoiding high notes on awkward syllables.
(b) *Melodic Line* Follow the suggestions given in Section 7, part 1.
(c) *Phrase length* Keep to two-bar or four-bar phrases. (Study Section 6, part 1.)
(d) *Repetition* Your melody should contain some repetition, in order to make a satisfactory tune. It may be in the form of simple repetition, following a phrase plan such as A B A C, as illustrated in Section 6, part 2; or it may contain varied repetition, perhaps developing an idea in one of the ways shown in Section 6, part 3.

The words will frequently suggest the best method. For example, in ' Ring out wild bells ', exercise 80, 2(a), below, the rhyming lines can perhaps use the same melodic idea; and ' The flying cloud, the frosty light ' may suggest the use of a sequence. Lines which have the same number of strong accents may pair off together—look at exercise 80, 2(b), ' The night is come ', below, with this in mind. ' To grass or leaf ', exercise 80, 2(c), below, suggests an extension at the end of the verse.

Exercise 80

1 Write melodies to the rhythms you have already written to the verses given in exercise 79. (By attending to the rhythm first you are more likely to write a satisfactory tune.)

2 Write a melody to each of the verses given below:

(a) Ring out, wild bells, to the wild sky,
The flying cloud, the frosty light:
The year is dying in the night;
Ring out, wild bells, and let him die.

Tennyson

(b) The night is come, but not too soon,
And sinking silently,
All silently the little moon
Drops down behind the sky.

Longfellow

(c) To grass, or leaf, or fruit, or wall,
The snail sticks close, nor fears to fall,
As if he grew there, house and all
Together.

W. Cowper

(d) The rivers rush into the sea
By castle and town they go;
The winds behind them merrily
Their noisy trumpets blow.

Longfellow

(e) How beautiful is the rain!
After the dust and heat
In the broad and fiery street
In the narrow lane,
How beautiful is the rain.

Longfellow

9 Transposition

1 *Definition of transposition*

When a piece of music is completely raised or lowered into a higher or lower key, it is said to be transposed.

2 *Uses of transposition*

Transposition has many uses.

Sometimes a *singer* wishes to sing a song in a higher or lower key. It is easy for him to do this, but harder for the accompanist, who has to find and play a different set of notes from those printed on the copy.

Sometimes a *choir* wishes to sing in a higher or lower key. A resourceful teacher or choir trainer may raise the pitch of a song, hymn tune or anthem without telling the choir on a dull or foggy day, or in a stuffy room, if the choir is tending to sing flat. Or he may perhaps lower it, to suit adolescent boys' or men's voices, who find it too high. Again it is easy for the choir, but difficult for the accompanist, if there is an accompaniment.

Some *wood wind and brass instrumentalists* read music in one key and play it in another. This is due to the historical development of the particular instrument, which is explained in part 6 of this section. It is easy for the players, as the composer does the transposing for them. But the score reader has to transpose their part back into the key of the piece, if he wishes to know exactly what notes they are playing. For *score readers*, then, an understanding of transposition is essential.

3 *How to transpose*

For all musicians except singers, who have no keys to manipulate, transposition means seeing the music written in one key and realising what the notes should be in another key. A few gifted instrumentalists may be able to transpose straight on to their instrument. But most people need to have the transposition written out.

But whether you try to transpose directly on to an instrument, or whether you work it out on paper, the method is the same. You must think of the notes in their *relationship* to the original key, and then think of them with the same relationship in the new key. If, for example, you see  in key C, you must think of them as tonic, mediant and dominant (or doh, me soh, which is quicker and easier) and then think of them as tonic, mediant, dominant, doh me soh, in the new key. Therefore in the key of D they would be  and in key E♭ .

When writing out the transposition, the best method is to write the sol-fa names under each note of the tune to be transposed, and then translate them into the pitch names of the new key, writing each note exactly under its own sol-fa name.

4 *Transposing a diatonic melody*

Look at the following example:

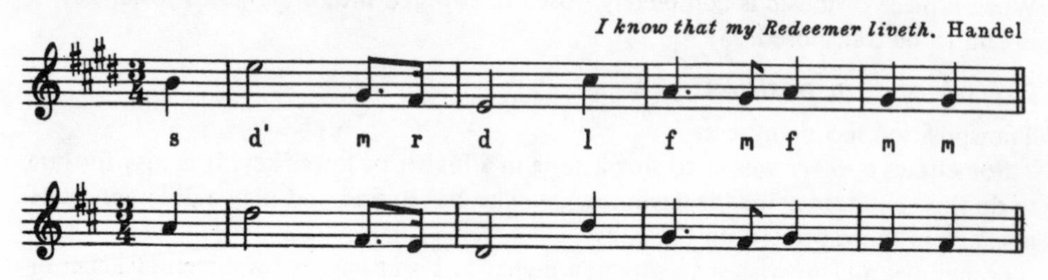

Exercise 81

Work any of the following exercises which are appropriate to your needs. Exercises (a) to (f) are diatonic major; (g) and (h) are diatonic minor; and (i) and (j) use alto and tenor clefs.

(a) Transpose this tune into the keys of (1) E♭; (2) G; (3) C.

(b) Transpose this tune into the keys of (1) D; (2) G; (3) A♭.

(c) Transpose tune (a), ‘ Polly Oliver ’, into the key (1) a minor third higher; (2) a major third lower. (Find the new key by carefully naming the required interval above or below D; and then think in the new key, as before.)

(d) Transpose tune (b) ‘ Some Talk of Alexander ’ into the key (i) a perfect fourth higher; (ii) a major second lower.

(e) Transpose this tune into the key (i) a major third higher; (ii) a minor third lower. In each case use a key signature instead of accidentals. (Name the original key first. Then write the sol-fa names underneath each note and from these write out the tune in the new key.)

(f) Transpose this tune (i) a minor third lower, using a key signature; (ii) into the key of B♭ without a signature. Name the original key first.

The Minstrel Boy

(g) Transpose this tune (i) into the subdominant key; (ii) into D minor; (iii) into the key a tone lower.

Sonata in C minor Mozart

(h) Transpose this tune (i) a perfect fourth lower, using a key signature; (ii) a major third higher, without a key signature.

The Miller of the Dee

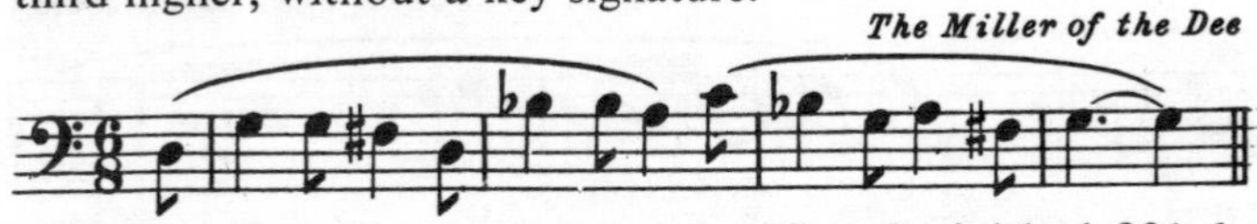

(i) Transpose tune (e) ' Fairest Isle ' (i) a diminished fifth lower and use the tenor clef; (ii) into the key of D♭ major and use the alto clef.
(j) Transpose tune (h) ' The Miller of the Dee ' (i) into the dominant key, using the alto clef; (ii) into the subdominant key, using the tenor clef. Name the new key, and use a key signature, in each case.

5 *Transposing a chromatic melody*

Study the following example, with particular reference to the notes at (a), (b), (c) and (d):
(a) F♯ in key C becomes E♮ in key B♭. A sharp does not always remain a sharp in another key.
(b) B♭ in key C is taw, the flattened leading note. In key B♭ it must be written as A♭, not G♯, because A♯ is the sharpened submediant and not the flattened leading note. If you are transposing by interval and not thinking in a key, you might make this mistake.
(c) B♮ in bar three has a natural before the B because it is contradicting the B♭ in the previous bar. But it is te, a diatonic note in the key of C, not a chromatic note. When you write this out in key B♭ you may forget that it requires an accidental. Realise that where there is an accidental in the original tune there is bound to be an accidental in the transposed version—provided that both use key signatures—though it may not be the same kind of accidental. Compare (a) above, where a sharp becomes a natural.
(d) D at the end of bar three is top ray, r' not r. Mark the correct octave by the sol-fa

name, and there is less chance of writing a note in the wrong octave by mistake. But always make a final check that the tune is following the same contour.

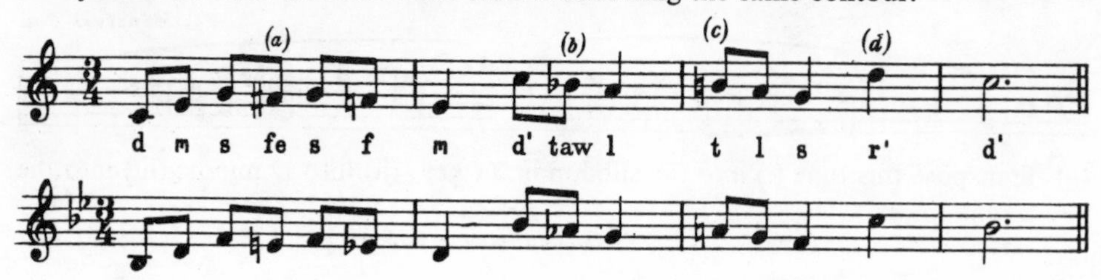

Exercise 82

(a) Transpose this tune (i) into the key of B major; (ii) a tone lower.

Spring Song Mendelssohn

(b) Name the key of the following passage. Then transpose it a major tenth lower and use the bass clef. Name the key of the transposed version.

Dance of the Sugar Plum Fairy Tchaikovsky

6 *Transposing instruments*

(a) *Woodwind Instruments* At one time it was difficult or impossible for clarinets to play in keys with many sharps or flats. To overcome this difficulty clarinets were made in many different sizes, which transposed the melody into different keys. The composer chose the size that would give the player an easy key, and transposed the part accordingly, so that the result would sound in the same key as the rest of the orchestra.

But so that players could play different sizes of clarinets equally well they always associated a certain finger and key-hole with the same note on the staff, even though it sounded different on different instruments.

The clarinets in regular use today are made in B♭ or A for orchestras, and military bands use the smaller, E♭, size in addition. In each case their notation assumes that C is their natural scale. So a clarinet player with a B♭ instrument, seeing

will play what he calls C E G, though the resulting sound will be

Similarly these notes played on an A clarinet will result in  and on

an E♭ clarinet will result in

In order to allow for this, clarinet parts for a B♭ instrument are always written, with the key signature of the new key, a tone higher than they sound; clarinets in A a minor third higher; and clarinets in E♭ a minor third lower. In this way they will sound in the same key as the other instruments in the score.

Orchestral music in sharp keys is usually written for the A clarinet and in flat keys for the B♭ clarinet, because this results in fewer sharps or flats in the key signature, and is therefore easier to play.

The score reader should realise that in a symphony in E the clarinet player plays in E, though the part, for the A clarinet is written in G; and that in a symphony in E♭ the clarinet plays in E♭ though the part, for the B♭ clarinet, is written in F. In each case the clarinet is really playing in the same key as the violins, so look at the violins' key signature, in order to see what transposition is required. In other words, as long as you can see the whole score, it is relatively easy to realise what the clarinet is really playing. But if you are asked to write a part for clarinet in isolation or to read a clarinet part at the pitch it really sounds, then you must fall back on the principles given two paragraphs above.

You will realise that what makes things easier for the clarinet player makes it harder for the composer, and for anyone who wants to read an orchestral score.

Fortunately flutes, oboes and bassoons do not transpose. But piccolos play an octave higher than their part is written, partly because this means the piccolo player can use the same fingering as he uses for the flute, and partly to avoid leger lines, as the range of the piccolo is very high.

Similarly a cor anglais part is written a fifth higher than it sounds so that an oboe player can use the same fingering, because a cor anglais is built a fifth lower than an oboe.

A bass clarinet part is written on the treble stave as if it were meant for an ordinary clarinet in B♭ or A. But the instrument is pitched an octave lower, so the resulting sound is a ninth or tenth lower.

(b) *Brass Instruments* The natural sounds that any brass instruments can play are the notes of the harmonic series. Here they are in the key of C.

The part of the series that the instrument actually plays depends upon the pitch of the instrument: the trumpet plays the high notes, the horn the middle notes.

Formerly horn and trumpet players who wished to play notes that were not in this natural harmonic series used to add or remove pieces of tubing, called *crooks*, to alter the length of the instrument and so produce a harmonic series in another key; and this took a little time to do. They were therefore unable to play

The player was told by the composer at the beginning of the score what crook he was to use: for example, horns in D, trumpets in E. But his part was written without key signature, as if it were in the key of C, and his transposing was done for him by means of the crook.

Horns always transposed downwards. But trumpets transposed up or down, according to which was the nearest to C. So trumpets in D transposed upwards, trumpets in B♭ downwards. Therefore a part written thus: would sound thus: (a) horn in B♭ ; (b) trumpet in B♭ ; (c) trumpet in D ; (d) horn in D

In older scores horn and trumpet parts were usually crooked in the key of the piece. For example, horns in E♭ were used for a symphony in E♭, which meant that they played the harmonic series of E♭, resulting in sounds a major sixth lower than the series shown above in the key of C.

But in the nineteenth century a simpler method was discovered, that of adding *valves* to pieces of tubing which were permanently attached to the instrument. These valves could be opened or closed immediately, and so alter the harmonic series from one note to the next. From now onwards, horns and trumpets could play a complete scale in any part of their range.

So it should no longer be necessary for horns and trumpets to transpose. But unfortunately they still usually do so, because composers prefer to write for horns in F and trumpets in B♭. So a horn part in F sounds a fifth lower than it looks, and a trumpet part in B♭ sounds a tone lower. Accidentals are usually added as required, and not put in the key signature.

Fortunately trombones and tubas do not transpose. Trombones have always had a slide mechanism by which they could easily change the pitch of the harmonic series; and tubas are comparatively recent instruments which never went through a stage of using crooks, so exact sounds have always been written for these valve instruments.

Exercise 83

(a) This tune is written for horn in E. Rewrite it at the pitch it actually sounds.

New World Symphony Dvorak

(b) This tune is written for flute. Rewrite it (i) for clarinet in B♭, (ii) for clarinet in A, so that it sounds the same as in the flute, in each case.

New World Symphony Dvorak

(c) This tune is written for clarinet in A. Rewrite it for violin so that it sounds the same.

Hebrides Overture Mendelssohn

10 Modulation

(Lack of space prevents the inclusion of as many examples and exercises in this section as are desirable. But as examination requirements are all different it is advisable, in any case, to make use of questions set in previous papers of the examination concerned, and to let these be the main source of supply.)

1 *Definition of modulation*

When music changes key during the course of a piece the result is called *modulation*. If you listen to the following tune, which begins and ends in key C, you will realise that it is not in the key of C at the end of the second phrase: it has modulated to the key of G. You will notice that there is an F♯ in place of an F, so that, in the second phrase, the tune is using the notes of the key of G, and not C. But the essential thing to realise is that the musical centre of gravity has shifted—the tonic is C during the first phrase and G during the second.

2 *Uses of modulation*

Only the shortest and simplest pieces of music stay in one key all the time. Any longer piece would become very monotonous without modulation. Composers make skilful use of modulation to give variety and interest to their music.

3 *Modulation from a major key to its dominant major*

The most natural modulation for a piece of music in a major key is to modulate to its dominant major—for example, from C major to G major, as in 'Polly Oliver' above. You will realise that only one note needs to be changed—F has to become F♯. But the music does not sound finished until it has returned to the tonic key.

If you wish to modulate when composing tunes decide first *where* you wish to modulate. In a twelve-bar tune the middle four-bar phrase can be entirely in the new key. In a sixteen-bar tune either the second or the third phrase can be in the new key, but not both, because too long in the new key might make you lose the sense of the tonic key as being the key centre. In any tune you must first establish the tonic key; and you must give yourself time to re-establish the tonic key at the end.

The method is simple: get the new tonic into your head and think in the new key. In, for example, ' Polly Oliver ' sing G after the first phrase, thinking of it first as soh in key C and then mentally change it to doh in key G. Sing d m s m d in the new key to yourself, to establish the key, if necessary. Then sing the next phrase in the new key. Make a similar adjustment in your head when you return to the tonic key. Sing ' Polly Oliver ' to the sol-fa names given above the tune, to help you to feel the process.

It is helpful to move towards a perfect cadence at the end of the phrase in the new key—probably te doh or ray doh. It will not sound too finished, because it is obviously not the home tonic.

It is also easier if, when writing your first tunes which modulate, you return straight away to the tonic key at the beginning of the next phrase, by using melody notes which imply V I in the tonic key.

Exercise 84

Write (a) twelve-bar melodies; (b) sixteen-bar melodies beginning thus, including a modulation to the dominant in each case.

4 *Modulation from a minor key to its relative major*

When in a minor key the most natural key to which to modulate is the relative major. Sing the air from ' Susanna ' given below to sol-fa names, in order to feel the change of key.

The process of working is exactly the same as when writing a tune which modulates to the dominant from a major key. But realise that, in this case, instead of adding an accidental, you take one away. In the above tune G minor requires an F♯ in addition to the signature; but B♭ major coincides entirely with the signature.

Exercise 85

Write (a) twelve-bar melodies; (b) sixteen-bar melodies, beginning thus, including a modulation to the relative major in each case.

5 *Modulation from a major key to its three most closely related keys*

If music in a major key contains more than one modulation the other two most likely modulations, in addition to the dominant major, are to the relative minor and to the subdominant major. The main modulation will probably still be to the dominant major, which will very likely occur half way through, and end with a perfect cadence. Modulation to the relative minor might occur before or after this; but modulation to the subdominant major usually occurs towards the end.

Study the Bach Gavotte given below, which is a typical example of a key scheme in binary form.

Gavotte from French Suite in G. Bach

Modulation to the relative minor and to no other key is comparatively rare—'Come lasses and lads' is an illustration of it; and modulation to the subdominant as the only key is practically unknown.

A piece of music containing modulation to two or three keys will probably be longer and more elaborate than you are likely to be asked to compose. But you should be able to recognise and enjoy the modulations in other people's compositions.

(a) *Visual Recognition* If you are required to recognise changes of key in a written melody first name the keys to which it is likely to modulate. Then look for the accidentals which would produce these changes of key, and also for the melody notes implying perfect cadences in these keys. A modulation may occur without an accidental being present in the melody, but you should be able to feel the change of key at the cadence. A melodic line falling by step often leads to a new tonic. Compare bars four and eight in exercise 86(c).

Exercise 86

Name the modulations which occur in these melodies, giving the bar number in each case.

(b) *Aural Recognition* You may also be required to recognise these three modulations from a major key centre in a piece of music which is played to you, by aural recognition only.

Modulation to the dominant sounds bright and natural; and there is a strong desire to return immediately to the tonic key. Therefore, if you sing soh doh of the original key to yourself after you have heard this modulation, it will follow on very naturally.

Modulation to the subdominant sounds rather heavier and it is very much less common. There is no great desire to return to the tonic key immediately, as you will discover if you apply the soh doh test mentioned above.

Modulation to the relative minor is easy to recognise, if it is the only minor key you expect to be given: you will hear a minor tonic chord at the end.

You will soon learn to recognise these three modulations by their general effect, as each is so different. But you can also check by keeping the original tonic in your mind and then mentally singing up or down from it by step to the new tonic.

Exercise 87

Recognise modulations from a major key to the three most closely related keys, in passages which are played to you by your teacher. (They may modulate to a single key, or one passage may contain several modulations, according to examination requirements. Previously set examination papers are the best source of material for this test.)

6 *Modulation from a minor key to its three most closely related keys*

The three most closely related keys to a minor key centre are its relative major, its dominant minor and its subdominant minor.

All three together occur comparatively rarely in a short piece, but here is a simple example:

Modulation to the relative major is most likely to be the main modulation and to carry the main cadence in the middle of the piece, though it may actually occur anywhere. Modulation to the dominant is much rarer than when starting in a major key; and modulation to the subdominant is more common towards the end of the piece.

(a) *Visual Recognition* Accidentals and cadences will help you to recognise a modulation visually, as before.

Exercise 88

Name the modulations which occur in these melodies, giving the bar number in each case.

(b) *Aural Recognition* Modulation to the relative major is very much more common than the other two, and is easy to recognise aurally because it is the only one of the three which ends in a major key. But a modulation to the dominant minor sometimes ends with a major chord (a Picardy third), because by this means it can more easily return to the tonic key.

If you keep the original tonic in your mind and then sing up or down from it to the new tonic you should be able to state the new key.

Exercise 89

As for exercise 87, but the passages will start from a minor key.

7 *Modulation from a major key to its five most closely related keys*

Music can modulate from any key to any of the other twenty-three major or minor keys, but some are much more closely related than others. Modulation to the nearly-related keys sounds natural and it is easy to get home again to the original key; whereas modulation to remote keys always comes as a surprise—though sometimes a very delightful one—and unless skilfully managed by the composer there is a danger of losing the feeling of the original tonic key.

It is generally considered that the five most closely related keys from any major or minor key are those which have not more than one sharp or flat more or less in the key signature. When starting from a major key these keys are the dominant and subdominant major and the relative minors of all three keys. Here are the related keys from C major:

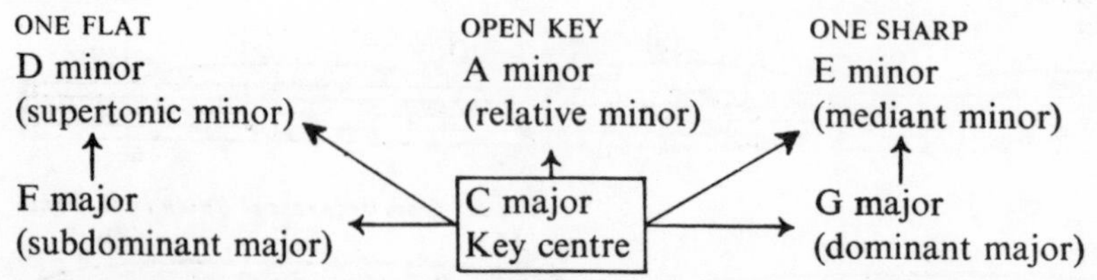

It is easy to think of these as: fah and soh major; ray, me and lah minor. This can be applied to any major key centre. Make a list of the related keys to other major keys, for practice.

Here are examples of modulation to the supertonic minor and the mediant minor, the two relationships which are new. They would be unlikely to occur as the only modulation in a piece of music, but would be part of a scheme including several modulations.

Bach and Handel rarely modulated to any key other than the five related keys mentioned above. Haydn and Mozart occasionally ventured further afield; and Beethoven and Schubert sometimes produced beautiful effects by means of unexpected modulations. Wagner wandered freely over the 24 keys; and some modern composers no longer write with a key centre at all.

(a) *Visual Recognition*

Exercise 90

Name the modulations which occur in these melodies, giving the bar number in each case.

(b) *Aural Recognition*

Exercise 91
Recognise modulations from a major key to any of the five most closely related keys in suitable passages played by your teacher.

8 *Modulation from a minor key to the five most closely related keys*

The five most closely related keys to a minor key centre are the dominant and sub-dominant minor and the relative majors of all three keys. Here are the related keys from C minor:

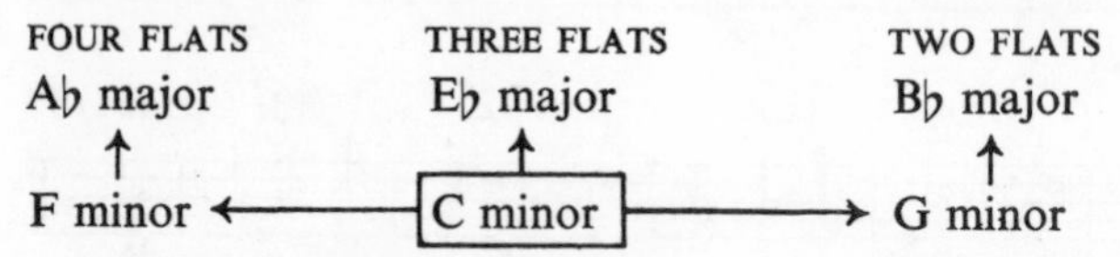

Make a list of the related keys to some other minor keys, for practice.

Here are examples of the two modulations which have not been illustrated before:

(a) *Visual Recognition*

Exercise 92
Name the modulations which occur in these melodies, giving the bar number in each case:

(b) *Aural Recognition*

Exercise 93

Recognise modulations from a minor key to any of the five most closely related keys in suitable passages played by your teacher.

11 Ornaments

1 *Definition of musical ornaments*

As their name implies, ornaments in music decorate a melody by adding extra notes to it. Another name for them is ' grace notes '. Some of them are written in smaller print than the main notes of the melody; others are shown by means of special signs. In all cases, the note values of the main melody notes are written as if the ornaments were not there, and the extra notes comprising the ornament are taken from the length of the main note which is being ornamented.

Each ornament has a precise meaning, as far as the additional *notes* required are concerned, But the *speed* at which they are played or sung depends upon the speed and style of the music, and sometimes it is impossible to show it in exact note lengths. Also the performer is allowed a certain amount of latitude, and different performers may play or sing the same ornament in different ways. A modern composer who wishes his ornaments to be performed in a particular way will write the ornament out in full. Also many editions write out the ornaments in full in a footnote, as a suggestion to the performer.

An ornament, then, is meant to be performed rather than written out on paper. But, in spite of this, some Examining Boards require candidates to write out onaments in full. So questions of this type are given here.

2 *The appoggiatura*

An appoggiatura is a ' leaning note '. It is written as a small note before the melody note on which it leans. Its stems are often written the opposite way to the main note, and the two notes are joined with a slur, thus: 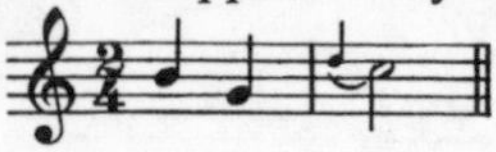 . The appoggiatura usually takes half the length of the main note, provided the main note is not dotted, but it frequently takes two-thirds of a dotted note. So  =  and  =  but  would be

Ultimately the performer should judge what is musically right.

Composers of the seventeenth and eighteenth centuries wrote appoggiatures thus, so as to show that the large note was the main, chord note. But modern editions of old music and modern composers usually write out appoggiatures in full.

Exercise 94

Write out the following in full:

(*a*) (*b*) (*c*)

3 *The acciaccatura*

The only differences between the appoggiatura and the acciaccatura are that the acciaccatura is written with a line through its stem, thus: , and it is performed as quickly as possible. So would be performed approximately if *presto*, and if *largo*. Another way of writing the latter is , in which the second note has as many dots as the first has extra hooks. Both methods of notation are correct, so use tied notes or dots, whichever you prefer. But be sure that the total length adds up to the length of the main note.

Although an acciaccatura is *written* as if it occurs at the beginning of the beat, in performance it is usually played just before the beat, and the principle note therefore retains the accent.

Acciaccaturas are still written as grace notes by modern composers, probably because it is frequently impossible to write them in full in notes of exact length. Also writing out in full often looks clumsy.

Exercise 95

Write out the following in full:

4 *The mordent*

There are two forms of mordent: (a) the upper mordent or *pralltriller*, written thus, and performed thus: and (b) the inverted mordent, written thus: and performed thus: .

Again, the speed of performance of the added notes depends upon the speed and style of the music, and the judgment of the performer, though the alternation is always rapid. Again, the last note can be written as a dotted or a tied note: or

Sometimes an accidental is written above or below the ornament, as an indication of a required modification of the added note: =

Exercise 96

Write out the following in full:

5 *The turn*

There are also two forms of the turn: (a) the ordinary turn, written thus: and performed thus: and the inverted turn, written thus: and performed thus: . The speed of the turn, and the length of the first note before the turn is started, again depend upon the speed and style of the music, and the judgment of the performer. But a turn is usually a leisurely kind of ornament, and there is no hurry to start it.

It is, however, usual to end the turn on the dot, if a note is dotted, in simple time, thus:

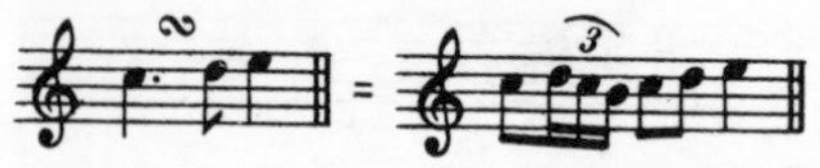

Accidentals above or below the turn affect the upper or lower note, as with mordents.

Sometimes a turn is placed *over* a note, instead of *after* it; and, in that case, the main note is not sounded at the beginning: the turn starts straight away:

Exercise 97

Write out the following in full:

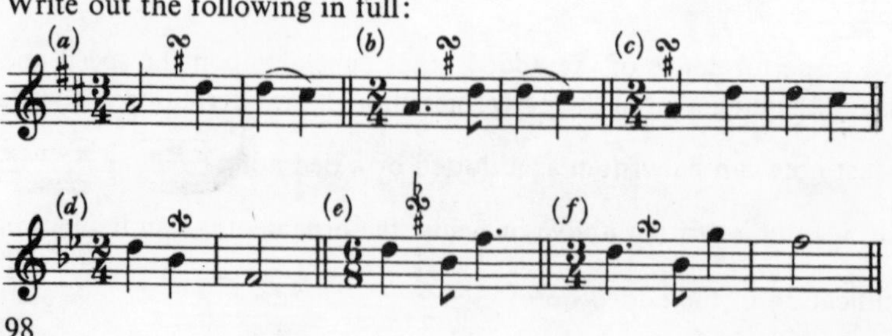

6 *The trill*

The trill, or shake, is written thus: [note with *tr*] and consists of the rapid alternation of the written note with the next scale note above, ending with the written note. The number of alternations depends upon the speed of the music and the skill of the performer. A trill over a short note, performed at a quick speed, may consist of nothing more than a mordent [example] might be performed: [example], whereas [example] might be [example].

A trill very often ends with a turn and this is usually indicated thus: [example], performed [example] or [example].

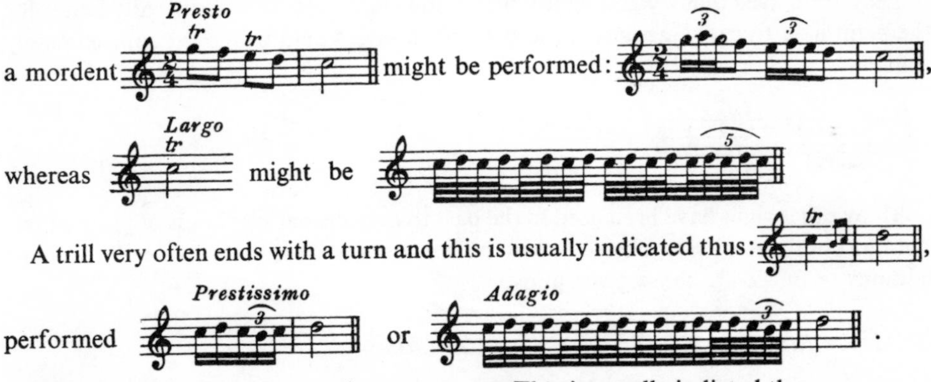

Sometimes a trill begins on the upper note. This is usually indicted thus:

If the note to be trilled is preceded by another note of the same pitch, and particularly if the music is by an early composer, such as Bach, it is usual to start with the upper note, whether it is indicated by a preliminary acciaccatura or not. Eighteenth century composers usually intended their trills to begin with the upper note, wherever they occurred.

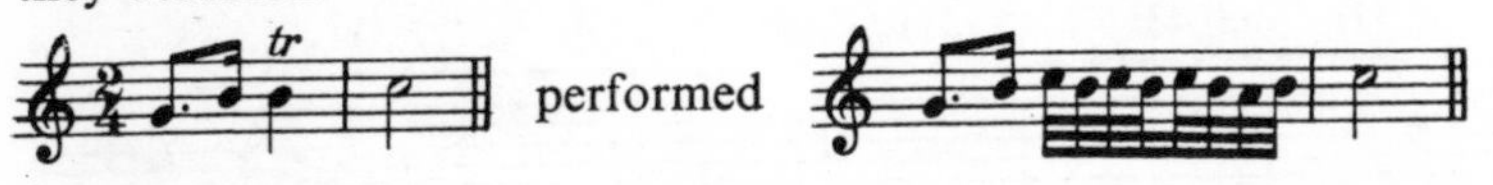

Exercise 98

Write out the following in full:

7 *Other grace notes*

Groups of two or three small notes are often written before a melody note, thus:

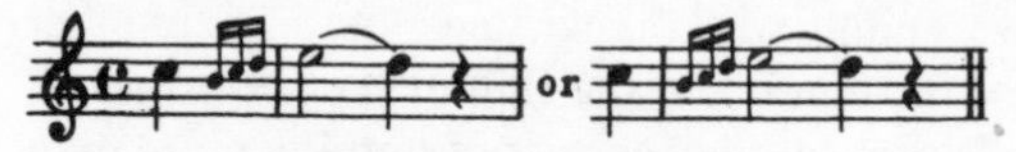

They are played quickly and lightly before the main note, and it is usually better for the main note to carry the accent. So both the above would be played approximately thus:

Many other signs have been used in the past to indicate various kinds of grace notes, but most of them are now obsolete; and the only ones you are likely to meet in modern editions of music are those given above.

8 *Miscellaneous exercises on ornaments*

If you are asked to write out passages containing ornaments in full take care that your note grouping is correct and that you have written the right number and length of notes to equal the main note. It is mainly a question of arithmetic.

Exercise 99

(a) Copy the following tune and add ornaments at the places marked: (1) turn; (2) trill; (3) acciaccatura; (4) appoggiatura; (5) mordent. Then write out the tune again, in full.

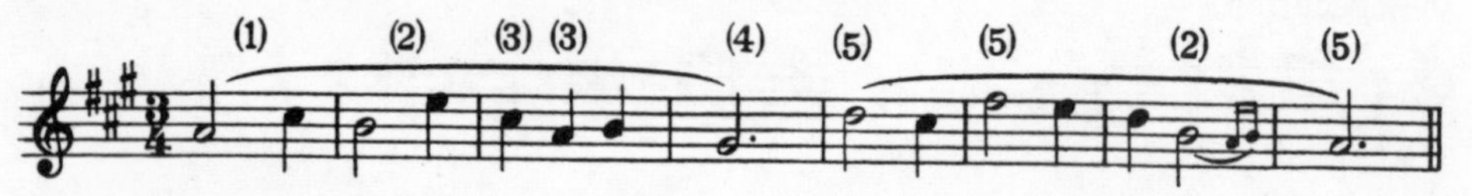

(b) Write out the following in full:

(c) Rewrite the following passages, substituting signs for ornaments wherever possible:

12 Harmony

The teacher should decide which parts of this section are necessary for his pupils or for a particular examination. These parts can then be studied and the appropriate exercises on them can be worked with little or no reference to the intervening material, if wished.

1 *Triads in root position*

A triad is a chord of three notes consisting of a root (the note from which it takes its name) and a third and a fifth above it. Here are some examples of triads on C:

A moment's thought will tell you that (e) and (f) above, though technically triads, are not usable chords, because they could not occur in any major or minor key. The ear recognises them as , not as a root, third and fifth at all.

So, in practice, only four kinds of triad are available:
1 A major triad, having a major third and a perfect fifth above the root. (See (a) above.)
2 A minor triad, having a minor third and a perfect fifth above the root. (See (b) above.)
3 An augmented triad, having a major third and an augmented fifth above the root. (See (c) above.)
3 A diminished triad, having a minor third and a diminished fifth above the root. (See (d) above.)

2 *Major and minor triads*

Notice the following points about major and minor triads:
1 They take their name from the kind of *third* they contain.
2 They both contain a perfect fifth.
3 They are so commonly used that they are often called ' common chords '.
4 They are concords.
5 The tonic triad of a major key is a major triad; the tonic triad of a minor key is a minor triad.

Exercise 100

(a) Write a major and a minor triad on each of the following notes. Build it up by using the required intervals. Then, if you know all the major and minor scales and arpeggios, you can check it by seeing if you have written a tonic triad of a major or minor key.

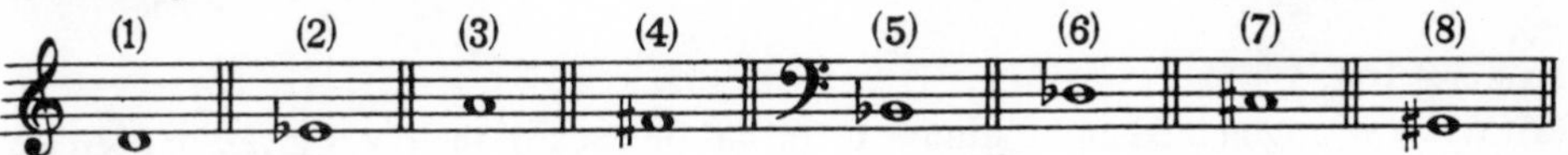

(b) State whether each of the following triads is major or minor:

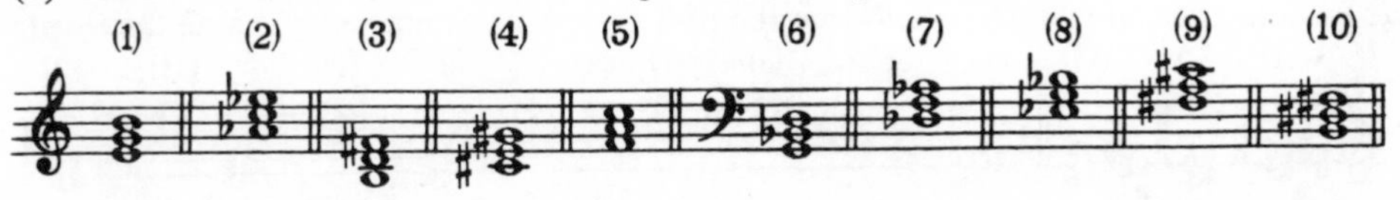

3 *Aural recognition of major and minor triads*

If you are required to recognise the difference between a major and a minor triad by ear, work as follows:

1 Mentally sing the notes of the chord downwards to the lowest note, the root.

2 From this note sing up the five notes of a major scale, d r m f s; then sing d m s, and see if what you are singing corresponds to the chord you have just heard.

3 If not, sing the first five notes of the minor scale, d r maw f s, followed by d maw s, to see if it corresponds with what you have heard.

4 Check your result by general impression. A minor triad has a heavier, sadder feeling than the brighter, major triad. If you mentally sing both a major and a minor triad on the same tonic you should be able to compare them and feel the difference.

If you have made such regular use of sol-fa names that you have learnt to associate the sound with the sol-fa name automatically, you will have no difficulty in recognising the difference between a major and a minor triad.

Exercise 101

State whether triads are major or minor, as they are played to you by your teacher.

4 *Diminished and augmented triads*

Notice the following points about diminished and augmented triads:

1 They take their name from the kind of *fifth* they contain:

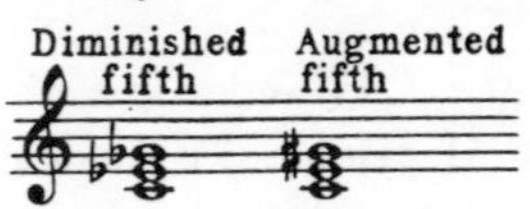

2 Because this fifth is discordant, they are both discords.

3 The triad with the larger fifth, augmented, contains the larger third, major; the triad with the smaller fifth, diminished, contains the smaller third, minor. (See above.)

4 They are comparatively rare chords, not ' common chords ', and they cannot form the tonic chord of any key.

Exercise 102

(a) Write an augmented and a diminished triad on each of the notes given in exercise 100 (a).

(b) Name the following triads. Name the fifth first; then, if necessary, name the third.

(1) (2) (3) (4) (5) (6) (7) (8) (9) (10) (11) (12)

5 *Triads which can occur in major keys*

The following is a list of the triads in C major:

Notice the following points:

1 It is customary to use roman numerals corresponding to the degree of the scale, to describe the triads.

2 I, IV and V are major triads (concords).

3 II, III and VI are minor triads (concords).

4 VII is a diminished triad, and is the only diatonic triad which is a discord in a major key.

Exercise 103

(a) Name the following triads, and then name all the major keys in which each can occur. (If it is a major triad it can be I, IV or V, and by working down the scale from the root of the triad to the tonic of the scale, the key can be discovered in each case. Similarly, if it is minor it can be II, III or VI; if diminished, it must be VII.)

(1) (2) (3) (4) (5) (6)

(b) Write out (1) all the major triads in C, F, A and E♭ major (i.e. I, IV and V in each case); (2) all the minor triads in B♭, E, F♯ and A♭ major (i.e. II, III and VI in each case); (3) the diminished triad in D, C♯, D♭ and G♭ major (VII in each case).

6 *Triads which can occur in minor keys*

The following is a list of the triads which can occur in C minor (assuming that the harmonic form of the scale is used for harmonies):

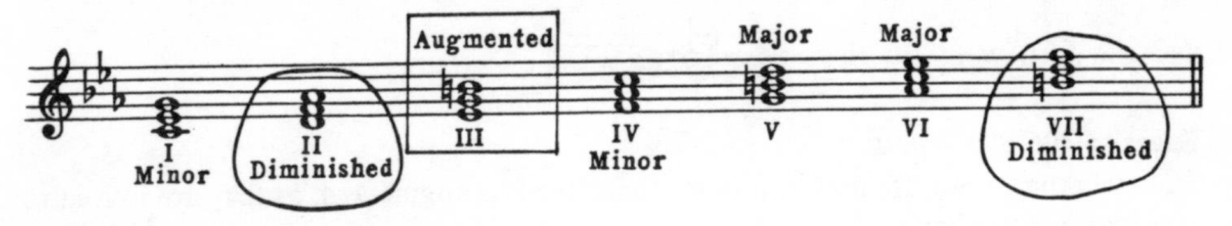

Notice the following points:
1 V and VI are major triads (concords).
2 I and IV are minor triads (concords).
3 II and VII are diminished triads (discords).
4 III is an augmented triad (a discord).

The melodic form of the minor scale is occasionally used for harmonies, and this will produce a different set of triads. If it is necessary for you to know them, you can work them out for yourself.

Exercise 104

(a) Name the following triads, and then name all the major and minor keys in which each can occur. (A major triad can be I, IV or V of a major key or V or VI of a minor key; a diminished triad can be VII of a major key or II or VII of a minor key; an augmented triad can only be III of a minor key.

(b) Write out (i) all the major triads in E, B, B♭ and D♭ minor; (ii) all the minor triads in D, F♯, E♭ and A♭ minor; (iii) all the diminished triads in C, F, G♯ and D♭ minor; (iv) the augmented triad in G, A, A♭ and C♯ minor.

7 *Aural recognition of all four kinds of triad*

If you are required to recognise whether a triad is major, minor, diminished or augmented work as follows:
1 Decide whether it sounds like a concord or a discord.
2 If it is a concord it is major or minor, and you will work as suggested in part 3 above.
3 If it is a discord, try singing t r f to it (i.e. VII). If it fits it is diminished. If not, sing maw s t to it (III in a minor key). If it fits, it is augmented.

4 Check your result by general impression. Major and minor have been compared in part 3 above. A diminished triad sounds weak and wants to collapse inwards:

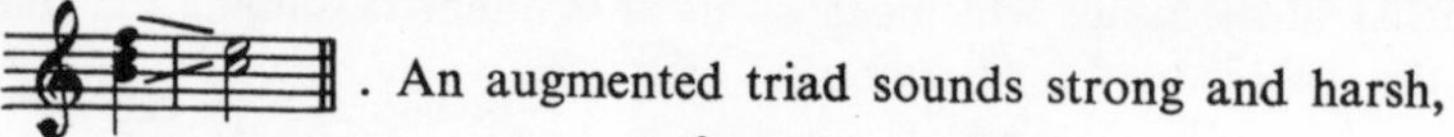

. An augmented triad sounds strong and harsh, and the fifth wants to rise: .

Exercise 105

State whether triads are major, minor, diminished or augmented, as they are played to you by your teacher.

8 *The inversions of major and minor triads*

Triads do not always have the root as the lowest sound, the bass, of the chord. They can be inverted, thus:

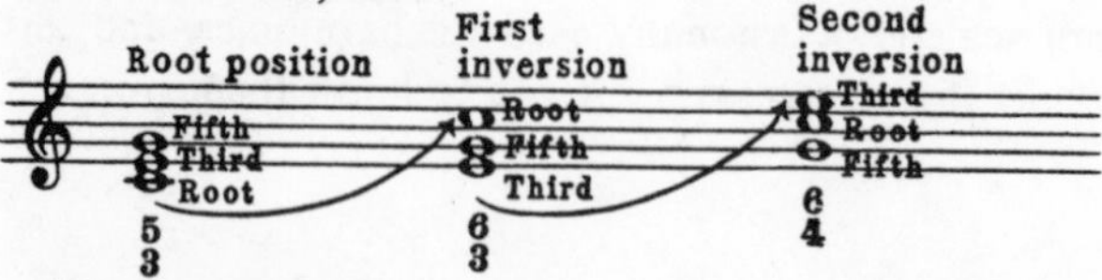

The figures underneath show the intervals from the *bass note* which are present in each chord.

Do not confuse a *root* with a *bass note*. The root in all three of the above chords is C, the third is E and the fifth is G. In the root position the root is the bass note; in the first inversion the third is the bass note; and in the second inversion the fifth is the bass note.

If you are asked to write a triad in its first or second inversion begin by writing the root position and then invert it, as necessary. For example, if you were asked to write the second inversion of the triad of G minor, work thus:

If you are asked to name written triads and their inversions, work thus:

1 Name the intervals from the bass.

2 If they are $\frac{5}{3}$ the chord is in its root position. Proceed to name it as you have done before. E.g. (a)

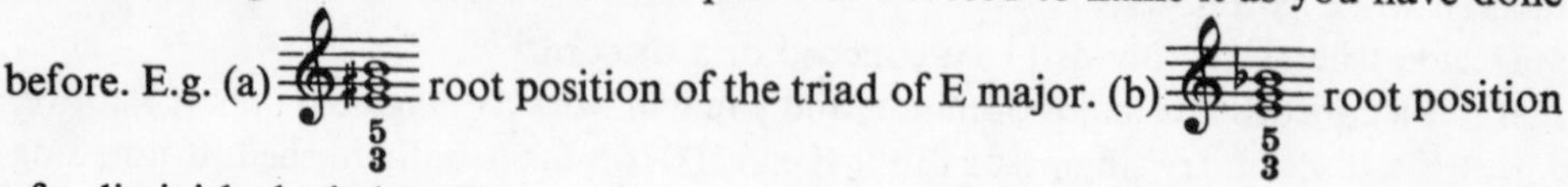

root position of the triad of E major. (b) root position of a diminished triad on E.

3 If the intervals from the bass are $^{6}_{3}$ the chord is in its first inversion. E.g. . F is the bass note, the third of the chord. The root is therefore a third below this, i.e. D♭. Rearrange the $^{6}_{3}$ chord so that D♭ is written below the F, thus: . Now you have the root position and you can proceed to name the chord: the first inversion of the triad of D♭ major.

4 If the intervals from the bass are $^{6}_{4}$ the chord is in its second inversion. E.g. . G♯ is the bass note, the fifth of the chord. The root is therefore a fifth below, i.e. C♯. Rearrange the three notes, moving downwards into lower positions, until finally you have the chord in its root position, making the intervals $^{5}_{3}$ from the bass, thus:

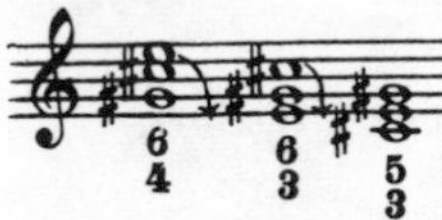

Now you have the root position, and you can proceed to name the chord: the second inversion of C♯ minor.

Exercise 106

(a) Write the following triads (all of which are major or minor); (1) the first inversion of F minor; (2) the root position of F♯ major; (3) the second inversion of E♭ minor; (4) the second inversion of B major; (5) the first inversion of D minor; (6) the first inversion of V in E major; (7) the second inversion of I in B♭ minor; (8) the root position of IV in E minor.

(b) Name the following triads, stating also their position. (All are major or minor.)

(c) Name all the major keys in which the triads given in exercise 106(b) can occur. (See part 5 above.)

9 *Aural recognition of major and minor triads and their inversions*

If you are asked to recognise by ear a major or minor triad in any of its three positions, work thus:

1 Sing the notes of the chord to be recognised, starting with the top note, downwards.

2 Does the bottom note sound like doh? If so, the chord is in its root position, and you proceed to decide whether it is major or minor, as before.

3 If the bottom note does not sound like doh, carefully sing the sound a third lower, moving downwards by step, and see if this sounds like doh. If it does, the chord is in its first inversion. E.g. you hear: .

You sing these three notes and then you add the lower D, thus: .

From this you can tell you have heard the first inversion of a major triad.

4 If the third below the lowest sound still does not sound like doh, carefully add another third below, moving downwards by step, as before. Now you should have reached the root position. E.g. you hear . You sing ,

and then, because the lowest note is still not doh, you add another third, thus:

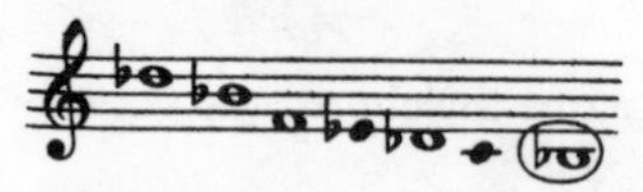

Now you can name the chord: the second inversion of a minor triad.

Another way of recognising the position of a triad is to sing down by step from the top note of the chord to the middle note, and on again to the bass, counting the steps between each note as you go. In this way you will discover the position of the fourth, and this tells you the position of the chord. There is no fourth in the root position; it is at the top in the first inversion; and the bottom in the second inversion. E.g.:

Exercise 107

Recognise major and minor triads and their inversions, when played to you by your teacher.

10 *The inversions of diminished and augmented triads*

When naming and writing the inversions of diminished and augmented triads follow the same methods as those shown in part 8 for the inversions of major and minor triads.

Exercise 108

(a) Write the following triads (all of which are diminished or augmented): (1) the first inversion of a diminished triad *of* D (i.e. D as root; (2) the first inversion of a diminished triad *on* D (i.e. D as bass note); (3) an augmented triad of F, in its second inversion; (4) the first inversion of an augmented triad which has G as its root; (5) the first inversion of the diminished triad which occurs in E major; (6) the augmented triad on the mediant of B minor, in its root position; (7) the first inversion of III in C minor; (viii) the second inversion of VII in G minor.

(b) Write the triads required in exercise 106(a) on the tenor stave; and those required in exercise 108(a) on the alto stave.

(c) Name the following triads, stating also their position. (They may be major, minor, diminished or augmented.)

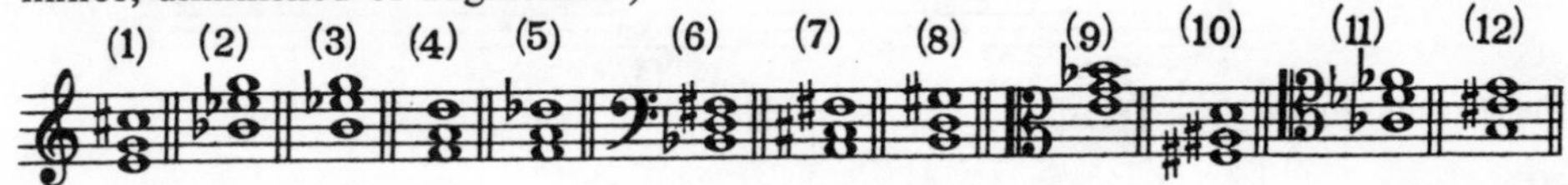

(d) Name all the major and minor keys in which the triads given in exercise 108(c) can occur.

11 *Aural recognition of diminished and augmented triads and their inversions*

If you are asked to recognise the first inversion of a diminished triad you should be able to recognise (a) a discord; (b) te at the top, e.g.

key C.

Second inversions of diminished triads are (a) discords; (b) have ray at the top and te in the middle. E.g:

key C.

You will not be asked to recognise inversions of augmented triads in isolation. The reason is that the root position, the first inversion and the second inversion all sound alike, if the chord is heard in isolation (i.e. not in relation to other chords in a key), because the intervals between the notes are the same every time—a major third. E.g.:

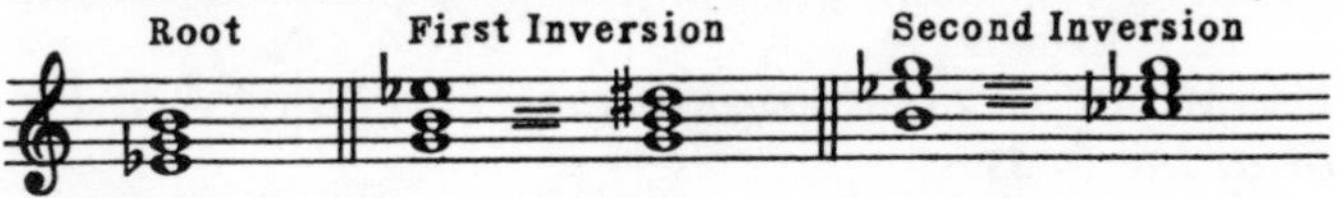

Exercise 109

Recognise any kind of triad and its position, when played to you by your teacher.

12 *The primary triads. Major keys. Root position*

Seven triads can be built on the seven sounds of the major scale, and three of these are more important than the rest. They are I, IV and V. Just as there are primary colours, so these are known as the primary triads.

It is possible to harmonise any note of a diatonic tune with one of these three chords, as every note of the scale comes in at least one of them.

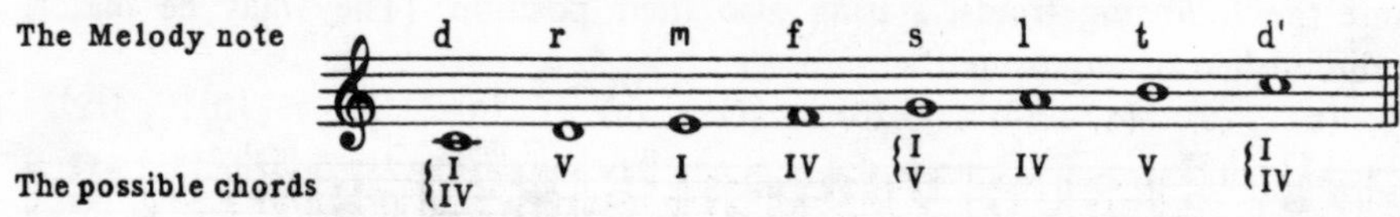

So:

doh can be harmonised by I or IV
ray can be harmonised by V
me can be harmonised by I
fah can be harmonised by IV
soh can be harmonised by I or V
lah can be harmonised by IV
te can be harmonised by V

Many simple pieces of music use only these three chords. For example, guitar players who can play them in the simpler keys can accompany a tune quite well.

Exercise 110

(a) Write out the three primary triads in the following major keys: G, B♭, D, F♯, A♭.
(b) Write (1) the tonic triads in the keys of A and F♭; (2) the dominant triads in the keys of G and D♭; (3) the subdominant triads in the keys of F and E.
(c) Name the following triads, which are all in major keys:

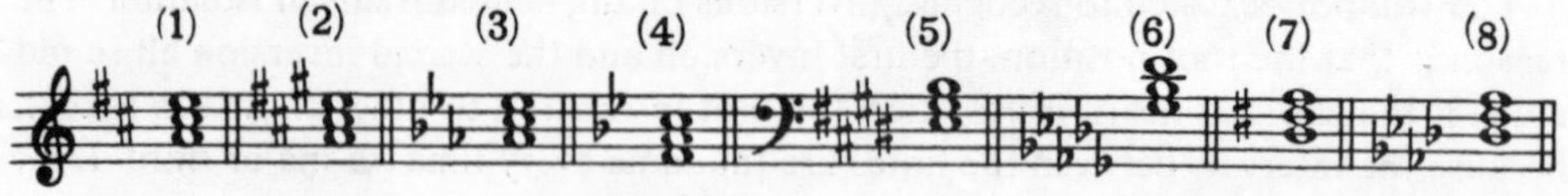

13 *The primary triads. Major keys. Root position. Three notes in the treble and the root in the bass*

Chords for the piano are very often written with one note, the root, in the left hand and all three notes of the triad in the right hand. If these three notes are written in close position, i.e. using the next nearest note in every case, three ways of arranging each chord are possible:

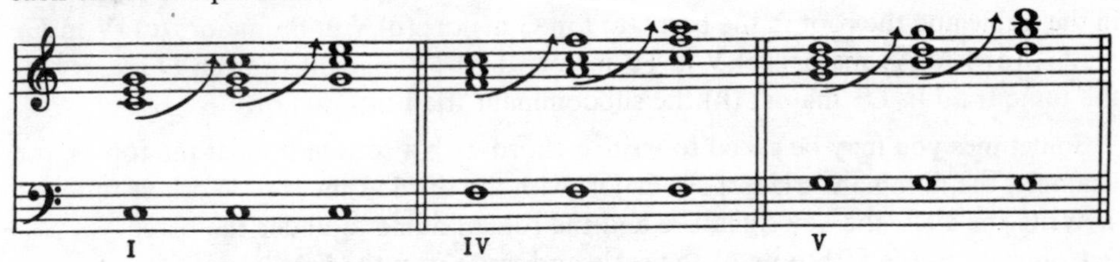

Note that none of these chords are inversions, because all have the root as the lowest sound heard. Do not think of right and left hands separately: the ear hears the chord as one composite sound.

Suppose you are asked to write the three positions of the subdominant triad in D major, work as follows:

1 Write the clef, the key signature, and the roman numeral under the bass.

2 Count up to the fourth note of the scale and write it in the bass three times, thus:

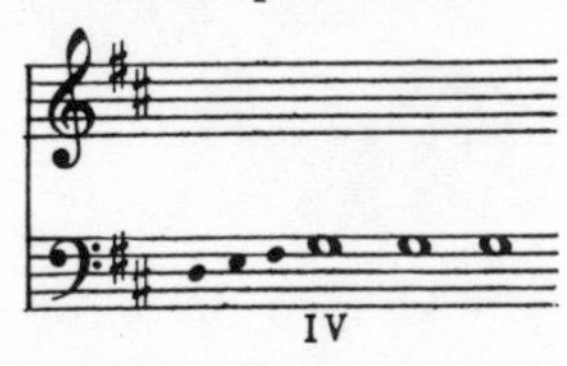

3 Write the letter names of the notes of the chord above the treble stave, counting upwards from the root: G B D.

4 Write these three notes, in close position on the treble stave:

5 Put the bottom note of the treble stave an octave higher for the second position, and repeat the process for the third:

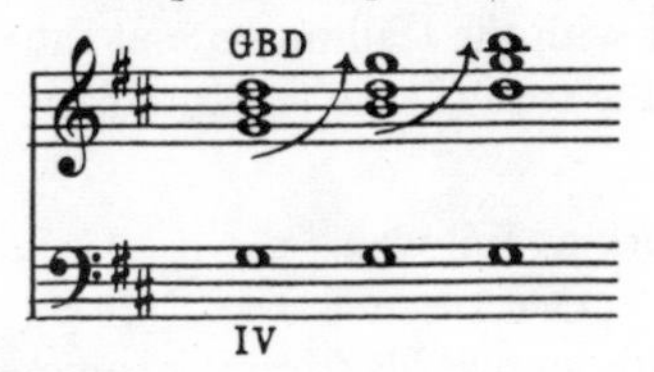

Exercise 111

Write three positions of each of the following triads, using three notes in close position in the treble and the root in the bass: (a) I in G major; (b) V in B♭ major; (c) IV in E♭ major; (d) I in A♭ major; (e) V in F♯ major; (f) the dominant triad in D major; (g) the tonic triad in D♭ major; (h) the subdominant triad in E major.

Sometimes you may be asked to write a chord with a certain note at the top as, for example, the dominant triad of B♭ major, with the third at the top. Work as follows:

1 Write the clefs, the key signature and the roman numeral under the bass.

2 Count up to the fifth note of the scale and write it in the bass, thus:

3 Write the letter names of the notes of the chord above the treble stave, counting upwards from the root: F A C.

4 Name the third: A. Write it on the treble stave, thus:

5 Finally, write the other two notes, in close position, *under* the A, thus:

Exercise 112

Using three notes in the treble in close position and the root in the bass write the following: (a) the tonic chord of A major with the root at the top; (b) the dominant chord of E major with the fifth at the top; (c) the subdominant chord of B♭ major with the third at the top; (d) the dominant chord of G major with the leading note at the top; (e) the tonic chord of B major with the mediant at the top; (f) the subdominant chord of A♭ major with the submediant at the top.

If you are asked to recognise primary triads visually, work as follows:

1 Name the key.

2 Write the roman numeral under the bass note, by counting upwards from the tonic.

3 Write the names of the chord above the treble, by counting upwards from the bass note.

4 From this information you should then be able to state what note is at the top of the chord, and any other information required.

Exercise 113

Name the following chords, in relation to the key, and state whether the root, third or fifth is at the top. They are all in major keys.

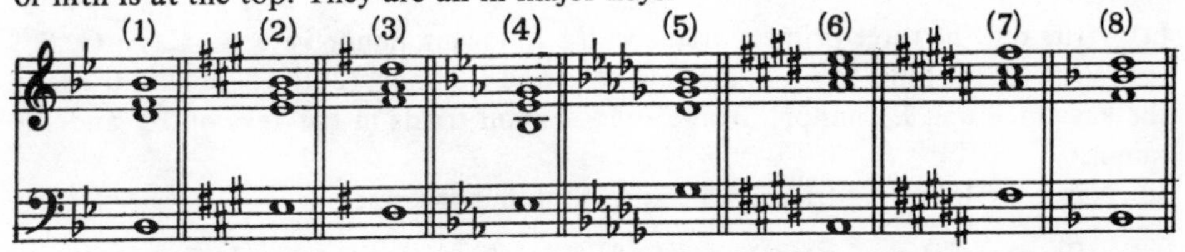

14 *Aural recognition of the primary triads in major keys, root position, in relation to a tonic*

Work as follows:

1 Memorise the tonic, as it is played to you.

2 Listen carefully to the chord, and then hum or sing to yourself the lowest sound you have heard. At first you may not be able to separate it from the rest of the chord; but if you wait quietly, it will begin to ' loom up ' above the other notes.

3 Sing from the tonic to the root of the chord, by step, and thus name the chord.

4 Check your analysis by the general impression. I with the tonic at the top sounds very finished; with the third or fifth at the top it is less finished, but it still feels like the tonic chord, the ' home ' chord of the key, and you should recognise the tonic in the bass. V sounds bright and unfinished; and if you sing te to yourself you will find it fits, as part of the chord. IV is also unfinished, but it is less bright than V; and if you sing te at the same time, you will find it clashes.

Exercise 114

Recognise the primary triads, major key, root position, as separate chords, in relation to a tonic, when played to you by your teacher.

15 *The primary triads. Minor keys. Root position*

Here are the triads of C minor, with the primary triads picked out:

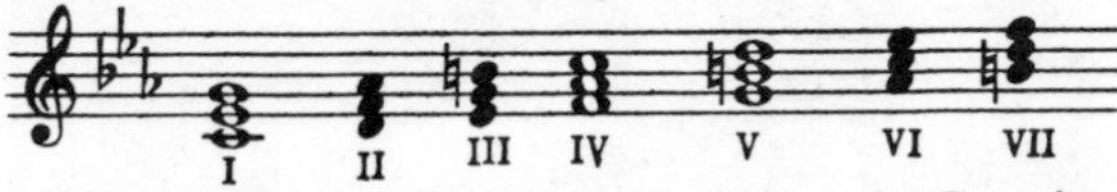

If you compare this list with the one in C major, shown in part 12, you may think that I and IV look alike; and that V, with its accidental, looks different. But, if you take the key signature into account, the opposite is true. I and IV sound different, because they are minor chords, instead of major as in C major; and V sounds exactly the same in C major and C minor: G B D, a major chord. But the B requires a natural in C minor to contradict the key signature. It is easy to forget this—the leading note *always* requires an accidental, when writing V in a minor key.

Exercise 115

(a) Write out the three primary triads in the following minor keys: E, C, A, G, B♭.

(b) Write (1) the tonic triads in the keys of D and F minor; (2) the dominant triads in the keys of B and E♭ minor; (3) the subdominant triads in the keys of F♯ and A♭ minor.

(c) Name the following triads, which are all in minor keys:

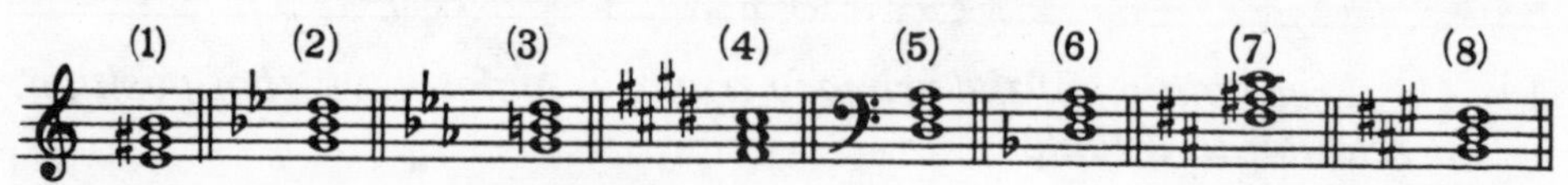

(d) Name the following triads. They are all primary triads, but they may be in a major or a minor key. (Note that [staff example] *could* be II in G major. But II is not a primary triad, so it must be IV in E minor.)

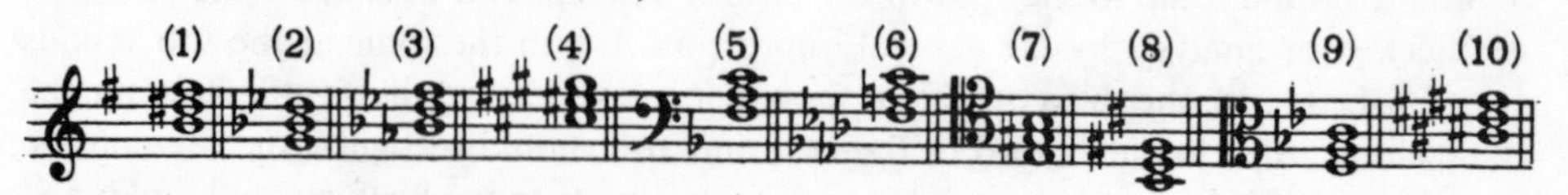

16 *The primary triads. Minor keys. Root position. Three notes in the treble and the root in the bass*

Here are the three close positions of the primary triads in C minor:

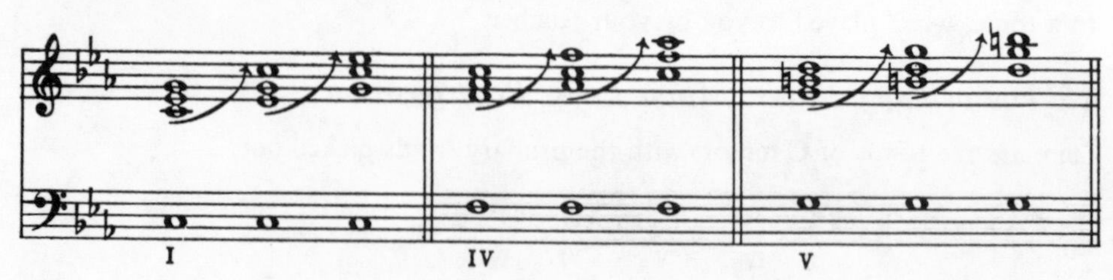

Exercise 116

Write three positions of each of the following triads, using three notes in close position in the treble and the root in the bass: (a) I in C minor; (b) V in A minor; (c) IV in E minor; (d) IV in B♭ minor; (e) V in F minor; (f) the tonic triad of G minor; (g) the subdominant triad of B minor; (h) the dominant triad of F♯ minor.

Exercise 117

Using three notes in the treble in close position and the root in the bass write the following: (a) the tonic chord of A minor with the fifth at the top; (b) the subdominant chord of E minor with the root at the top; (c) the dominant chord of C minor with the third at the top; (d) the dominant chord of E minor with the root at the top; (e) the tonic chord of C♯ minor with the dominant at the top; (f) the subdominant chord of G minor with the subdominant at the top.

Exercise 118

Name the following chords, in relation to the key, which may be major or minor, and state whether the root, third or fifth is at the top.

17 *Aural recognition of the primary triads in minor keys, root position, in relation to a tonic*

Work as suggested for the recognition of primary triads in major keys, in part 14 of this section. But in the minor key there is an additional aid to recognition. I and IV are minor chords, but V is major, so can easily be differentiated from the other two.

Exercise 119

Recognise the primary triads, root position, minor key, as separate chords, in relation to a tonic, when played to you by your teacher.

18 *Joining primary triads, three notes in the treble and the root in the bass, major keys*

When moving from one chord to another it is usually advisable to move as smoothly as possible. Compare (a) and (b) below. I and V have a note in common, soh. This note can be used as a ' binding note ', to bind the chords together, and the other two note can then move by step. See (b), (c) and (d) below. There are three ways of doing this, according to which note is at the top.

Similarly I and IV have a note in common, doh. This note can again be used as a binding note:

This is not the only way of joining these chords, though it is a good way in the early stages. If you wish to use other arrangements move as smoothly as possible. The following is a good arrangement, though there is no binding note, because there are no awkward jumps: no part moves more than a third, except the bass.

IV and V do not possess a binding note in common. If you should be required to write this progression it is wise to let the treble notes move in the opposite direction to the bass: (a) is better than (b) below.

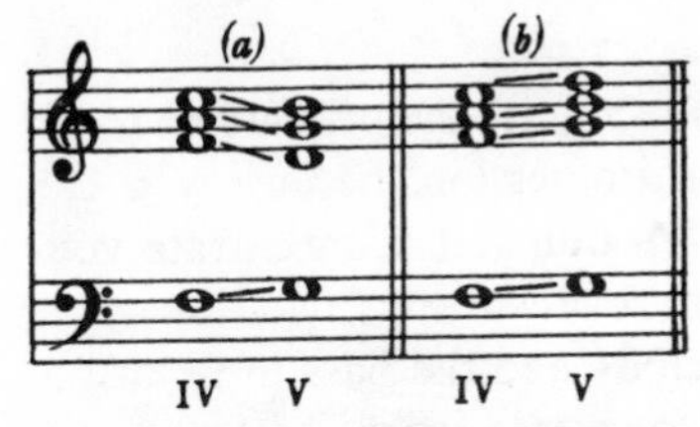

V moving to IV is rarely found, and it will be wise to avoid it in the early stages.

If you are required to write a progression of two or more primary triads with three notes in the treble and the root in the bass, work as follows:

1 Write treble and bass clefs, the key signature and the Roman numerals under the bass stave.

2 Write in the bass notes (roots).

3 Write the treble notes of the first chord in close position, building up from the root in the bass. (If you are required to write a particular note at the top, put this in first, and add the other two *below*. But still think upwards from the root, in order to find the right notes.)

4 Write the treble notes of the second chord in close position, keeping a binding note if possible, and otherwise moving as smoothly as you can. If you use IV–V move contrary to the bass.

5 If more than two chords are required, continue in the same way.

Exercise 120

Write the following progressions, using three notes in the treble and the root in the bass: (a) I V in G major; (b) IV I in D major; (c) I V I in B♭ major; (d) I IV I in A major; (e) I IV V I in F major; (f) I IV in C major, starting with the mediant at the top; (g) V I in E♭ major, starting with the leading note at the top.

Visual recognition of a progression of primary triads requires no new knowledge or skills. Name each chord separately in the way recommended for exercise 113.

Exercise 121

Name the following primary triads, in relation to their key:

19 *Aural recognition of a progression using primary triads in root position, major keys*

Refer to part 14 of this section, which tells you how to recognise the primary triads in isolation. It is rather easier to hear several chords in progression, because you can hear the bass part making a tune, for example: doh fah doh soh. Concentrate your listening on to the bass part, and you will certainly improve with practice.

Sometimes you may be asked to write down the melody and the bass in notation. This is really easier, as the melody checks the bass, and vice versa. Listen to the melody and the bass as separate tunes, using sol-fa, and write them down on the staff. Then see that they fit. If you have fah (IV) in the bass and te in the melody, obviously something has gone wrong. Think again, deciding which of the two you are more sure is correct. Even when you are only asked to name the chords you may find it helpful to write down the tune of the melody and the bass. If you have not been told the key you can write the sol-fa names only, letting one part check the other.

Exercise 122

(a) Name the chords of a progression of primary triads, major key, as played to you by your teacher.

(b) Write down the melody and the bass of a progression of primary triads, major key, as played to you by your teacher.

20 *Joining primary triads, three notes in the treble and the root in the bass, minor keys*

This is no more difficult than writing these chords in a major key, provided that you are sure of the minor key and its notation. But remember, when using V, that the leading note always requires an accidental.

Exercise 123

(a) Write the following progressions, using three notes in the treble and the root in the bass: (1) I IV I in G minor; (2) I V I in D minor; (3) V I in A minor; (4) I IV I V in F minor; (5) V I IV I in E minor; (6) I IV V I in B minor; (7) I V in C minor, starting with the dominant at the top; (8) I IV V I in F♯ minor, starting with the tonic at the top; (9) IV I V I in B minor, starting with the submediant at the top; (10) V I IV I in B♭ minor, starting with the supertonic at the top.

(b) Name the following progressions, in relation to the key, which may be major or minor:

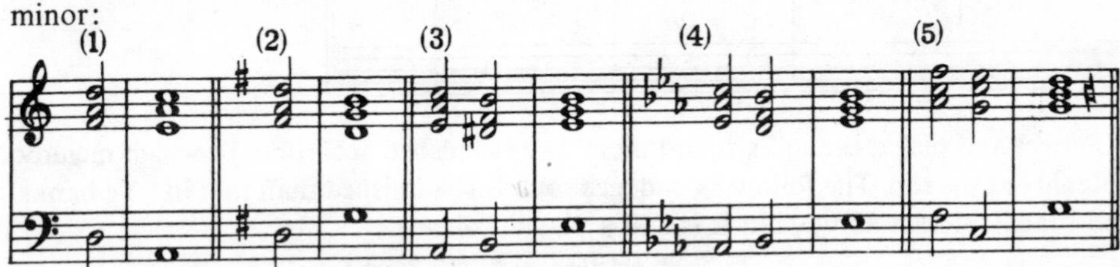

21 *Aural recognition of a progression using primary triads in root position, minor keys*

Refer to parts 14, 17 and 19 of this section.

In a major key the primary triads are all major chords. But in a minor key I and IV are minor and V is major, so it is easier to differentiate them in a minor than a major key.

Exercise 124

(a) Name the chords of a progression of primary triads, minor key, as played to you by your teacher.

(b) Write down the melody and the bass of a progression of primary triads, minor key, as played to you by your teacher.

22 *Cadences, using primary triads, major and minor keys*

The last two chords of a phrase make a cadence. There are four different kinds of cadence, and three of them can be built with the primary triads. The fourth kind, the interrupted cadence, requires a secondary triad, so consideration of it is deferred until part 25.

A phrase that ends with a tonic chord obviously sounds more finished than any other cadence. If the previous chord is V it is called a *perfect* cadence. Most pieces and main sections of pieces end with this cadence, and it sounds bright and final.

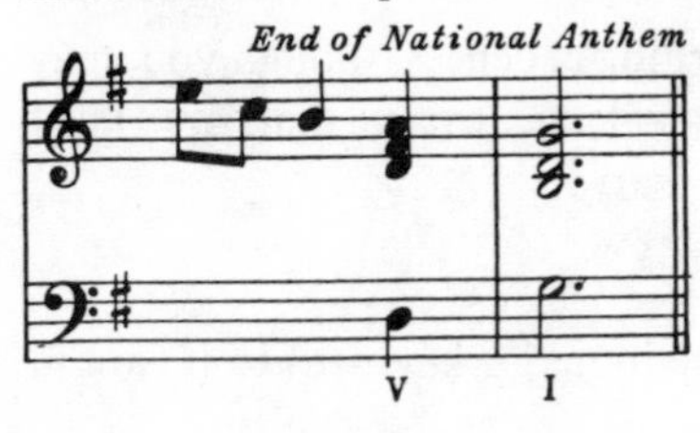

A *plagal* cadence consists of IV I. It, too, sounds finished, but is much more rarely used than a perfect cadence; and the use of IV, instead of V, gives it a heavier effect.

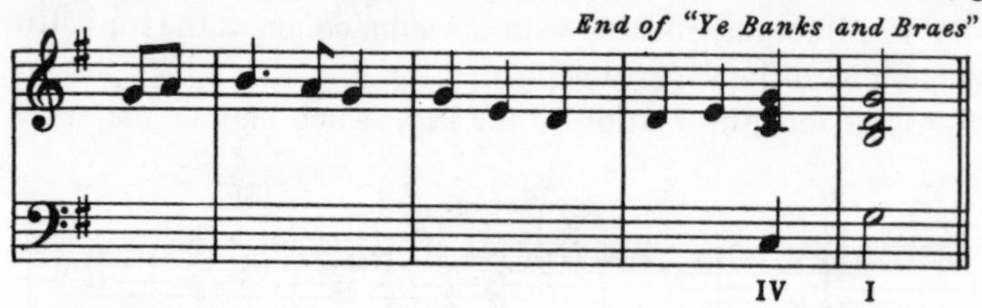

Perfect and plagal cadences sound more or less finished according to which melody notes are at the top. The following cadence sounds less finished than that in ' Ye banks and braes ', shown above, but it is still a plagal cadence.

Perfect and plagal cadences, in their less finished forms, can occur at the end of any phrase, even the first phrase, as in the example above.

Most cadences that do not end with I are called *imperfect*. (The exception is the interrupted cadence, described in part 25 of this section). An imperfect cadence nearly always ends with V, and almost any chord can be used before it. I V and IV V are quite common, and they make imperfect cadences which you can use and recognise, because they are formed by primary triads.

When you wrote exercises 120 and 123 you were writing cadences, though you may not have realised it. Exercise 125 requires no new knowledge, except that you must know what chords make which cadences.

Exercise 125

Write the following cadences. (Questions (a) to (c) are in major keys; (d) to (f) are in minor keys.) (a) perfect cadences in G and E♭ major; (b) plagal cadences in F and D major; (c) imperfect cadences in B♭ and A major; (d) imperfect cadences in A and F minor; (e) perfect cadences in E and B♭ minor; (f) imperfect cadences in B and E♭ minor.

Sometimes you may be asked to harmonise the melody notes at a cadence. Suppose you are to harmonise the cadence at the end of the following phrase:

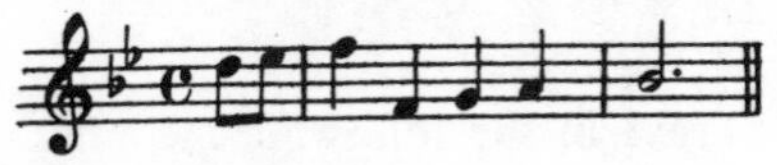

Work as follows:

1 Write the sol-fa names over the top of the last two notes: te doh.

2 Decide to which of the primary triads te can belong and write in the name and the bass note:

3 Decide to which of the primary triads doh can belong: I and IV. But V IV does not make a cadence, whereas V I does. So choose I, and write in its name and bass note.

4 Write the letter names of the two chords above the treble stave, counting up from the bass note:

5 The first chord already has A at the top. Proceed to place the other two notes in close position beneath it.

6 Build the second chord in the same way:

Sometimes the last two melody notes of a phrase can imply more than one cadence, and in that case you are free to choose, though one may be more appropriate than the other. For example could be I V, imperfect, or V I perfect; while could be IV I, plagal, or IV V, imperfect.

Exercise 126

Harmonise the melody notes at the end of each phrase in the following melodies. (Melodies (a) to (d) are in major keys; (e) to (h) are in minor.)

Exercise 127

Name the cadences made by the progressions given in exercises 121 and 123(b).

The only difference between the aural recognition of cadences using the primary triads and the aural recognition of chord progressions as in exercises 122 and 124 is that questions on cadence recognition usually contain one or more complete phrases, with or without harmonies in the course of the phrase, and that only the cadence chords need to be identified.

Work as follows:

1 Decide whether the last chord is I. Do not be misled by the melody, which may be relatively unfinished. Listen *down* to the bass.

2 If the last chord is I, then listen to the penultimate chord and decide whether it is the bright V or the heavier IV. V I will sound bright and natural, whereas IV I will sound heavier and form a much less common cadence. If you sing te doh it will fit with V I, but not with IV I.

3 If the last chord is not I then, if the question is confined to the primary triads, the cadence must be imperfect. But check by the general impression of an unfinished cadence, and by listening to hear if soh is the last bass note. (I IV is occasionally found as an imperfect cadence, but it is not usually given in ear tests.)

Exercise 128

Name the cadence in passages played by your teacher. (The cadences should only use the primary triads, in root position.)

23 *The inversions of primary triads*

Refer to parts 8 and 9 of this section which were concerned with the inversions of major and minor triads. As you know, I IV and V of a major key are major triads; and I and IV of a minor key are minor triads, while V is major.

The first inversion of any triad keeps to its same roman numeral, but adds ' b ' to it, while the second inversion adds ' c '.

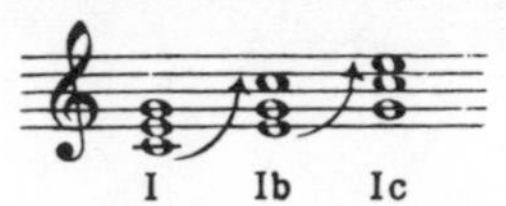

Here are the primary triads and their inversions in C major and C minor. The roman numerals and also the figuring showing the intervals from the bass note are given for each chord.

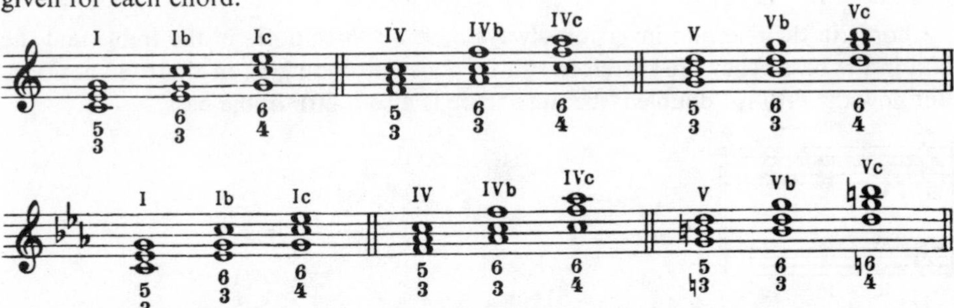

The only difference between the exercise which follows and exercise 106 is that now you are required to write or name all the chords in relation to a key.

Exercise 129

(a) Write the following triads. (Those in minor keys can be omitted, if wished.) (1) IVb in F and B♭ major, D and G minor; (2) Ic in C and C♯ major, E♭ and D minor; (3) Vb in A and E♭ major, A and E♭ minor; (4) IVc in G and A♭ major, E and B♭ minor; (5) Ib in D♭ and F♯ major, C and E minor; (6) Vc in D and G♭ major, B and A♭ minor.

(b) Name the following primary triads in relation to their key, which may be major or minor. State the position of each triad. (The chord can be described as either IVb or the first inversion of the subdominant triad of G minor. Note that the answer is not IIb of B♭ major, because II is not a primary triad.)

When chords in their first inversion are written with three notes in the treble and one in the bass, the bass note, the third, is rarely repeated in the treble because it sounds too thick. It is better to have two roots or two fifths. So (a) and (b) below are better than (c), even though they are no longer in 'close position'. They are still playable on the piano, as the right hand keeps within the range of an octave; and they use the nearest notes that avoid 'doubling' the third.

Chords in their second inversion always have all three notes in the treble and the fifth in the bass. They are therefore still in 'close position', as in the root position. But now the fifth is 'doubled' because there is also a fifth in the bass.

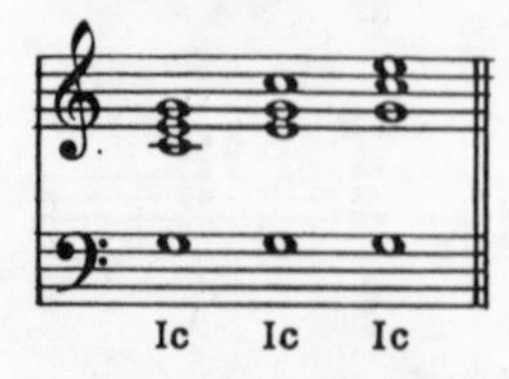

You may be asked to write a primary triad, in root position or inversion, with three notes in the treble and one in the bass.

Suppose the chord is the second inversion of the subdominant triad of B♭ major. Work as follows:

1 Write the treble and bass clefs, the roman numeral under the bass, and the names of the required notes above the treble stave, thus:

2 Add the required bass note, the fifth of the chord; and choose any of the three notes as the melody note, thus:

3 Add two more notes below the G, in close position, thus:

Suppose the chord is the first inversion of the dominant triad in E minor. Work as follows:

1 Write the treble and bass clefs, the roman numeral under the bass, and the required notes above the treble stave, thus:

2 Add the required bass note, the third of the chord, not forgetting to insert the accidental; and choose either the root or the fifth as the melody note, thus:

3 Add two more notes below the F♯, as close as possible, provided that you do not use another third, the D♯, thus:

Exercise 130

Write the chords given in exercise 129(a) with three notes in the treble and one in the bass.

You may be asked to name a primary triad, in root position or inversion, with three notes in the treble and one in the bass. It may even be arranged with two notes in the treble and two in the bass, as in a hymn tune for soprano, alto, tenor and bass voices. This is no more difficult, as far as naming is concerned, and the method of working is the same.

Suppose you have to name:

Work as follows:

1 Add the figuring showing the intervals from the bass: $\frac{6}{3}$ in this case. (There are two sixths, but this does not affect the figuring.) This tells you that the chord is a first inversion.

2 C♯ is therefore the third of the chord. The root must be a third below this, A; and the triad must be A C♯ E.

3 Write out the roots of I IV and V in D major and I IV and V in B minor, thus:

4 From this you can tell that the chord is V in D major, in its first inversion, Vb.

Suppose you have to name:

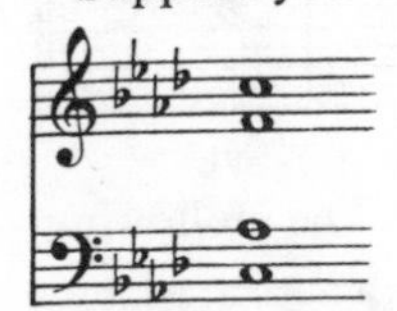

Work as follows:

1 Add the figuring showing the intervals from the bass: $\frac{6}{4}$ in this case. This tells you that the chord is a second inversion.

2 C is therefore the fifth of the chord. The root must be a fifth below, this, F, and the triad must be F A♭ C.

3 Write out the roots of I IV and V in A♭ major and I IV and V in F minor, thus:

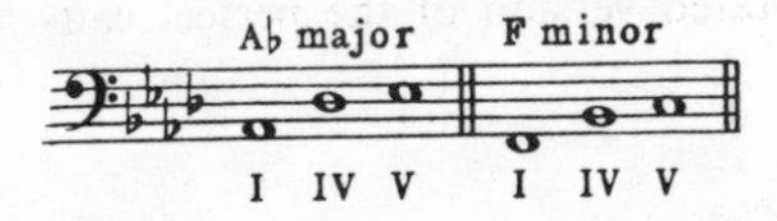

4 From this you can tell that the chord is I in F minor, in its second inversion, Ic.

5 If you should be asked to state which note is at the top, refer again to the root F. The triad is F A♭ C, and the fifth, the C, is at the top. It is the dominant of the key.

Exercise 131

Name the following primary triads, in relation to their key, which may be major or minor. State the position of each chord, and also which note is at the top.

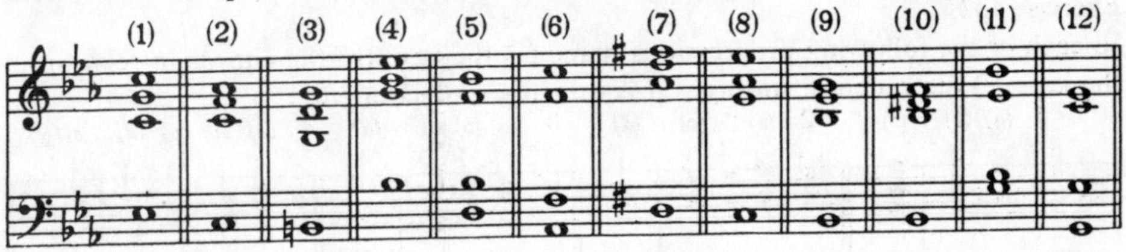

(1) (2) (3) (4) (5) (6) (7) (8) (9) (10) (11) (12)

If you are asked to name two or more chords in progression, this is no more difficult than naming the chords in isolation. You may also be asked to state the cadence they make.

A cadence in which one or both of the chords is inverted is called an inverted cadence. The following are all inverted cadences:

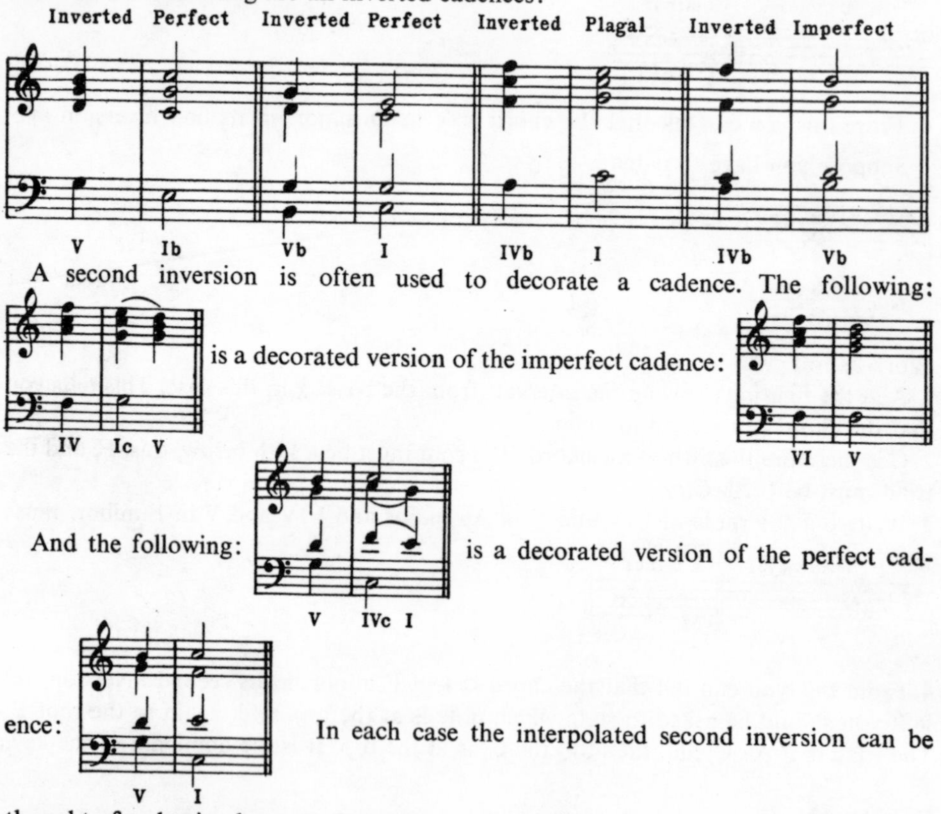

A second inversion is often used to decorate a cadence. The following: is a decorated version of the imperfect cadence:

And the following: is a decorated version of the perfect cadence:

In each case the interpolated second inversion can be thought of as having been produced by appoggiaturas. This kind of second inversion is called a *cadential* $^6_4$.

Exercise 132

In each of the following progressions name (a) the key; (b) the chords in relation to the key; (c) the cadence, stating if it is inverted or decorated.

It is assumed that you will not be asked to write a progression of chords involving the inversions of triads at this stage: it requires greater knowledge than is given in this book.

You may, however, be asked to recognise primary triads and their inversions by ear, either as isolated chords or in progressions.

In order to do this you must be able to hear the bass.

Let us assume that you are required to recognise progressions using I, Ib, Ic, IV and V, as is required for some examinations. Here is a progression using all these chords:

Realise the following:

(a) Doh in the bass must be I.
(b) Me in the bass must be Ib.
(c) Fah in the bass must be IV.
(d) Soh in the bass can be Ic or V.

If there is only one chord with soh in the bass it must be V, given a progression which is limited to these five chords. If there are two different chords, one after the other, with soh in the bass, Ic will be the first of the two, followed by V. V Ic is never used. The progression Ic V (the cadential $\frac{6}{4}$) is frequently found at a cadence. You will soon get to know the sound of it.

If you are required to recognise aurally all three primary triads in all three positions, work out what each chord will have as its bass note. If you then put these bass notes in scale order, you will discover the following, which you should memorise.

The only bass notes which can carry two different chords are doh and soh, and in each case they can have a cadential $\frac{6}{4}$ progression above them: IVc I and Ic V. The $\frac{6}{4}$ chord always comes first, in both progressions:

Second inversions can occur elsewhere, as passing $^{6}_{4}$s:

But in these progressions the bass moves by step. The only cases of a *repeated* bass note with two different chords are the cadential $^{6}_{4}$ progressions shown above.

Exercise 133

Recognise chords and cadences using primary triads and their inversions, either as isolated chords, or in progressions, as they are played to you by your teacher.

24 *Secondary triads*

Here is a list of all the secondary triads, with their first inversions, in C major and C minor. Their second inversions are practically never used.

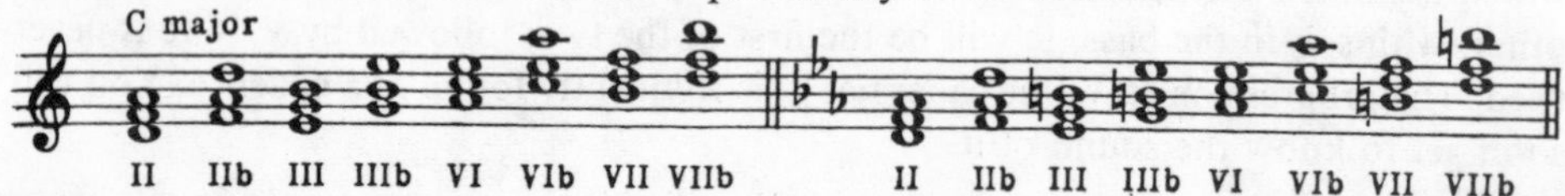

If you need to know which of these triads are major, minor, augmented or diminished, refer to parts 5 and 6 of this section.

Parts 5, 6, 8 and 10 showed you how to name and write secondary triads in their simplest form, i.e. one of each note in close position.

The secondary triads and their first inversions, like the primary triads, can be arranged with three notes in the treble and one in the bass, or with two in the treble and two in the bass, as in a hymn tune. But it is assumed that, for the elementary purposes dealt with in this book, you will not be required to write them in these ways, either separately or in progression. Nor are you likely to be asked to recognise them aurally.

You may, however, be asked to recognise them visually. Let us assume that you are asked to name the following chords:

Work as follows:

1 Name the key.

2 Put figures showing the intervals from the bass note underneath each chord. The figures will be $^{5}_{3}$ for root position, $^{6}_{3}$ for first inversion and $^{6}_{4}$ for second inversion. There is no need to show **8** for an octave, and you can ignore repeated notes. For example, chord (a) is $^{5}_{3}$, not $\substack{8\\5\\3}$; and chord (c) is $^{6}_{3}$, not $\substack{6\\6\\3}$. Also you can ignore the quaver between chords (f) and (g), which is a passing note, and does not affect the harmonies.

3 On another music stave under the bass stave write the roots of each chord. It will be the same as the bass part if the figures are $^{5}_{3}$, a third below if they are $^{6}_{3}$, and a fifth below if they are $^{6}_{4}$.

4 Now add roman numerals under these bass notes, thus:

5 Add ‘ b ’ to every chord which has the figuring $^{6}_{3}$, and ‘ c ’ to the one which has $^{6}_{4}$, and you get this: I VIIb Ib IIb Ic V VI.

6 The answer may be accepted in this form. Or you may write it out in full: (a) Root position of the tonic triad. (b) First inversion of the leading note triad, etc.

Exercise 134

Name the chords in the following progressions:

25 *The interrupted cadence*

An interrupted cadence is one which has V as its penultimate chord and leads you to expect I and a perfect cadence, but some other chord is used in place of I; and it creates an element of surprise, according to how unexpected the chord is.

V VI is the most frequently used form of interrupted cadence. See (a) below. But the second chord may be chromatic and therefore create much more surprise. See (b) below.

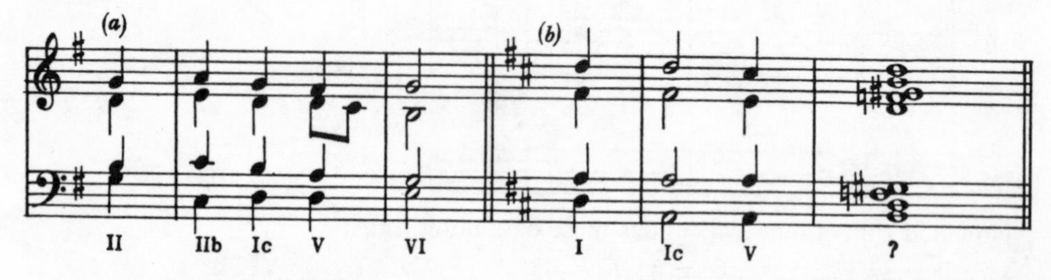

The interrupted cadence is perhaps the easiest of all cadences to recognise. The ear is expecting the perfect cadence and hears the penultimate V, followed by an unexpected chord. Compare it with the imperfect, which merely sounds unfinished, and contains no element of surprise.

Exercise 135
Recognise any of the four cadences in progressions played to you by your teacher.

26 *The dominant seventh*

This section on harmony finishes with a brief reference to a frequently used chord which is not a triad at all. It is the dominant seventh, and it consists of the dominant triad with the seventh from the root added:

It is frequently used in place of V at a perfect or interrupted cadence, thus:

It is often used in this way in cadence recognition tests, but it presents no problems as it is just as easy to hear as V, and has the same bass note. It is never used in place of V at an imperfect cadence, because it is a discord, and phrases do not usually have a discord for their *last* chord: a discord always requires another chord to complete it.

As the dominant seventh has four different notes it has three inversions:

The inversions are frequently used in the course of phrases; and they are also used to make inverted cadences, thus:

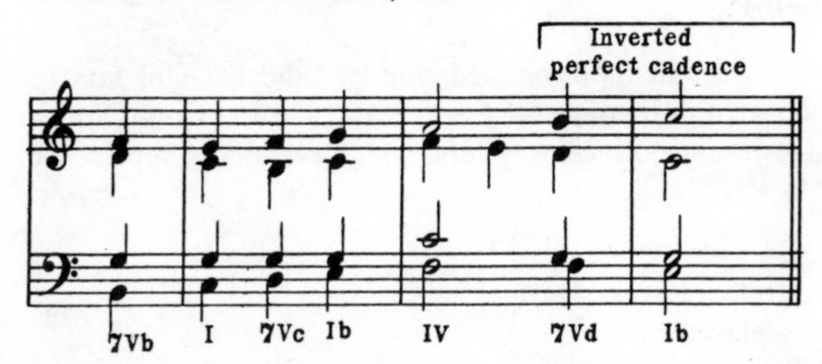

The chord consists of exactly the same notes in C major and C minor, though it is written differently because of the key signature:

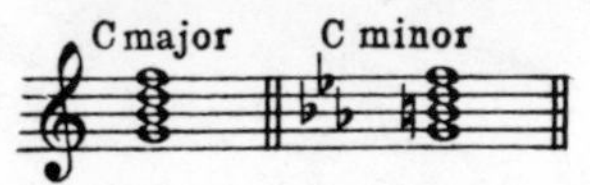

Exercise 136

Write the following dominant sevenths, four notes in close position: (a) the dominant seventh and its inversions in the keys of G, B♭, E and F♯ major, and F, D, E♭ and B minor, all with key signature; (b) 7Vc in B minor, 7Vd in E major, 7Vd in G♭ major, and 7V in C♯ minor, all without key signature.

13 Musical Instruments

1 *Acquiring a knowledge of musical instruments*

There are a number of interesting and informative books on musical instruments to which students may have access. Copies are to be found in school music libraries or other reference libraries.

Also far more students are familiar with the sound and look of orchestral instruments than was the case even a few years ago. Not only do many more young people attend orchestral concerts but many schools now have more or less complete orchestras. Some readers of this book may play orchestral instruments, while others can see and hear a friend playing one. It is much better to know an instrument by personal acquaintance than merely to read about it.

Most schools possess wall charts showing large-scale reproductions of instruments; and records can be obtained which illustrate their sound, either separately or in combination.

So all that a book such as this needs to do is to summarise the main features of each instrument, for purposes of reference.

2 *Bowed string instruments*

Two families of bowed string instruments developed side by side: the viol family, whose instruments were much used in the days of Elizabeth I; and the violin family, which grew to perfection in the seventeenth century, and which eventually superseded the viol family.

(a) THE VIOL FAMILY

The viol had six strings and a fretted finger board (like a guitar) and was played by a bow which was held from underneath instead of from above like a violin. The instrument was not unlike a violin in shape, but its shoulders had more of a downward curve, and it had a flat back, like that of a guitar.

Viols were made in a number of sizes, but a ' consort ' of viols usually consisted of four: treble, alto, tenor and bass or viol da gamba. They were all, even the smallest (which was roughly the size of a violin) held downwards like a 'cello.

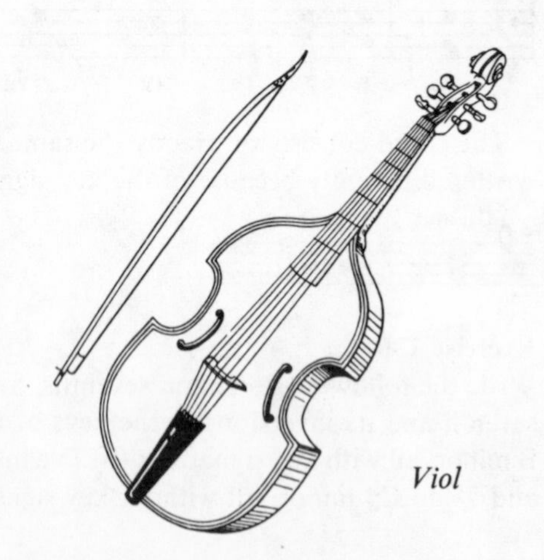

Viol

Bowed String Instruments

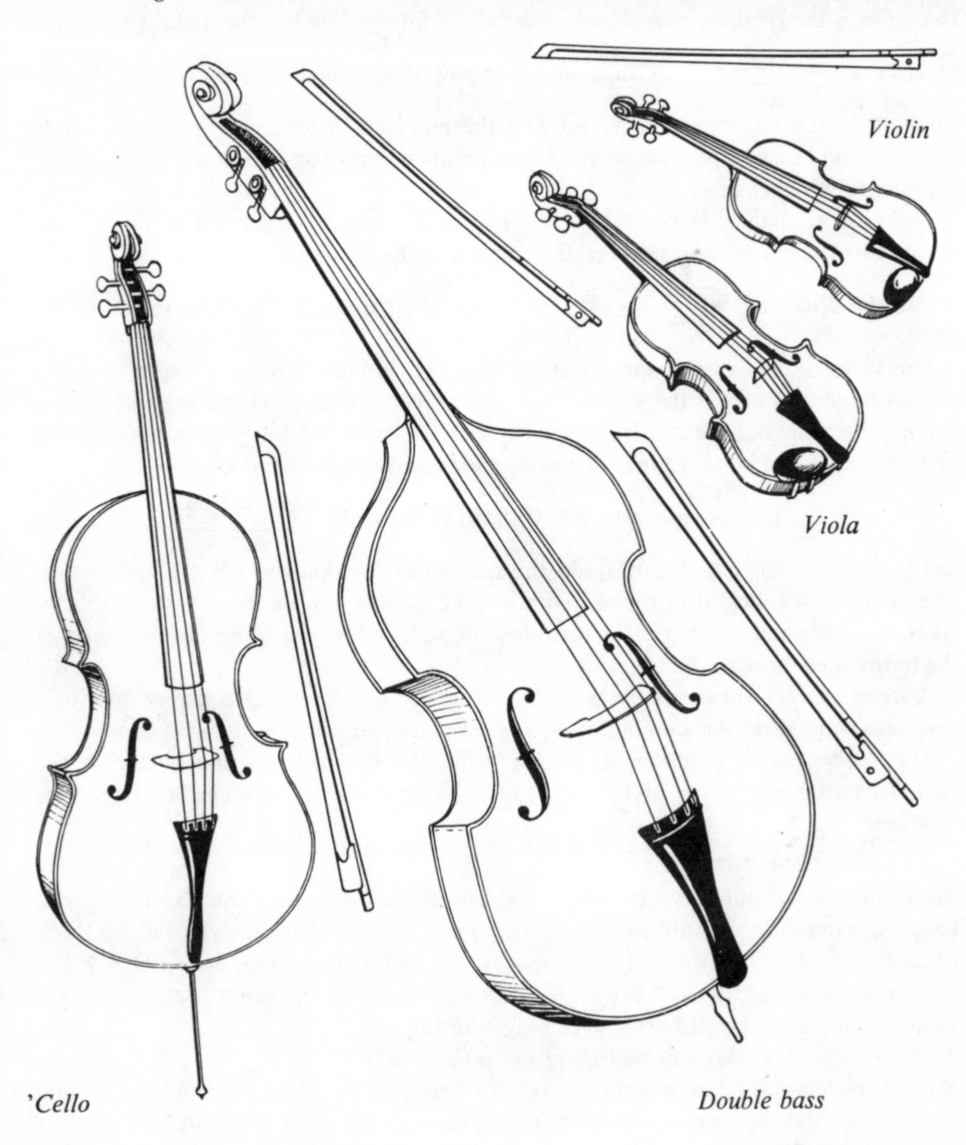

(b) THE VIOLIN FAMILY

The *violin* is the smallest instrument of the violin family, and has the highest pitch. Its strings are:  . Other notes are played by pressing the fingers of the left hand on to the finger board. By moving the hand up into higher 'positions' it is comparatively easy to play an octave above an open string; and good players can play considerably higher than this.

The *viola* is slightly larger than a violin and has strings which are a fifth lower. Because its range comes in between the treble and the bass stave it is more convenient to use the alto clef:  . But its highest notes are written on the treble stave.

The viola is held in the same way as a violin, but the stretch between notes is slightly larger. Its tone is thicker and lacks the brightness of the violin, even when it is playing the same note. But it is indispensible in the orchestra for playing notes of the middle range; and certain types of rather melancholy melody suit it admirably.

The '*cello* has strings an octave below those of the viola:  . The tenor clef is used for fairly high notes and the treble clef for notes which are higher still. The instrument is held downwards, with a spike pushed into the floor to keep it firm. Its tone is rich and it often plays melodies, in addition to providing the bass part of the harmonies most of the time.

A *string quartet* consists of two violins, a viola and a 'cello, which together provide a very satisfying harmonic combination, a great favourite with the classical composers.

The *double bass* is much bigger than a 'cello, and its chief function is to play the 'cello part an octave lower, and thus to provide a firm bass to the orchestra. Its strings are written:  , i.e. a fourth apart, not a fifth like the other members of the violin family, but they actually sound an octave lower than this. So the double bass is a transposing instrument. (It may help you to remember the strings if you think of them as in the opposite order to those of the violin: E A D G, not G D A E.)

In modern scores the double bass sometimes plays an independent part, i.e. not the same as the 'cello; but it hardly ever plays the tune.

Various ways of playing instruments of the violin family

Various effects can be obtained on string instruments by using the bow in different ways. A separate movement of the bow can be used for every note. Or two or more notes can be played by one movement of the bow, and this is indicated by a slur. The combination of legato and staccato, as for example in produces special effects of phrasing. *Pizzicato* means pluck the strings with the fingers; and *arco* is written to show that the bow is to be used again.

Two notes played at the same time produce *double stopping;* and occasionally chords of three and four notes are seen. A mute placed over the strings by the bridge produces a softer, different kind of tone. This is shown by the term *con sordino;* and *senza sordino* indicates a return to normal.

In an orchestra, the violins are divided into two sections: violin I and violin II. Their parts are written on different staves and they normally play different parts. If further divisions of parts, in any of the string instruments, are required they are indicated by the term divisi or à 2, à 3, à 4, as the case may be; and *unis* shows that they are to play in unison again.

3 *The wood wind instruments*

(a) INSTRUMENTS WITHOUT A REED

The *recorder* is a very old instrument that has recently been revived. It is comparatively easy to play and, for this reason, is popular in schools. It is held vertically, with the top of the instrument in the mouth, ' end-blown '; and fingers cover the open holes to provide the different notes.

Recorders, like viols and members of the violin family, are made in various sizes; and a consort of recorders was just as popular in the days of Elizabeth I as was a consort of viols. Descant, treble, alto, tenor and bass recorders are all made and used, but the highest one, the descant, is the most popular.

The *flute* is held horizontally, ' side-blown ', and the player blows into a hole at the side of the ' end-piece '. (All orchestral wood wind instruments divide into three pieces, for ease of transport, and for cleaning purposes.) The earliest flutes had holes which had to be covered with the fingers, to make the various notes, but modern flutes have keys to cover the holes.

The range of the flute is: 8va . Its tone is very soft, but it is sweet and very agile. By blowing harder a sound an octave higher can be produced with the same fingering. This is called ' overblowing ' at the first harmonic. (See Section 9, part 6, under brass instruments, for information about the harmonic series.) The third, highest, octave is produced by the use of higher harmonics.

Flutes are not made in as many sizes as are recorders because one cannot hold a very long instrument horizontally. A *bass* or *alto flute*, very occasionally used in orchestras, is made a fourth lower than an ordinary flute, and is a transposing instrument. (See Section 9, part 6.) But a smaller, ' octave ' flute is quite frequently used, and this is called a piccolo.

The *piccolo* is an octave higher than the flute. Its range is written as [music: 8va], but it actually sounds an octave higher than this, so it is a transposing instrument. Its tone is very shrill, and its top notes are easily heard above quite a large orchestra.

(b) SINGLE REED INSTRUMENTS

Some wood wind instruments, such as the clarinet, have a single reed inserted at the back of a shaped mouthpiece, and the player inserts the reed and the mouthpiece into his mouth and blows between the two. The resulting sound has more ' edge ' to it than an instrument without a reed, like a flute, but less than an instrument with two reeds, like an oboe.

Although the *clarinet* has older ancestors, the instrument itself is a comparatively recent one, dating from about 1700. Mozart was the first great composer to use it. Its range is written as: [music: 8va], but nearly all clarinets transpose. (See Section 9, part 6 for information about the transposition of clarinets.) Clarinets in B♭ and A are the sizes most used in the orchestra.

The clarinet overblows at the second harmonic—in other words, the player uses the same fingering for the sound a twelfth higher. (See the harmonic series in Section 9, part 6.)

Clarinets are nearly as agile as the flute, but their tone is fuller and more powerful, and they have an extra octave at the bottom of their range which has a peculiar, rich and, at times, menacing quality. They are very versatile and can play melodies, accompanying arpeggios, or brilliant runs equally well.

The *Bass Clarinet* is twice as long as the ordinary clarinet and therefore sounds an octave lower. Its part is written on the treble stave, as if it were meant for an ordinary clarinet in B♭ or A, so the resulting sound is a ninth or tenth lower. But only the bass clarinet in B♭ is used today. Its range is written as: [music]. Sometimes its part is written on the bass stave, and so it transposes a second instead of a ninth.

Its tone is very rich and velvety, but it is not often used.

The *Saxophone* came into existence about 1840. It is not unlike a clarinet, and it can easily be learnt by a clarinet player. But its tube is made of brass, so it is a cross between a wood wind and a brass instrument. It has a single reed, like the clarinet, but it overblows at the octave, like the flute and oboe.

There is a complete saxophone family of various sizes, but the usual sizes are pitched in B♭ and E♭, transposing like the clarinets in B♭ and E♭. The written range is:

Wood Wind Instruments

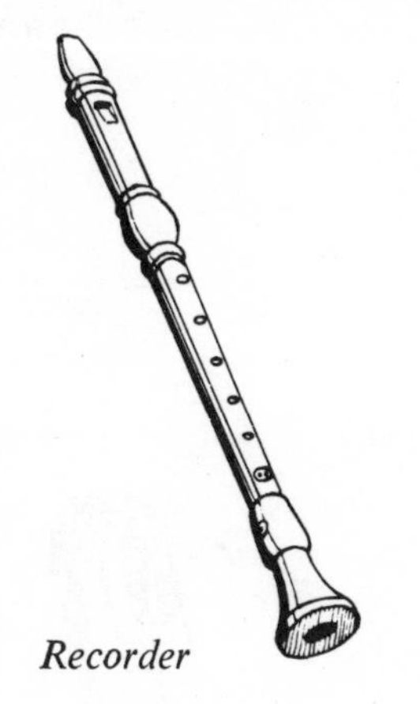

Recorder

Flute

Piccolo

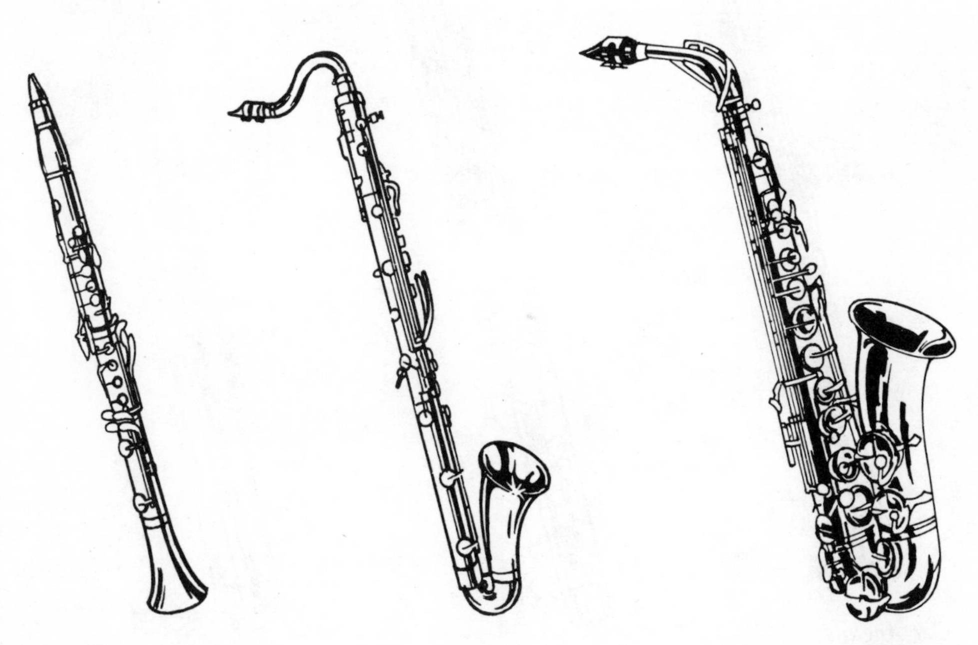

Clarinet *Bass Clarinet* *Saxophone*

Wood Wind Instruments

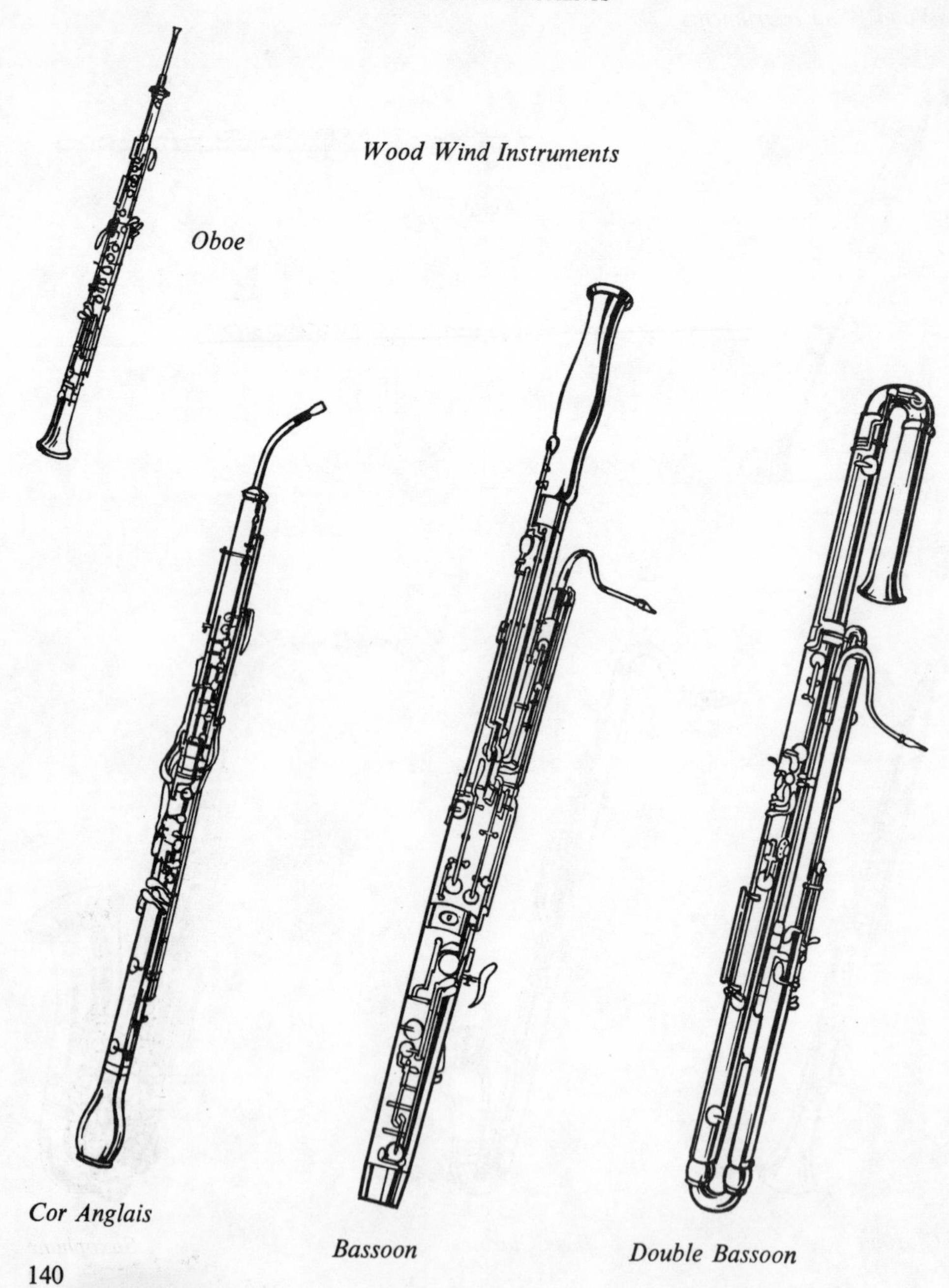

Although the saxophone is rarely used in the orchestra it is frequently found in military bands. And all readers will be familiar with its sound because of its regular use in dance bands.

(c) DOUBLE REED INSTRUMENTS

The double reed instruments are an old family of instruments and have been used in the orchestra much longer than have the single reed instruments. Two reeds are fastened together and inserted into the top of the instrument. The player puts the reeds (and not the instrument) into his mouth; and his breath, passing between the two, produces a characteristic edge which is called a ' reedy ' tone.

The *Oboe* is the highest of the family. Its range is narrower than that of the flute or the clarinet though, like them, it is a treble instrument. The range is  , and it does not transpose. It overblows at the octave.

It is particularly suited to plaintive or pastoral melodies, though it can also sound humorous, if played quickly and staccato. On first acquaintance some people dislike its reedy, rather harsh tone, but they soon get to appreciate its characteristic, astringent quality, and the contrast it provides to the flute and the clarinet.

The *Cor Anglais* is a transposing instrument. It is a fifth lower than the oboe, and its part is written a fifth higher than it sounds, so that the fingering is similar on the two instruments. Its range is less than the oboe and is written as:  .

It is not used very frequently, but it is admirably suited to very plaintive or tragic melodies.

The *Bassoon* corresponds to the 'cello in the oboe family. Its range is:  ; like the 'cello, it uses the tenor clef for its higher notes. Its tone is naturally deeper than that of the oboe, but otherwise it is very similar. At times it sounds very ' throaty '.

The *Double bassoon* is an octave below the bassoon, having the same relationship to the bassoon that the double bass has to the 'cello. Its range is written as: 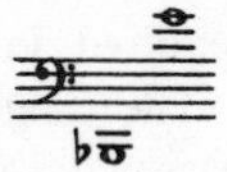 , but, like the double bass, it sounds an octave lower than it is written. It provides a gruff and powerful bass to the wood wind group when necessary.

4 *Brass instruments*

See Section 9, part 6 for a description, under ' brass instruments ', of how they use the harmonic series, a definition of crooks and valves and how they work, and an account of the methods of notation used.

The *Trumpet* is the highest of the brass instruments, and everyone knows the sound of its noble and powerful tone.

Before valves came into use trumpeters could only play the notes of one harmonic series at a time, so they added crooks, extra pieces of tubing, to make the harmonic series coincide with the key of the piece.

The earlier symphonic composers rarely wrote orchestral music in keys with more than three sharps or flats, so trumpet crooks were made in all these keys. The music was written in the key of C, and directions were given to the player as to which crook he was to use.

Today the valve trumpet is usually pitched in B♭ or A and then its transposition is the same as for clarinets in B♭ or A; and it uses the appropriate key signature in the same way. But some modern composers write a non-transposing part, for trumpets in C, which therefore has the same key signature as the key of the piece.

The range of the trumpet is written as: [music notation].

The *Cornet* is very similar to the trumpet and has the same range. It is always written in B♭ or A, therefore transposing like the clarinet. But it is a cheaper instrument than the trumpet, with a much less noble tone. It is mainly used in brass and military bands, and is rarely required in the orchestra.

The *Horn* is a middle-ranged instrument which is quite indispensible in the orchestra. When playing softly it has a poetic tone which blends beautifully with the wood wind instruments, but it can also produce a powerful tone which blends well with the other brass instruments. Many slow movements of the classical composers do not use trumpets and drums, but they still require horns.

Until the middle of the nineteenth century, and even later, natural horns were always used, with crooks available for the key of the piece. The parts were written in the key of C, like those of the trumpet, and the performer was told which crook to use.

The modern valve horn is built in F, so it is always written a fifth higher than it sounds, whatever the key of the piece. This means that it is no longer necessarily in the key of C, but it *appears* to be so, because accidentals are usually put in as they are required, instead of being written as a key signature.

The range of the modern valve horn is written as: [music notation], but notes on the bass stave and above the treble stave are seldom used.

The *Trombone* has a different mechanism from the other brass instruments. The production of the notes is still based on the harmonic series, but it can change from one harmonic series to another on adjacent notes, simply by using its slide. (Everyone has seen the slide being pushed in and out as the trombones are played.) It has, therefore, never had any need to transpose.

Trombones are made in several sizes. The alto trombone is now obsolete, and its part is played on the tenor trombone.

The modern orchestra usually contains two tenors and a bass trombone, which may play in unison or in three part harmony.

Brass Instruments (Orchestral)

Trumpet *Cornet*

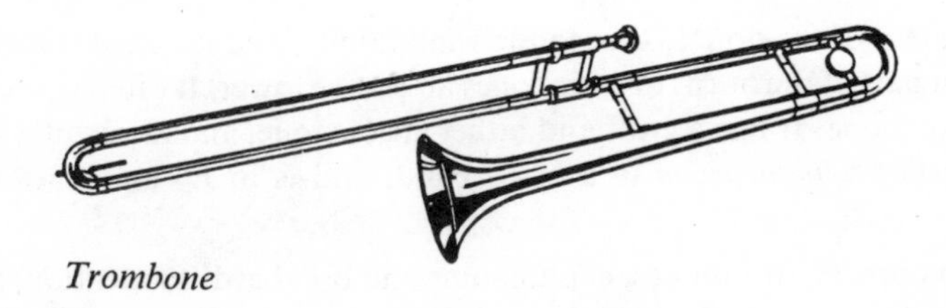

Trombone

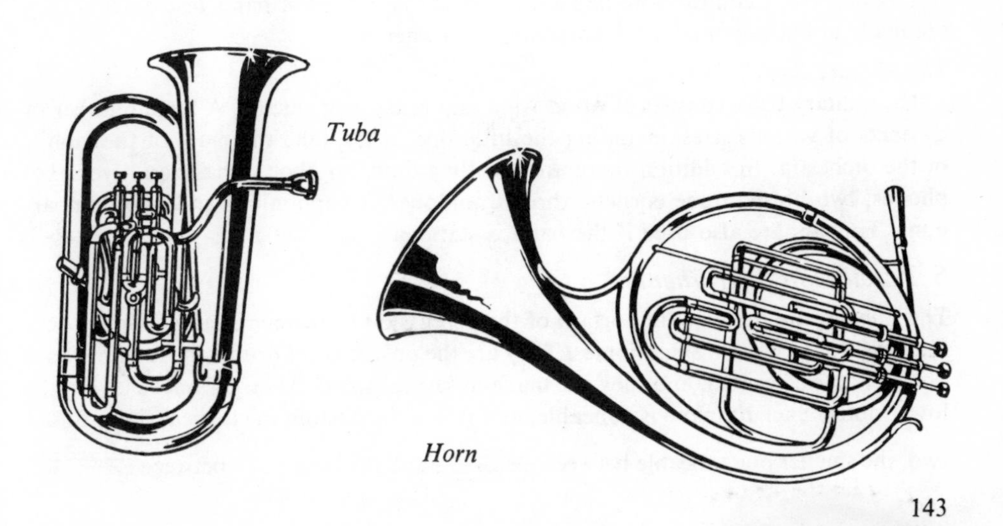

Tuba

Horn

The range of the tenor trombone is: , and that of the bass trombone is:

Modern composers sometimes use the bass clef for all three.

Trombones have a noble, powerful tone, very similar to the trumpet but at a lower register, and they are very effective at an orchestral climax.

The *Tuba* came into existence about the same time as the invention of valves, so it has always been a valve instrument. It looks a little like a horn, except that its bell points upwards instead of outwards.

There is a whole family of tubas. The small ones are called *euphoniums*, and are found in brass bands. But the only one that is regularly used in the orchestra is the bass tuba in F. It is a non-transposing instrument, and its range is: .

It is the equivalent of the double bass in the wind family, and its usual function is to double the lowest part of the horns or trombones an octave lower. It often shares a stave with the bass trombone. It has a gruff and rather coarse tone, and rarely plays a tune.

The tuba is called a *bombardon* in a brass band, and is in E♭ and B♭.

The Brass Band

In addition to cornets, trombones, euphoniums and bombardons mentioned above, a brass band also contains various members of the saxhorn family: the *flugel horn*, the *tenor horn* and *the baritone*. They all have cup-shaped mouthpieces like trumpets and trombones, but a conical bore like a horn. And like all brass band instruments they are made in flat keys and are transposing instruments.

The Military Band

The military band consists of wood wind and brass instruments. A large number of clarinets of various sizes, including the little one in E♭, take the place of the violins of the orchestra. In addition there are usually a flute, an oboe, a bassoon, two saxophones, two horns, three cornets, three trombones, a euphonium and two bombardons. Timpani are also used if the band is stationary.

5 *Percussion instruments*

The *Timpani* are the most important of the percussion instruments, and the only ones that are always used in symphonies. They are the only kind of drums that can produce notes of an exact pitch, and they are made in several sizes, the larger ones playing the lower notes. Each timpano is tuneable, and it was the custom in classical times to use two, the smaller one tuneable between and the larger one between .

Brass Instruments (*Brass and Military Bands*)

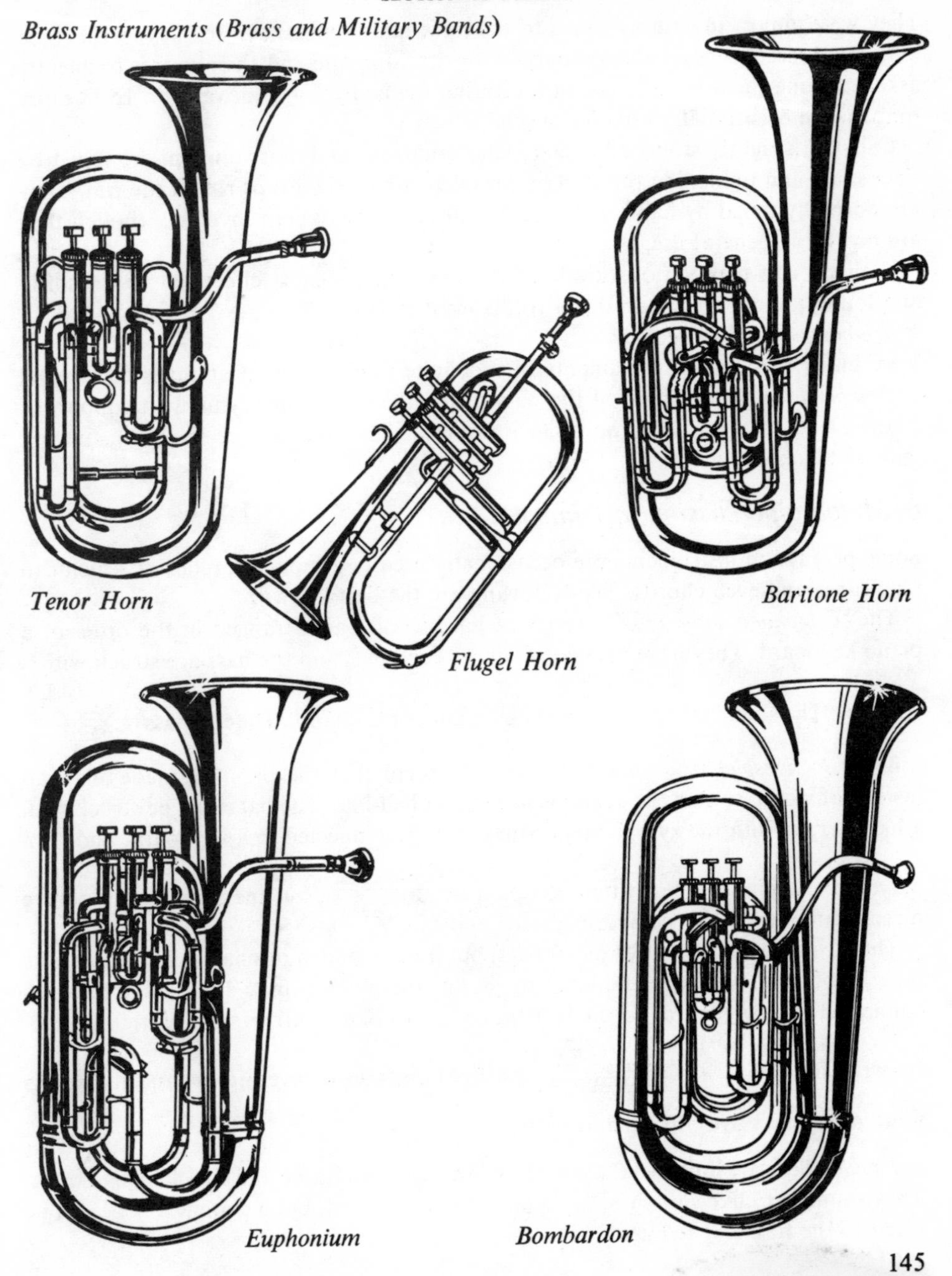

Tenor Horn

Flugel Horn

Baritone Horn

Euphonium

Bombardon

They were almost invariably tuned to the tonic and dominant of the key.

In more recent times it is customary to use three timpani and the player is frequently asked to tune them to different notes during the course of a movement. Even more timpani are occasionally used for special effects.

Calfskin is tightly stretched over a metal cauldron; and most timpani are tuned by slackening and tightening the skin by means of six or eight taps round the rim. They are normally tuned by hand, but mechanical tuners have been invented, though they are not yet in general use.

Timpani can play various kinds of rhythmic figures most effectively, both softly and loudly; and a crescendo drum roll is most exciting.

Instruments of indefinite pitch

Very many percussion instruments of indefinite pitch are used at times for special effects. The look and sound of the bass drum, the side drum, cymbals, tambourine, triangle and castanets are known to everyone. Less common are the gong, jingles, chinese block and whip.

6 *Melodic percussion instruments*

Some percussion instruments are occasionally used in a modern orchestra which can play tunes and even chords. The following are the best known:

The *Xylophone* consists of a series of hard-wood bars arranged in the order of a piano keyboard. They have resonators under each bar, and the bars are struck with a hammer. The sound is hard, with a clicking kind of brilliance. The compass is: 8va.

The *Glockenspiel* is a similar instrument except that the bars are made of metal instead of wood, so that the sound is liquid and bell-like. The bars may be struck with a hammer, as with the xylophone, or they may be connected to a keyboard, and then played like a piano. The written compass is:  , but the sound is an octave or sometimes even two octaves higher.

The *Celesta* also consists of metal bars, but it has wooden resonators as well, and its tone is soft and even more liquid than that of the glockenspiel. The bars are always connected to a keyboard, so the instrument looks like a rather small upright piano. Its written compass is:  8va, but it sounds an octave higher, and its part is written on two staves, like piano music.

Tubular Bells are long metal tubes hung in a woooden frame and struck by hammers. They sound very like church bells. Often only one is used, but a complete scale can be fitted to the frame, if required.

Melodic Percussion Instruments

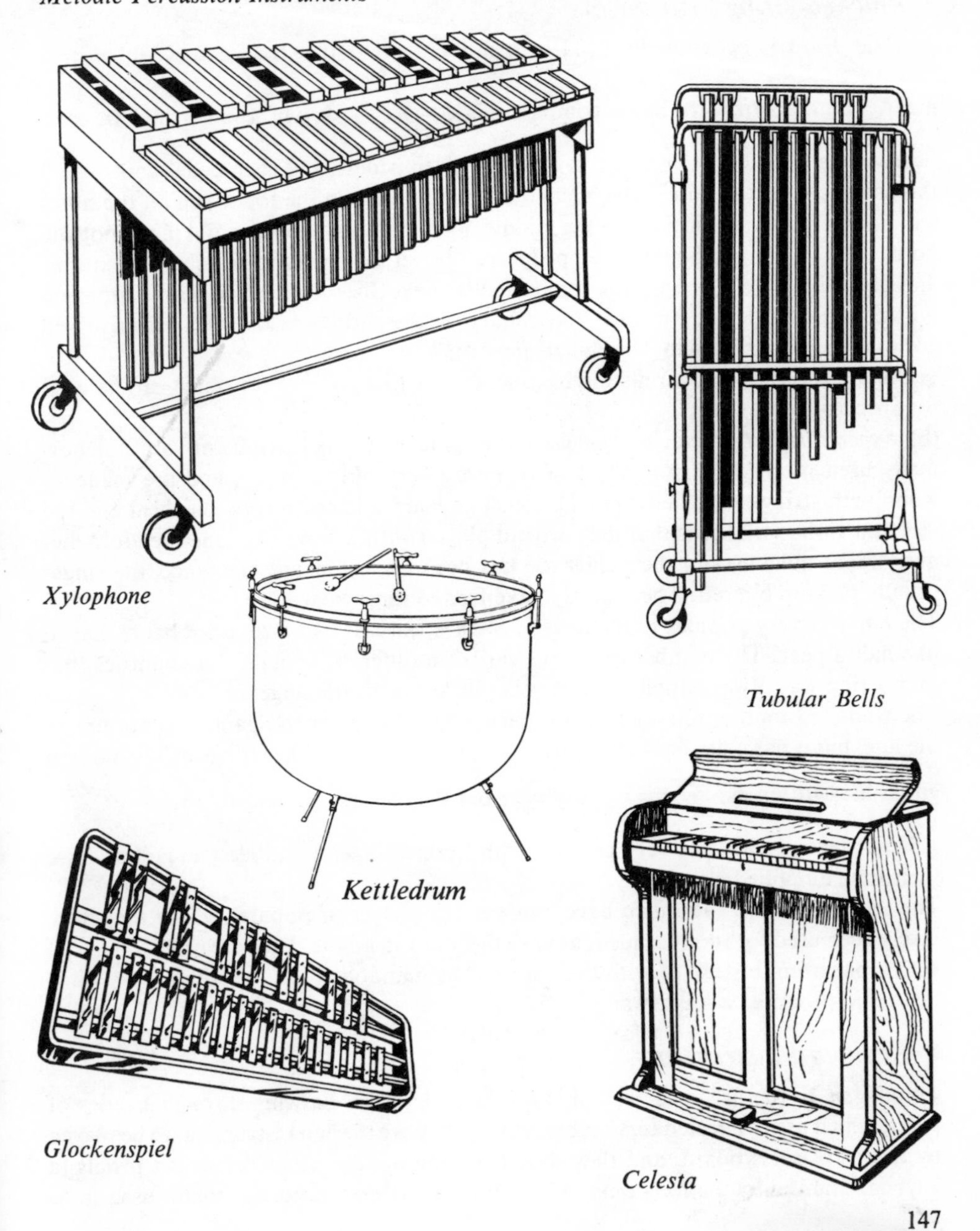

Xylophone

Tubular Bells

Kettledrum

Glockenspiel

Celesta

7 *Plucked string instruments*

(a) The *Harp* is occasionally used in a modern orchestra. It is a very old instrument. The modern form has a compass of:  . It has seven strings to each octave, one for each letter name. It also has seven pedals, and each pedal controls all the sounds with the same letter name. When a pedal is in the top notch all the notes with that letter name are flats; in the middle notch they are naturals; and in the bottom notch they are sharps. So the seven pedals can be set to provide all the sharps, naturals and flats which are necessary for any particular key. Chords are often played arpeggio on the harp: ' arpeggio ' means ' like a harp '. Glissandos are also very effective and are easy to play over many combinations of notes.

One or two harps add a distinctive tone colour to an orchestra, which can be used for special effects.

(b) *Other Plucked String Instruments* Other plucked string instruments are not normally used in an orchestra. Most of them are very old in origin, and are made of wood with strings stretched over the top. The main difference between them and the viol and violin families is that they are not played with a bow. The tone therefore dies away more quickly, and their chief use has been to accompany the voice, the singer usually playing himself. They mostly have fretted fingerboards.

The *lute* was very popular in the days of Shakespeare. It had a rounded back, shaped like half a pear. The number of strings varied in different periods and countries, but each string was always duplicated. It was plucked with the fingers.

The *Guitar* is another old instrument, particularly linked with Spain. It is not unlike the lute, but it has a flat back. It is plucked in the same way. The strings of the modern guitar are written as:  , but they sound an octave lower.

It has recently become very popular with ' pop ' singers; and electric guitars have their tone amplified electrically.

The *Mandoline* and the *Banjo* have had passing phases of popularity, but they have rarely been used for serious music, as have the lute and guitar. They are usually plucked with a plectrum, instead of with the fingers. The mandoline has the softer tone, while the banjo produces a loud twang.

8 *Keyboard instruments*

The *Organ* In the organ the sound is produced by wind blowing through a series of pipes, which are connected to a keyboard. Organs were the first instruments to be played by means of a keyboard, and they date from the middle ages. The organ pedals (a keyboard played by the feet) were invented in the fifteenth century. Organs used to be

SECTION 13 PART 8

Plucked String Instruments

Harp

Lute

Guitar

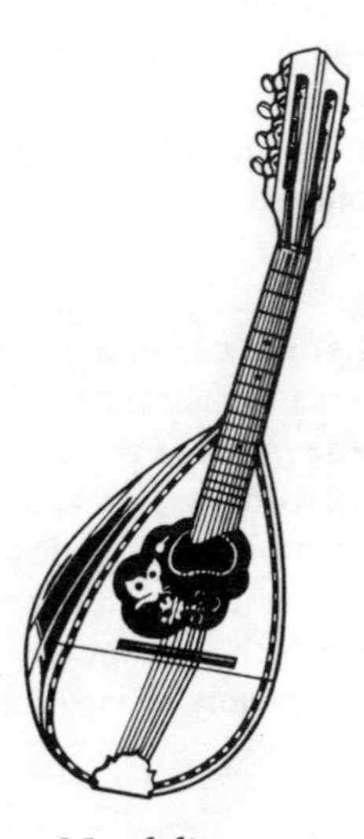

Mandoline

Banjo

blown by hand bellows but now they are mostly powered by electricity.

An organist can pull out a number of ' stops ' which connect up with different series of pipes to create tonal effects, and they are often imitative of orchestral instruments. But the fundamental organ stop, the diapason, is the sound that we associate with the noble effect of a large organ in a cathedral.

Organs nearly always have at least two keyboards, and the very large ones have as many as five, so that five different tonal combinations, using different stops, can be available at the same time.

The modern electric organ does not have pipes at all: the sound is produced by a series of small metallic plates or tone wheels, activated and amplified by electricity. This means it is a great deal smaller and cheaper than a pipe organ.

The Virginal, Spinet and Harpsichord These keyboard stringed instruments all operate on the same principle. When a key is depressed, a quill which is connected to it jumps up and plucks the string.

The virginal was in use in the days of Elizabeth I, while the spinet was popular in the seventeenth and eighteenth centuries. The harpsichord was the most highly developed instrument of the three, and was the keyboard instrument for which Bach and Handel wrote. Harpsichords are still made today, in order to play seventeenth and eighteenth century music on the instruments for which the composers wrote it.

A harpsichord often had two or even three keyboards; and stops, a little like those of an organ, could be pulled out to produce various effects.

A harpsichord was in almost continuous use in accompanied vocal, chamber and orchestral music in the days of Bach and Handel, and for this reason its part was called the ' continuo '. The harpsichord player directed the performance from his instrument and took the place of the modern conductor.

The Clavichord This is another old instrument, and was contemporaneous with the harpsichord. But the sound was produced by a metal tangent rubbing against the string. The tone was much softer than that of the harpsichord, so it was mainly used in the home. Bach used it in this way.

The Piano The piano was invented at the beginning of the eighteenth century. The strings were struck by a wooden hammer connected to a key, and each key was also attached to a damper which silenced the string as the finger left the key. Although the earliest instruments must have sounded rather crude, rapid improvements were made. When Haydn and Mozart wrote their keyboard sonatas they were probably played more often on a harpsichord than on a piano. But in Beethoven's lifetime the sustaining pedal of the piano was invented, which added considerably to the tonal effects available; and eventually the piano completely superseded the harpsichord.

Keyboard Instruments

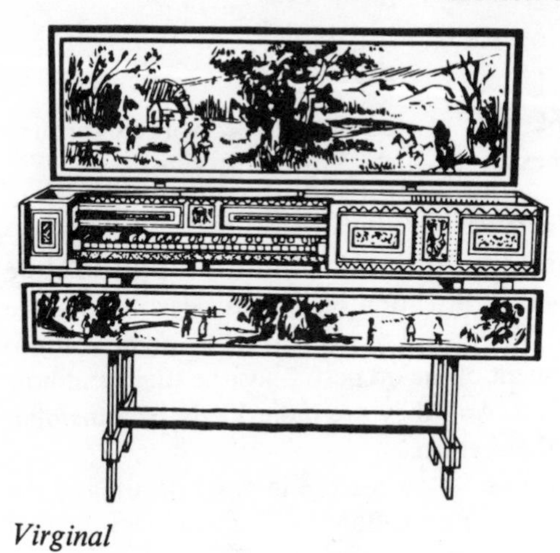

Virginal

Spinet

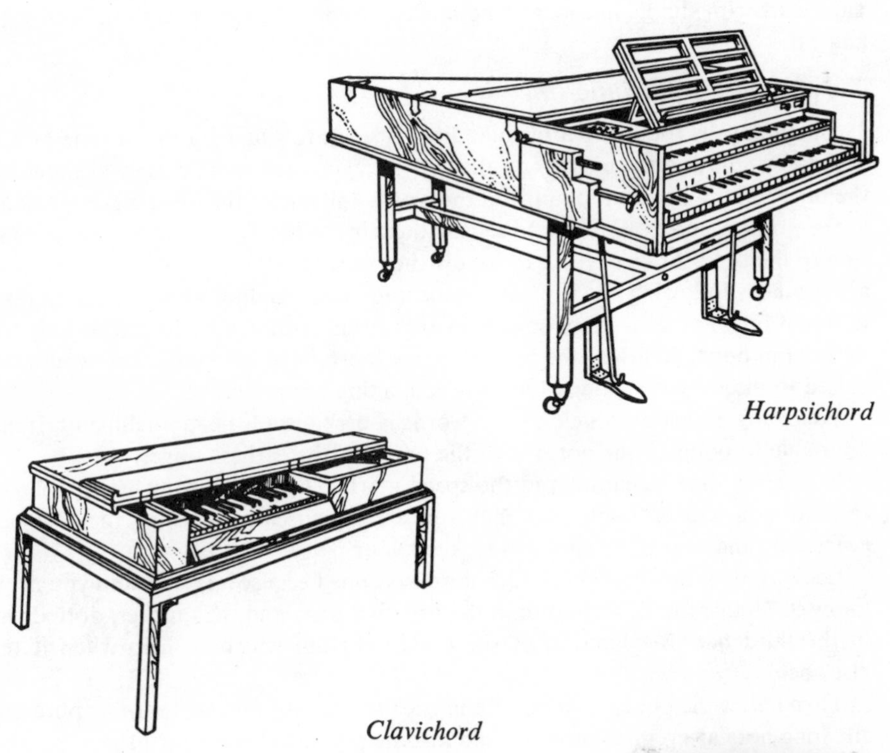

Harpsichord

Clavichord

14 Following a Score

Unlike many other sections of this book, this section should be worked through progressively, as each stage leads to the next.

1 *The advantages of being able to follow a music score*

Many musical people derive great pleasure from being able to follow a printed score while listening to music. It helps to focus their attention on the music; and they are better able to follow the composer's ideas, with regard to musical form, orchestration, and so on. They enjoy seeing which instrument of the orchestra has the tune, and how the accompanying texture has been built up. And they are more likely to remember the themes, and to recognise them when they return.

A highly qualified professional musician can follow a score in great detail, and the link between the eye and the ear will be very strong. But the amateur who, at first perhaps, can follow little more than the main rhythm, can still derive pleasure and profit from following the score, and he will certainly improve with practice. But he must start with simple music, and he must give concentrated attention, both with eye and ear.

2 *Following a melodic line*

The first stage is following a melodic line. If you are singing a hymn tune or a song, with the words and the melody on the copy, do you look more closely at the words or the tune? Many people look only at the words and ignore the tune. Yet a quick glance at the words is surely all you need to take them in; so you should be paying more attention to the tune. At least you can follow the rise and fall of the tune. Choir boys who are regularly following music print tumble into music reading, almost without realising it; and if boys and girls in schools, who are fortunate enough to have a melody edition of a hymn book, followed the melody every morning at assembly they would be surprised to discover how much their music reading improved.

Following a melody which has no words is perhaps a little more difficult. It may be advisable to point to the notes with the finger at the earliest stages.

Notice the time signature and the speed mark. Then, while your finger follows the rhythm, you will probably find that you are unconsciously feeling the first beat of every bar, and that this helps you to keep your place.

Look at the following tune, which is an easy one because it is slow and you probably know it. Notice the slow rhythm in the first two bars, and the quicker, dotted rhythm in the third bar. Recognition of the dotted rhythm will be a help when it returns elsewhere.

Then notice the phrase marks. The music divides into regular four-bar phrases, and the long note at every cadence should also help you to keep your place.

Having had this preliminary glance at the music, follow it, note by note, and bar by bar, as suggested, while it is played or sung to you.

The next example is rather harder. The first part is a mixture of quavers and semiquavers; and the repeated semiquaver figure in bars 3 and 4 is easily recognizable.

Notice the repeat marks at the end of bar 8, and be prepared to go back to the beginning.

Bar 9 starts a new figure. At first it consists of repeated Gs, in varied rhythm. Be prepared for the ornament, the turn, which occurs three times.

Then, at bar 15, it moves up to repeated Cs.

Bar 19 has a return to the quaver and semiquaver rhythm of the opening.

Notice the repeat marks again at the end, and quickly find the place to which you have to return.

Now follow the music, bar by bar, while it is played to you. Having heard it as a melody you may perhaps be able to hear it on a record, in the form that Haydn wrote it, with three other instruments playing underneath it at the same time.

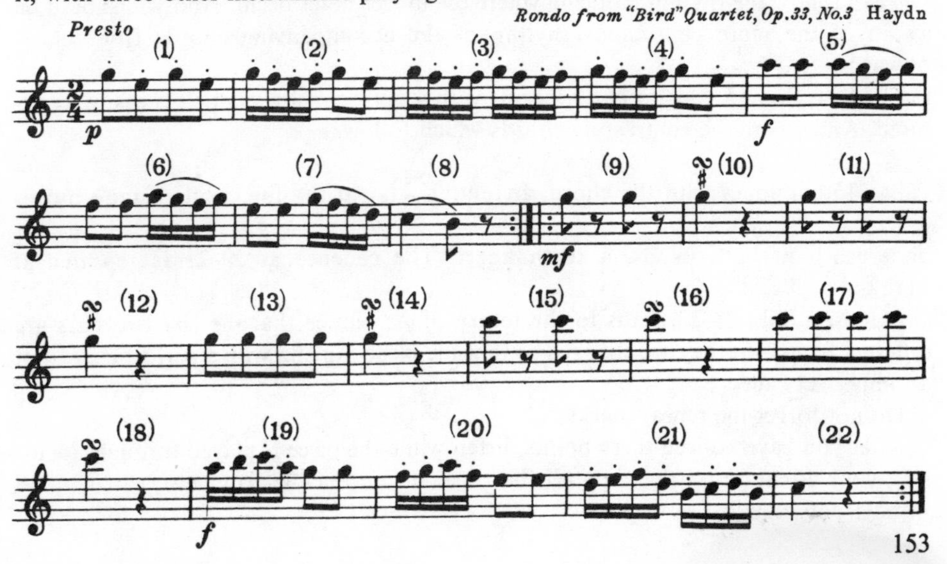

Exercise 137

Follow melodies from the score as they are played or sung to you. Some of the melodies given in Section 6, particularly those given in exercise 74, may be used as examples.

3 *Following a piano score*

Following a piano score means reading from two staves at once, and often from many more than two notes at once, if the music is chordal. But, in practice, you may find it easier than reading from a single melody. Two staves are not particularly difficult to take in at once, and your eye can easily glance from one to the other, according to what your ear tells you is more important. Often one stave helps the other in telling you where you are.

When you first follow a piano score you may prefer to keep your eye on the top part, particularly if it is the melody; and this is then no different from following a melody. But if there is a melody in the bass you can hear it, and your eye should then follow this, rather than the top part. You can hear and see if there is a change of texture, from single notes to chords, and so on.

In the following piece by Schumann a number of comments are made on the copy, in order to help you to follow the music. Study them before the piece is played.

There is a melody in the right hand from bars 1–8, which is rather complicated and chromatic. Probably you will not be able to hear the pitch of the notes accurately, but you can follow the rhythm, noticing where the longer notes occur. And you should be aware of the more continuous rhythm of the accompanying chords from bar 4 onwards.

The B section, starting at bar 9, begins with a unison melody which is easily recognised. And so are the contrasting chords which follow.

Bar 16 continues with the chord rhythm, ♪. ♬ | ♩. at the top, while a tune moves underneath in both hands, a tenth apart. The cadence at 20–21 is repeated at 21–22.

A unison link, 22–23, leads to the return of A. Notice that the last two bars are different from 7–8: they are changed so that the piece can end with a perfect instead of an imperfect cadence.

Do not forget the repeat marks.

After you have noticed these points, listen while the piece is played through, focussing your attention on the copy all the time. If you once let your eye, ear or mind wander you may lose your place.

Un poco agitato
Impressions of the Theatre Schumann
A
R.H. melody
(1)
(2)
(3)
mf
L.H. Accompaniment
(4)
(5)
(6)
(7)
cresc.
f
(8)
B
(9)
(10)
(11)
f Unison. Same notes in both hands
Notice
repeat
marks
Imperfect
cadence
(12)
(13)
(14)
(15)
ff Chords in both hands

(16)
rhythm above
(17)
(18)
(19)
Tune in 10ths in R.H. and L.H.
(20)
(21)
(22)
Unison link to A
(23)
A
f
f
f
f
dim.
p
Imperfect
cadence
cadence
repeated
(24)
(25)
(26)
(27)
(28)
(29)
(30)
(31)
cresc.
f
Changes from here to end
Perfect
cadence

Now listen to the piece by Handel given in the appendix, part 4, while it is played to you. It is perhaps rather easier to follow than the Schumann piece above, but there are no comments on the copy to help you. Listen for the semiquaver scale, which frequently occurs in both right and left hands, as it should help you to keep your place.

Exercise 138

Follow simple piano pieces as they are played to you. A book of miscellaneous easy piano classics will provide plenty of suitable material, and a set of such books are a useful addition to any school music library.

4 *Following a string quartet score*

In a string quartet score there are four staves, instead of two. In some of Haydn's earlier string quartets the first violin has the tune most of the time, so they are relatively easy to follow. But in most quartets all the four instruments ' have a turn '; and you must learn to glance quickly from one stave to another, as your eye and ear tell you which is the most important part. In practice you may still be following only one part at a time, at any rate in the earlier stages, but it is a different part from moment to moment.

Here is the complete score of the Haydn extract of which the first violin part was quoted in part 2, above. You should find it a little easier to follow the four parts because you already know the sound of one.

Notice that at bar 9 the second violin and viola take over the theme, while the first violin part is quite subordinate. Then, at 15, the 'cello takes over; while, at 19, the theme is transferred to the first violin again.

(6)
(7)
(8)
(9)
(10)
(11)
mf
mf
mf
(12)
(13)
(14)
(15)
(16)
mf
(17)
(18)
(19)
(20)
(21)
(22)
f
f
f

Exercise 139

Now follow any string quartet scores that you happen to have available, while the music is played on records. Haydn minuets are fairly easy, though you must be prepared for all the repeat marks. Slow movements are usually easier to follow than quick ones. And modern quartets are generally harder than those of the early classics.

5 *Following an orchestral score*

General hints on following a score

All modern editions of scores are published with the wood wind instruments at the top, then the brass, then the percussion, then the strings. Any extra instruments, such as harp or piano or a solo instrument in a concerto, are placed immediately above the strings. But vocal parts are usually placed immediately above the 'cello part, thus splitting the string section into two.

The strings are the most important part of the orchestra and the violins carry the main melody much more often than any other instrument. So you may think it a little strange that they are not at the top of the score. But it is an advantage to have all the instruments of one family grouped together, and it is important to have the 'cellos and basses at the bottom of the score, as they carry the bass part most of the time.

When you make your first attempt at following a full score you will be wise to follow the first violin part all the time. This means that you must learn to find the violin part quickly on every page. The following general points about score lay-out will be a help:

1 Most, but not all, scores start with a stave for every instrument required in the work on the first page, whether the instruments actually play on the first page or not.

2 The instruments are all labelled on the first page, but their names may be in a foreign language. Refer to the list of foreign terms found in orchestral scores at the end of this section, if necessary.

3 After the first page the instruments are not usually labelled, so you must find your way about by some other means.

4 Early classical works usually have two sets of staves (scores) on the first page, while modern works, which are written for more instruments, usually have only one set or score on the first page.

5 But, after the first page, it is customary to print staves for only those instruments that are actually in use in those particular bars. So the number of scores may vary from page to page, some pages having only one score while others may have three or even four.

6 A mark like this, //, usually divides one score on a page from the next. But sometimes the only indication that there are two or more scores to a page is that there is a

break in the vertical line at the beginning of the page connecting all the staves together.

7 Therefore one of the first things you must do is to learn to recognise how many scores there are on a page. Take as many different works as you can and look over the pages to see how many scores there are on each page.

8 Next you must learn to recognise the different groups within the score. In some of the most helpful editions a thicker vertical line joins each family of instruments together. And even if this does not happen there will be a break in the bar lines between each group of instruments.

9 Frequently two staves for the same kind of instrument, such as two staves of horns, trombones or violins are bracketed together; and this, too, provides a useful guide. In a modern score, flutes and piccolos, and oboes and cor anglais, and other similar pairs, may be bracketed together in the same way.

10 Transposing instruments help in the recognition of which instrument is playing each line. In a classical score containing two flutes, two oboes, two clarinets and two bassoons, you can distinguish the clarinet from the flute and the oboe because it will have a different key signature. In a modern work, scored for a larger orchestra, you can distinguish the oboe from the cor anglais in the same way.

11 In older works the horns and trumpets are written without a key signature and this, also, provides a useful guide. In more modern works the trumpets frequently have a key signature, though they may be transposing like the clarinets. But in most modern works the horns are still without a key signature. All this makes the brass parts easy to see at a glance; and in older scores you can usually find the violin part by looking for it just below the instruments without a key signature.

Now look at a variety of scores, to see if your eye can follow the violin part throughout.

THE STRING GROUP

Now your eye has learnt to locate the violin part you should be ready to follow the string parts of a score while listening to a record. It is similar to following a string quartet, except that a bass part is added. This may share a stave with the 'cello in an older work; but it is usually on a separate stave in a modern work.

A minuet from a Haydn symphony would be a suitable work for a start, though you must be prepared to find the correct place to which to return when a section is repeated.

A slow movement of a Haydn or Mozart symphony is a little more difficult to follow. It may look very ' black ' with notes, but it is usually so slow that you are unlikely to get lost. If the violin part is very ornate it may be helpful to follow the rhythm of a slower-moving 'cello part, to help you to keep your place.

An *allegro* movement, such as an overture or the first movement of a symphony, is harder to follow because it moves more quickly. And you will have to be very alert to keep your place in a *vivace* finale.

Gradually you should learn to keep your eye on all the string parts, letting it travel from one part to another, according to which is the more important.

Exercise 140

Follow the string parts of orchestral works while you listen to them on records or at a concert. (In the classroom the teacher can help by calling out the page number occasionally.)

THE WOOD WIND GROUP

While you were following string parts there must have been occasions when you realised that, maybe, an oboe part was momentarily more important than the violin part; and perhaps your eye has already learnt to glance up towards it. The next stage is to follow the wood wind parts throughout a work, whether they happen to be important or not.

The standard classical orchestra consists of two flutes, two oboes, two clarinets and two bassoons, always placed in that order. But an early Haydn work may contain only oboes and bassoons, while most Haydn and Mozart works do not contain clarinets. It was only at the end of Mozart's life that he had clarinets available; and sometimes he used them instead of oboes. Haydn's later symphonies, which were composed after Mozart's death, used both oboes and clarinets. And, from Beethoven's time onwards, the 'double' wood wind combination mentioned above became the standard classical orchestra.

A modern orchestra usually contains 'triple' wood wind. The third flute player plays the piccolo, the third oboe plays the cor anglais, the third clarinet the bass clarinet and the bassoon the double bassoon. Works written in the last 100 years may contain some or all of these extra instruments.

Notice whether the clef is treble or bass and whether a transposing instrument has resulted in a different key signature, as this all helps in the quick recognition of which instrument is playing each line.

Start with a classical work which uses few wood wind instruments. Look at the copy before you listen to the music, noticing how the wood wind instruments are used, when the oboe or the clarinet has the melody, and so on. You will notice that the flutes frequently play the same tune as the violins, and you may be surprised to discover, when you listen to the work, that you cannot hear the flute parts. But they are brightening the tone, and the sound would be different if they were silent. Now follow the wood wind parts while the work is played.

Next, go on to more elaborate, modern scores, containing more wood wind instruments, and learn to follow their parts, again letting your eye travel from one to another, according to which is the most important.

Exercise 141

Follow the wood wind parts of orchestral works while you listen to them on records or at a concert. Start with classical works, and then go on to such works as Grieg's ' Morning ' from ' Peer Gynt Suite ' and Wagner's ' Siegfried Idyll '. Gradually the eye will help the ear to become familiar with the sound of the different instruments.

THE BRASS GROUP

In early classical works the only brass instruments in regular use were two horns and two trumpets. The trumpet is a higher instrument than the horn but it is always placed below it in the score. This is because the horns so often play with the wood wind that it is an advantage to have them as close to each other as possible. Horns play a great part of the time, even in the softest music, whereas trumpets are confined to the louder passages. They were rarely used in the slow movements of earlier classical symphonies.

In a classical work horns and trumpets were always written in the key of C and transposed by the player, using crooks, into the key of the piece. This has the advantage that it is easy to find their position on the page; but the reader has to transpose the part, in order to realise the exact sound.

Look at a classical score to see where the horns and trumpets come in. Then follow the parts while the music is played.

Composers such as Weber and Berlioz found the limitations of being confined to the notes of the harmonic series such a disadvantage that they began to write for four horns, two in one key and two in another. By this means they had more notes available. Two scores which it would be helpful to follow, as they illustrate this, are Weber's overture to ' Der Freischütz ' in which the horns are in F and C; and Berlioz's ' Carnaval Romain ' in which the horns are in C and E.

With the invention of the valve horn all horn parts began to be written for horn in F, therefore sounding a fifth lower than they look. But even today the accidentals are usually inserted as they are required, instead of being put into a key signature. Brahms, a conservative, continued to use the natural horn; but Wagner, a radical, adopted the valve horn. You can tell which is intended by looking at the beginning of the piece to see what key the horns are in. Of course, all parts today are played on valve horns, no matter what keys they are written in. The player has to transpose them yet again if natural horn parts are in the wrong key for his horn in F.

If you have followed any of these scores containing four horns you will have realised that they usually also contained trombones. Mozart occasionally used trombones in his stage works, and Beethoven even brought them into some of his symphonies. Since his time they have become a regular part of the symphony orchestra.

Composers always write for three trombones. Beethoven, in the last movement of his fifth symphony, uses an alto trombone with an alto stave, a tenor trombone with a tenor stave and a bass trombone with a bass stave, though some modern editions let the alto and tenor trombones share a tenor stave. Composers writing a little later, such as Weber, Berlioz and Dvorak, usually had two alto trombones using an alto stave, and a bass trombone. Wagner and Tchaikovsky wrote for two tenors and a bass trombone, and this has since become the accepted custom. The alto trombone is now obsolete. Some present-day composers now write for the tenor trombone on the bass stave.

Various attempts have been made to provide a really low bass instrument for the brass group. Mendelssohn wrote for the serpent and the ophicleide, two instruments which are now obsolete. Wagner and Tchaikovsky began to use a tuba, and this is now a normal member of the modern orchestra. It usually shares a stave with the bass trombone, its stems going down while those of the trombone go up.

So the standard orchestra of today contains four horns in F; two or three trumpets, usually in B♭ or A; three trombones and a tuba.

Exercise 142

Follow the brass parts of orchestral works while you listen to them on records or at a concert. Start with works by Haydn and Mozart; then go on to works by Beethoven and Schubert; then look at Weber and Berlioz when they are experimenting with four horns in two keys; then on to Wagner in such works as the overtures to ‘ The Flying Dutchman ’ and ‘ The Mastersingers ’, and ‘ The Ride of the Valkyries ’. The finale of Dvorak's ‘ New World ’ symphony, the *andante* of Tchaikovsky's E minor symphony, and Moussorgsky-Ravel's ‘ Pictures from an Exhibition ’, particularly ‘ The Great Gate of Kiev ’ are other works which will repay study of the brass parts.

THE PERCUSSION GROUP

The earlier classical composers used two timpani, tuned to the tonic and the dominant of the key, though they rarely used them for slow movements. Beethoven, while still using only two, experimented by tuning them to the upper and lower tonics in his last two symphonies; and Weber, in his overture to ‘ Der Freischütz ’, has them in C and A, effectively using A as the bass of a chromatic discord in the introduction.

Berlioz, the experimentalist, used a varying number of timpani, with several players, and even wrote chords for them, as in his ‘ Symphonie Fantastique ’. Other composers have used four timpani with two players. But the usual number today is three, with one player. Frequently the player is required to change the pitch of his drums during the course of a movement.

Other percussion instruments are rarely used in symphonies, even today. But many other kinds of percussion instrument are used in programme music. If the instrument has no exact pitch its part is sometimes written on a one-line staff instead of five.

Exercise 143

Follow the percussion parts of suitable works while you listen to them on records or at a concert. Any works by Berlioz are interesting in this connection. Britten's 'Variations on a theme of Purcell' (The Young Person's Guide to the Orchestra) has a section in which the percussion instruments are heard by themselves. Ravel's 'Bolero', Walton's 'Façade' and 'Portsmouth Point', and Britten's 'Four Sea Interludes' from 'Peter Grimes' are other works with interesting percussion parts, though they are quite difficult works to follow with a score.

THE COMPLETE SCORE

Normally, when you listen to a work while following the score, you do not listen solely to one instrument or to one group of instruments. Having had this preliminary training, your eye and your ear should now jointly tell you which are the important parts to follow at any particular moment. You will still tend to keep your eye mainly on the violin part, but it should move to another part of the score immediately you hear a solo in another instrument, or whenever you realise that the violin part is comparatively unimportant.

In quick, loud music you may find it easier to follow the trumpet or trombone parts at a climax rather than quick string passages in which you may more easily get lost.

If you do get lost it may pay you to skip a few pages ahead, fasten on to some passage that you can feel sure you will recognise, and then wait for it to arrive.

Exercise 144

Listen to orchestral works and follow them with a score, as often as you can.

SECTION 14 PART 6

Foreign terms found in orchestral scores

English	*Italian*	*German*	*French*
Piccolo	Flauto piccolo	Kleine Flöte	Petite flûte
Flute	Flauto	Flöte	Flûte
Oboe	Oboe	Oboe	Hautbois
Cor anglais	Corno Inglese	Englisch Horn	Cor anglais
Clarinet	Clarinetto	Klarinette	Clarinette
Bass clarinet	Clarinetto basso	Bass Klarinette	Clarinette basse
Bassoon	Fagotto	Fagott	Basson
Double bassoon	Contrafagotto	Kontrafagott	Contrebasson
Horn	Corno	Horn	Cor
Trumpet	Tromba	Trompete	Trompette
Trombone	Trombone	Posaune	Trombone
Tuba	Tuba	Tuba	Tuba
Timpani	Timpani	Pauken	Timbales
Bass drum	Gran cassa	Grosse Trommel	Grosse caisse
Side drum	Tamburo militaire	Kleine Trommel	Tambour militaire
Cymbals	Piatti	Becken	Cymbales
Tambourine	Tamburino	Tamburin	Tambour de Basque
Triangle	Triangolo	Triangel	Triangle
Tubular bells	Campanelle	Glocken	Cloches
Glockenspiel	Campanette	Glockenspiel	Jeu de timbres
Celesta	Celesta	Celesta	Celesta
Xylophone	Zilafone	Xylophon	Xylophone
Harp	Arpa	Harfe	Harpe
Violin	Violino	Violine	Violon
Viola	Viola	Bratsche	Alto
'Cello	Violoncello	Violoncello	Violoncelle
Double bass	Contrabasso	Kontrabass	Contrebasse
Major	Maggiore	Dur	Majeur
Minor	Minore	Moll	Mineur
A	La	A	La
B	Si	H	Si
C	Do	C	Ut
D	Re	D	Re
E	Mi	E	Mi
F	Fa	F	Fa
G	Sol	G	Sol
Sharp	Diesis	" is " added to letter. Eg, C♯=Cis	Dièse
Flat	Bemolle	" es " is added to letter. Eg. C♭=Ces, except B♭, which is called " B "	Bémol

15 Musical Form

1 *Terms used in musical form*

For terms used in the construction of melodies refer to Section 6, where definitions of the following will be found: phrase; cadence; masculine and feminine endings; decoration; sequence; rhythmic development; inversion; augmentation; diminution; phrase extension and contraction.

For information about modulation refer to Section 10. Change of key is an essential factor in musical form, just as important as change of theme.

The following terms also need to be understood, in relation to musical form:

(a) MELODY A single line of music, forming a tune. It is frequently at the top of the texture, but it can be in the middle or at the bottom.

(b) HARMONY A series of chords which sound well in succession. They are often used to ' harmonise ' a melody.

(c) COUNTERPOINT Two or more melodies performed at the same time. Bach was a great master of ' contrapuntal ' writing. He interweaved his melodies so skilfully that they produced good harmony as well as good counterpoint.

(d) DOUBLE AND TRIPLE COUNTERPOINT If two contrapuntal parts are so written that they sound equally well whichever is at the top or the bottom they are said to be in double counterpoint. In triple counterpoint three contrapuntal melodies can be interchanged in the same way.

(e) VOICE PARTS Contrapuntal parts are called voice parts, whether they are played or sung.

(f) THEME An important musical idea. It may be no more than a melody, but usually it consists of the complete texture: melody and harmony combined.

(g) SUBJECT A theme which occurs more than once. There may be more than one subject in a piece of music; for example, a movement in sonata form has a first and a second subject.

(h) EPISODE A theme which only occurs once. Its purpose is to provide contrast. In harmonic forms, such as episodical, rondo and sonata-rondo, described below, it is completely new material in a new key. But in fugue, a contrapuntal form, it is usually built on a figure taken from the subject or the counter subject, though its purpose is still to provide contrast, in this case a rest from hearing the complete subject.

(i) FIGURE. RHYTHMIC PATTERN. IDÉE FIXE. LEITMOTIV All these terms describe a short theme which may be used frequently but is hardly long enough to be called a ' subject '.

(j) LINK A short connecting passage between two themes, used so as to prevent the music being too broken up into separate sections.

(k) TRANSITION OR BRIDGE PASSAGE A longer, connecting passage whose purpose is to change from the key and mood of one theme to the key and mood of another. It merges smoothly from the one to the other.

(l) INTRODUCTION A slow, introductory section, usually played before a quick movement or piece.

(m) CODA The end of a movement or piece, coming after the other parts of the structure. Its purpose is to round the music off and make a final peroration.

(n) CODETTA A little coda, rounding off a section of a movement or piece.

(o) CADENZA A brilliant passage for a solo instrument, intended to show off the capabilities of the performer.

(p) PEDAL One note is held or repeated, either in plain or decorated form, while the music continues with harmonies of which the pedal may play no part.

Tonic and dominant pedals are the most common. A dominant pedal produces a desire to return to the tonic, and is often found at the end of the development section in sonata form. A tonic pedal often occurs at the end of a piece, and helps to make it sound more finished.

Pedals are usually in the bass, and in orchestral music the timpani are often effectively used for them. If a pedal occurs in an upper part it is called an inverted pedal.

2 *Binary form*

A piece of music is said to be in binary form if it divides into two parts. It is formulated thus: A : || : B : || or I : || : II : ||. The latter method is perhaps preferable, as letters such as A and B are usually thought of as implying contrasted ideas, whereas the second part of a piece in binary form is not usually completely different from the first, and it may even contain a repetition of some of the first part.

In the simpler examples of binary form, such as 'Barbara Allen' and 'The Bailiff's Daughter of Islington', part I may consist of no more than four or eight bars ending with an imperfect cadence, while part II continues with the same idea and ends with a perfect cadence. In such simple examples there will be no modulation and the parts may not be repeated.

In a movement from a Bach suite part I is usually at least 16 bars and ends with a perfect cadence in a related key, usually the dominant if the piece is major, and either the dominant or the relative major if the piece is minor. Part II frequently starts rather like part I but in the complementary key in which the first part ended, perhaps with the melody inverted or put into the bass. It is usually longer than part I and may touch on several other keys before ending with a perfect cadence in the tonic key. Frequently the two endings are alike, except for key.

In a piece containing several modulations they will tend to be on the sharp side of the tonic in the first part and the flat side of the tonic in the second part. (See Section 10, parts 7 and 8.)

A minuet in a Haydn or Mozart chamber work or symphony may also be in binary form. Part II may end with a complete repetition of part I or part of I, but with the ending modified so as to finish with a perfect cadence in the tonic key. Some people call this a hybrid form, because it is a mixture of binary and ternary (see below). It could be formulated thus:

$$\begin{cases} \text{I} : \| : \text{II I} : \| \\ \text{A} : \| : \text{B A} : \| \end{cases}$$

Many short modern pieces, or sections of longer pieces, are in binary form. The two parts are still usually repeated, but the repeated parts may be written out in full.

3 *Ternary and aria da capo form*

Ternary form is formulated thus: A B A. ' Charlie is my darling ' is a short and simple example. Songs such as ' All Through the Night ', which is on the plan A A B A, are also usually said to be in ternary form in spite of containing four phrases, because they consist of a complete statement, A, a digression, B, and then a restatement of A.

Ternary form is rarely found in the instrumental works of the classical composers. But it is often seen in their longer solo vocal pieces called ' airs ', ' ayres ' or ' arias ', and is then sometimes called *aria da capo* form. At the end of B will be found the instruction ' da capo al fine '.

The essential difference between binary and ternary form is that in binary form the first section could not possibly be the end of the piece: either it ends with an imperfect cadence in the tonic key or a perfect cadence in a related key. But in ternary form A ends with a perfect cadence in the tonic key and could therefore be complete in itself. The repetition of A after B can therefore be exact and usually is so, whether it is shown by ' da capo ' as in aria form or whether the repeat is written out. Both A and B may contain a number of modulations.

Some minuets and scherzos in chamber works and symphonies are in ternary form even though, because of repetitions, the plan appears to divide into two parts and is formulated thus: A : ‖ : B A : ‖, apparently similar to a plan shown above for binary form. But if the first A ends with a perfect cadence in the tonic key it is usually considered to be in ternary and not in binary form. However, as there is disagreement about the terminology of A : ‖ : B A : ‖, whatever the key scheme may be, examiners must perforce accept both binary and ternary as possible descriptions of this form.

Ternary form is often found in short and simple modern pieces, or as a section of a longer piece.

4 *Minuet and trio, and episodical form*

A minuet is usually on the plan A : ‖ : B : ‖ or A : ‖ : B A : ‖, that is, it is a complete piece in binary or ternary form. But as it is rather short to be a complete movement, balancing other movements of a longer work, such as a sonata, quartet or symphony, it is followed by a second minuet in such works. This second minuet is called a trio. In the minuets of seventeenth century operas a trio was contrasted with the first minuet by being written for three instruments instead of the whole orchestra, hence the term ' trio '. Its form is the same as that of the minuet.

So the complete plan can be expressed thus:

MINUET TRIO MINUET

A : ‖ : B(A) : ‖ C : ‖ : D(C) : ‖ A ‖ B(A) ‖. It is ternary form on a large scale.

The trio is usually in some related key that has not been used in the minuet, and is contrasted in style. At the end is found the instruction ' minuetto da capo '. Sometimes ' ma senza repetizione ' is added; but it is customary to omit the repeats of the sections of the minuet, on its second appearance, whether this is expressly stated or not.

Beethoven and later composers began to write the quicker, often humorous, *scherzo*, in place of the sedate minuet. But the form usually remained the same.

Minuet and trio form can be used for other dances besides minuets and scherzos. For instance, gavottes and waltzes may be built in the same way.

The plan of minuet and trio form is also frequently used for pieces and movements which are not dances, and in which the sections merge into each other, instead of being in clear-cut divisions, with repeats. The middle (trio) section is called an episode, because it only occurs once, and the term ' episodical form ' is generally used for this plan.

5 *Rondo form*

Rondo form is expressed by the formula A B A C A. The main theme, A, is usually tuneful and often in binary form. It begins and ends in the tonic key every time, though it may be varied or decorated in its later appearances. The episodes, B and C, are well contrasted and are in related keys. The sections are sometimes joined by links.

6 *Variation form and the ground bass*

A short theme, which may be a melody or a bass, is frequently made into a longer piece by being repeated several times in a varied form, often with decorations added. If a *melody* is decorated in this way it becomes an ' air with variations '. If a *bass* has varied harmonies and textures above it it is called a ' ground bass '. A chaconne or passacaglia is a dance in triple time on a ground bass. A ' basso ostinato ' is another name for a ground bass. The ground bass was very popular with Purcell and is occasionally used by more modern composers.

Haydn and Mozart were fond of writing an air with variations. Usually each variation became more elaborate than the previous one. Often one variation changed the mode from major to minor, or vice versa, and sometimes there was even a variation in a completely different key.

With later composers the variations became further and further removed from the original theme. A well-known example is the ' Variations on a Theme of Haydn ' (St. Antony Variations) by Brahms.

7 *Sonata form*

The general plan of sonata form is as follows:

EXPOSITION	DEVELOPMENT	RECAPITULATION
First subject, in tonic; usually rhythmical, short and assertive.	The composer develops any material from the exposition in any way he likes, and in any key. He may also introduce new material, i.e. an episode.	*First subject*, in tonic; as before.
Transition, leading to the key and the mood of		*Transition*, modified so as to lead to
Second subject, usually in dominant or relative major; melodious, and often in several sections.		*Second subject*, now in tonic.
Codetta, to round off the exposition.		*Codetta*, as before, but now in tonic.

A slow introduction or a coda may be added.

' Sonata form ' and ' first movement form ' are both misleading titles, but one or other is always used for this plan. It should be realised that the form is not the form of a whole sonata, but merely of one movement of it; also that it is not confined to either first movements or sonatas. It is often found in second and last movements, and in symphonies, concertos, all kinds of chamber music, and even in one-movement forms, such as the overture.

It is a highly dramatic form, offering great contrasts between the two main subjects, and considerable freedom in the details of its working out.

8 *Modified sonata form*

Modified sonata form is sonata form without a development section. It is used where sonata form itself would be too long, such as in slow movements, or in an overture to an opera. The exposition and recapitulation are frequently joined by a short link.

9 *Sonata-rondo form*

The plan of sonata-rondo form is as follows:

EXPOSITION	MIDDLE SECTION	RECAPITULATION
A *First subject*, in tonic. *Transition.* B *Second subject*, usually in dominant or relative major. *Transition.* A *First subject*, in tonic.	C Usually an episode in another related key. But it may contain some development.	A *First subject*, in tonic. *Transition* (modified). B *Second subject*, now in tonic. *Transition* (modified). A *First subject*, in tonic. (May be considerably shortened, or may merge into a coda.)

Sonata-rondo form is like rondo in that it has clearly defined, dance-like sections, but it usually has transitions joining the sections. And the second theme, B, occurs twice, so it is called a second subject, instead of an episode. Sonata-rondo is A B A C A B A, whereas rondo is A B A C A.

Sonata-rondo form is like sonata form in that it divides into three main sections. But the exposition and the recapitulation end with a return to the first subject, or at least a reference to it; and the middle section is usually an episode, though it may consist partly, or even entirely, of development.

10 *Contrapuntal forms. Canon and fugue*

One of the earliest contrapuntal forms was that of *canon*. In a canon two or more voices sing or play the same tune throughout, one after another. The music has to be so composed that they will fit in this way.

If the last bars of the canon are made to fit with the first bars it is possible to return to the beginning and go ' round ' again. This kind of canon is called a *round*. Two well-known examples are ' Three Blind Mice ' and the thirteenth century ' Sumer is i-cumen in '.

A round with humorous words is called a *catch*.

Rounds and canons are often sung in schools as an introduction to part singing, because it is easier for the singers to sing the same tune than to sing different ones.

In contrapuntal writing the voices very often imitate each other by beginning with the same figure, though the imitation may not be exact and the parts will progress independently after the first few notes. This device is called *imitation*. It is continually used in Elizabethan madrigals.

A *fugue* is a contrapuntal structure which makes use of imitation. In the first part, the exposition, all the voices enter in turn with the same tune, called the 'subject'. The first entry is in the tonic key, the second, the 'answer', in the dominant; and the two keys alternate until all the voices have entered. If each voice goes on to another tune after it has finished the subject or answer and this tune also appears in all the voices in turn, it is called the 'counter subject'. It has to be written in double counterpoint because it must sound equally well above or below the subject. But when a voice goes on to sing or play a tune which, while fitting quite happily with the other parts, does not regularly recur, it is called a 'free part'.

In the second part of a fugue, called the middle section, the voices enter with the subject in other keys, and these entries are now called 'middle entries'. They may be separated by episodes, when no voice is having the subject, though fugal episodes are frequently based on figures from the subject or counter subject, unlike episodes in the harmonic forms described earlier, which are a complete contrast to the other material.

In the third part of the fugue, called the final section, the subject returns to the tonic key. Sometimes the music is made more exciting by the voices entering in 'stretto', i.e. one voice interrupting another before it has finished the subject. The subject may also be heard in shorter note lengths (diminution) or longer note lengths (augmentation) or by inversion (every interval moving in the opposite direction).

If the music continues after the last note of the last entry of the subject it forms a coda.

A *double fugue* is a fugue with two subjects. They may occur together at the beginning, or each may have a separate exposition before being combined.

Fugato describes a passage in fugal style, without its being a complete fugue.

11 *Works written in more than one movement*

(a) THE SUITE

The suite consists of a series of movements collected together to form one whole. Other names for it are 'lesson' (English), 'ordre' (French) and 'partita' (German).

The earliest suites consisted mainly, if not entirely, of dances.

The Elizabethans paired together a *Pavane*, a slow dance, and a *Galliard*, a quick dance.

Bach usually included the following dances in his suites, in this order:

1 An *Allemande*, a dance in moderate $\frac{4}{4}$ time, of German origin. It usually contained continuous semiquavers, beginning with one or three semiquavers before the first bar line (anacrusic rhythm).

2 A *Courante* or *Corrente*. The French courante was in running $\frac{3}{2}$ time with its cadences in $\frac{6}{4}$. The Italian corrente was quicker and in $\frac{3}{4}$ time.

3 A *Sarabande*, a Spanish dance in slow triple time, and in a more harmonic style than the other three dances. It often had a strong accent on the second beat of the bar.

4 A *Gigue* or *Giga*. This orginated in the British jig. It was quick and gay and usually in compound time.

In between the sarabande and the gigue several other French dances were often introduced, of a lighter and more harmonic style. The four most common were:

The *Minuet*, a slow, stately dance in triple time.

The *Gavotte*, a rather quicker dance in $\frac{4}{4}$ or $\frac{2}{2}$ time, with each phrase starting at the half-bar.

The *Bourrée*, again in $\frac{4}{4}$ or $\frac{2}{2}$ time, about the same speed as the gavotte, but with every phrase starting on the last quarter of the bar.

The *Passepied*, in triple time, beginning on the last beat of the bar.

Each of these extra dances could be followed by another dance of the same type. If the second gavotte was built on a pedal it was called a *Musette*, after the French bagpipe of that name.

Sometimes the suite began with some sort of a *prelude* which was not in dance form.

It was customary to write all the movements of a classical suite in the same key; and the movements were almost invariably in binary form.

After the death of Bach the classical suite almost died out. But more recent composers still group a collection of movements together to form a suite, though they are not necessarily all dances, and they are not all in the same key. Well-known examples are Tchaikovsky's ' Nutcracker ' suite (a series of dances from a ballet), and Grieg's ' Peer Gynt ' suite (taken from incidental music to a play).

(b) THE CONCERTO GROSSO

Concerti grossi were written by Corelli, Bach and Handel and their contemporaries. They were a collection of movements, usually three (quick, slow, quick), written for a string orchestra called the *ripieno*, usually contrasted with a group of solo instruments called the *concertino* or *concertante*. A harpsichord continuo part was used throughout.

The first movement, an allegro, began with an opening tutti called the *ritornello*, and this passage returned at intervals throughout the movement in different keys, contrasted with quieter passages in which the solo group of instruments took part. This plan is sometimes called *ritornello form*.

The concerto grosso was a forerunner of the symphony of Haydn and Mozart.

(c) THE SONATA

This word literally means a piece which is played (sounded) rather than sung. (A sung piece is called a cantata.) Sonatas by Purcell, Corelli, Bach or Handel were usually for one or two violins, accompanied by a continuo part played by the 'cello and the harpsichord. (See Section 13, part 8.) Like the suite, the movements were all in the same key, but they were not usually dances. There were usually four movements of contrasted speeds, and the majority of them were in binary form.

Domenico Scarlatti used the term 'sonata' for harpsichord pieces in one movement, in binary form.

By the time of Haydn and Mozart the term 'sonata' had come to mean a work in three or four movements for one or two instruments. The first movement was usually quick and in sonata form; the second movement was slow, and often in modified sonata form, episodical form, or an air with variations; the third movement (if there were four) was a minuet and trio; and the fourth movement, the finale, was often in rondo, sonata or sonata-rondo form. They were no longer in the same key, as in the suite. The second movement was in a different, though still a related key, and occasionally the third movement (of four) was in a different key, too. But the first and last movements were always in the same key.

Beethoven sometimes wrote a scherzo in place of a minuet, and from this time onwards the minuet gradually died out.

The rest of the works described below, in (d) to (h) are based on the form of the sonata as established by Haydn and Mozart, but they nearly always have four movements, whereas the actual sonata quite often has only three.

(d) THE TRIO

A trio is a sonata for three instruments. (But notice that the word has other meanings. It can mean a contrasted dance, as in minuet and trio. It can be applied to music for three singers or three choral parts, which is not, of course, in the form of a sonata. And three instrumentalists can form a trio without necessarily playing music in the form of a sonata. For example, they could be a dance-band combination.)

(e) THE QUARTET

A quartet (when the term is applied to a musical form) is a sonata for four instruments. The string quartet (two violins, viola and 'cello) is the most popular combination, but a number of other combinations are possible.

(f) LARGER CHAMBER COMBINATIONS

Music which is written for a small number of instruments is suitable for a small room or chamber, and is therefore called *chamber music*. It is assumed that, in chamber music, there is only one player to each part, whereas in orchestral music, there is more than one player to each of the string parts.

Other chamber groups, besides those described above, are those for five instruments (*quintet*), six instruments (*sextet*), seven (*septet*) and eight (*octet*). When the term is applied to the music the group plays, it is still in the form of a sonata.

(g) THE SYMPHONY

A sonata for orchestra.

(h) THE CONCERTO

A work for one (or occasionally more than one) soloist and an orchestra. Bach and

Handel built their solo concertos on the same plan as the concerto grosso. But they wrote relatively few.

Mozart was the founder of the modern solo concerto. From his time onwards concertos were built on the same plan as the sonata of the period described above, but with the following modifications:

1 In the first movement Mozart let the orchestra play right through the exposition without the soloist, and with the second subject in the tonic key. Then, when it was repeated, the soloist came in and decorated the themes, and the second subject was in the usual related key. But from Beethoven's time onwards this preliminary exposition with the orchestra alone began to die out, though Brahms still continued the practice.

2 At the end of the recapitulation of the first movement, before the coda, and sometimes elsewhere, the soloist played a *cadenza*, a showy solo passage giving him scope to show his brilliance, and based on the themes of the movement. In Mozart's time the soloist was supposed to improvise his own cadenza, but Beethoven began to write out the music he wanted the soloist to play, and this custom has continued since. The cadenza was usually preceded by an orchestral tutti ending with a $\begin{smallmatrix}6\\4\end{smallmatrix}$ chord on the dominant (Ic), and the soloist ended with a resolution of this chord on to the dominant triad (V), usually with a trill above it, though he might have wandered very far afield in the meantime. The trill was the signal for the orchestra to re-enter with the coda.

3 Most concertos contain only three movements, there being no minuet or scherzo.

12 *Other types of music*

ABSOLUTE MUSIC Music which is complete in itself, depending for its beauty upon its musical qualities, and not upon some external mood, story or idea.

ANTHEM A short, sacred choral work, sung in a church service, and usually accompanied by the organ.

ARIA, AYRE OR AIR A solo song which comes in a larger work, such as an opera, oratorio or cantata. Frequently in aria da capo form (ternary form) and accompanied by an orchestra.

ARIETTA. ARIOSO A short aria, with no contrasting middle section, as in the aria.

ART SONG An artistic setting of poetry for a solo voice, nearly always with a piano accompaniment. It is not part of a larger work, as is the aria, nor is it an unsophisticated folk song. The term is particularly associated with the classical lieder of Schubert, Schumann and Brahms. But many modern composers have written art songs.

BALLAD A poem with a story, often an old folk tale. Frequently set to a simple tune, which is the same for every verse (strophic).

BALLADE An instrumental piece of indeterminate form, usually dramatic, and sometimes based on a story.

BALLET Spectacular dancing, which became a feature of French opera in the seventeenth century. Sometimes it is a complete entertainment in itself.

BARCAROLLE A Venetian gondola song, or instrumental piece based on it, in compound time.

CANTATA A fairly long choral work, often with parts for solo voices, which may be either sacred or secular. Bach wrote many church cantatas.

CASSATION See Divertimento.

CHANT A choral sentence, usually of two or four phrases, to which verses of the psalms are sung in church.

CHORAL(E) A German hymn tune.

CHORALE PRELUDE A piece of organ music based on a hymn tune.

COLORATURA Ornate vocal passages, written to add dramatic colour to certain words and to show off the soloist's voice.

CYCLIC FORM A work in several movements. The term is sometimes reserved for those works in which a theme from one movement occurs in another.

DIVERTIMENTO A work for a small chamber orchestra, in several movements, often six, of a lighter character than a symphony, and frequently intended for performance in the open-air. The words ' serenade ', and ' cassation ' were used for the same kind of work. Popular with Haydn and Mozart.

ENTR'ACTE Incidental music meant to be played between the acts or scenes of a play.

FANFARE A short, introductory flourish of trumpets.

FANTASY. FANTASIE. PHANTASIE A work of free form, in which fantasy has full play.

FOLK SONG A song composed by simple ' folk ', often so long ago that the name of the composer is not known. Usually unaccompanied. Today the term is also applied to popular songs composed by present-day composers, perhaps with guitar accompaniment.

GLEE A short, unaccompanied, choral work for men's voices only. Composed in England, mostly between 1750 and 1830, i.e. after the madrigal and before the part song.

IMPROMPTU A short piano work, meant to sound rather casual and improvised. Schubert and Chopin wrote impromptus.

INCIDENTAL MUSIC Music used incidentally in a play.

INTERLUDE (a) An English term having the same meaning as entr'acte. (b) An instrumental passage played between the lines of a hymn.

INTERMEZZO A short instrumental movement, usually part of a longer work such as an opera or an instrumental work. But Schumann and Brahms wrote piano intermezzi, which were complete in themselves.

LIED The German word for song. The plural is LIEDER.

MADRIGAL A short, unaccompanied, secular, vocal work for two or more voices, which usually enter in imitation of each other. Popular in the days of Elizabeth I. The *Ballett* was a madrigal in dancing style, containing fa-las.

MASS The chief service of the Roman Catholic church, corresponding to the communion service of the Church of England. The words are in Latin, and they are usually sung in plainsong (see below). But choral settings of the congregational part of the mass, not unlike a series of motets (see below) have been written by many composers, such as Palestrina, Byrd and Bach. A *Requiem Mass* is a mass for the dead.

MAZURKA A fairly quick Polish dance in triple time, using frequent dotted notes, and with the phrases often ending on the second beat of the bar.

MOTET A short, sacred, contrapuntal, choral composition, usually unaccompanied, and with Latin words.

MUSIC DRAMA The name given by Wagner to his operas.

ODE A poem in praise of some important person or quality. In the days of Purcell and Handel, setting an ode to music provided an opportunity for giving a concert.

OPERA A large work for the stage, in which the actors (and chorus, if there is one) sing most or all of the time. Accompanied by an orchestra.

ORATORIO A large work for solo singers, chorus and orchestra with sacred words. Today oratorios are usually sung on the concert platform, but originally they were sung (and even acted) in church.

ORDRE The French term for suite.

OVERTURE A preliminary orchestral introduction to a longer work, such as an opera or oratorio. The seventeenth century *French overture* started with a slow introduction in dotted rhythm and was followed by a fugato. One or more dances occasionally followed this. The seventeenth century *Italian overture* consisted of three movements, quick, slow, quick. From the time of Mozart onwards overtures were usually in one movement, and in modified sonata or sonata form. Mendelssohn and later composers wrote *concert overtures* which were, however, complete in themselves. They were usually based on some ' programme ' or story.

PARTITA Another name for a suite.

PART SONG A short, modern, choral composition, accompanied or unaccompanied.

PASSION A setting of the words describing the Passion of Christ—a kind of oratorio.

PASTORALE A short, instrumental piece, of a countrified nature.

PLAINSONG OR GREGORIAN CHANT Traditional, unison settings of the words of the Roman Catholic church services, sung in Latin. They were written in the old modes, because they were written before the major and minor modes had come into use.

POLKA A Czech dance in quick duple time, often containing this or a similar rhythm:

POLONAISE A stately, Polish, processional dance, in moderate triple time, often containing this rhythm 3/4 ♩ ♫♬ ♩ ♫ ♩ ♫, or a similar one in the accompaniment, and with the phrases usually ending on the third beat of the bar.

PRELUDE A short work, intended as a preliminary to another, as in Bach's Preludes and fugues. But Chopin's preludes are complete in themselves.

PROGRAMME MUSIC Music which is based on a non-musical idea, such as a poem, a story or nature.

RECITATIVE Solo singing with the free rhythm and inflexions of speech. The voice part is often written in a series of quavers, but the singer is free to vary them to suit the words. It was much used in the earlier kinds of opera and oratorio. *Recitativo Secco* was accompanied by the harpsichord or organ continuo only, which merely played a few chords between the sung phrases. *Recitativo Stromentato* was accompanied throughout by the orchestra, and therefore the singer could not sing with the same freedom of rhythm. Recitative was dramatic and carried the story swiftly onwards, being a contrast to the more leisurely and formal arias and choruses in which the words were frequently repeated.

RHAPSODY An instrumental composition in a very free, rhapsodical style.

RITORNELLO (a) Orchestral tutti passages, a feature of the concerto grosso. (b) Instrumental passages played at the beginning, middle or end of a song.

SEA SHANTY A folk song sung by sailors.

SERENADE (a) See divertimento. (b) A love song sung outside a lady's window at night.

SINGSPIEL A light opera, with spoken dialogue.

SONG CYCLE A collection of art songs, written by one composer, and often one poet, with a common thought, or story, running through them, and meant to be performed as a group.

STABAT MATER A setting of an early Latin hymn, like a short oratorio.

STUDY A piece of music written to give practice in some technical difficulty.

SYMPHONIC POEM. TONE POEM A large orchestral work, usually in one movement, which depends upon an external programme for its musical ideas and shape, though it is frequently in a very loose kind of sonata form.

TANGO A Spanish-American dance of negroid origin in slow quadruple time. Cross rhythms are a feature as, for example, five notes in the melody against four in the accompaniment.

TOCCATA An instrumental piece written to show off the finger dexterity of the performer.

TONE POEM See symphonic poem.

VOLUNTARY An organ solo played in any part of a church service.

WALTZ, VALSE A gay Viennese dance in quick, triple time.

Exercise 145
Recognise the form or style of music which you hear. If it is a dance decide what kind it is by listening to its speed, time, and rhythm. You should be able to recognise many pieces, such as a quartet or a concerto, by the combination of instruments which you hear. When listening to a work to decide its form, remember its main themes, so that you can recognise them when they return.

Exercise 146
As exercise 145 but judging the music from the copy, with or without hearing a performance at the same time.

16 Summary of Musical History

1 *The value of a sense of period*

Music has varied very much at different stages of its history. It is no use trying to compare a Palestrina mass with a Beethoven symphony or a Chopin waltz, and saying you prefer one to the others. Not only are they for quite different mediums but they were written at different periods, when musical ideals were quite different; and each is a masterpiece of its own kind. No one has ever written a better mass than Palestrina, and you will learn to appreciate it if you understand something of the life and music of the period. After Palestrina music changed, but it did not grow better or worse, so do not think of the history of an art as a continual progress, as is the history of science. You will get most out of the enjoyment of music if you learn to understand the aims of the composers of each period, and to appreciate the best they have to offer.

It is possible that, at present, you enjoy one type of music, or music of one period, more than another. But keep an open mind and develop a catholic taste, then your enjoyment will continue to grow.

2 *Music before* 1550 *A.D.*

Man has always wanted to make music. You can see and hear examples of primitive music today if you watch television programmes showing life in primitive communities.

The earliest cultured peoples also made music. There are pictures of musical instruments on Egyptian friezes, and references to music in the Bible and in Greek literature. But although these peoples had invented a written language of words, they had not thought of a notation for music, so we do not really know what their music sounded like.

The first people to invent a notation for music were the monks of the middle ages, and it took some hundreds of years to grow, until it became the notation you see today.

Music was entirely melodic until about 900 A.D., when the monks first began to experiment with harmony; and this also took hundreds of years to grow until it was at all like the music you hear today.

The monks based their music on scales built of tones and semitones as we do, but they used more modes than our present-day major and minor mode. Their modes had two pairs of semitones, a fourth apart, as does our major mode, but they were not necessarily between the third and fourth, and seventh and eighth notes. The simplest way for you to think of their modes is to play a scale on the white notes of the piano, starting on each note in turn. From A to A was the aeolian mode, from D to D the dorian mode and so on.

These modes were used for plainsong (see Section 15, part 12); and composers as late as Palestrina and the English Tudor composers still used them. Music based on the old modes seems rather strange to us today, but it can be quite beautiful when you learn to appreciate it, provided that you do not expect it to sound like music in the major or minor mode.

Side by side with the growth of music in the church, ordinary folk sang and danced. They were not literate and could not write their music down, but some of it has survived and has since been written down, and we know it as folk music.

3 1550–1600

By 1550 music was being composed that we can still appreciate today; and by 1600 composers such as the Italian Palestrina and the English Tudor composers had written music which was as beautiful as anything which has been written since. It was based on the old modes, it was contrapuntal and full of imitation, and it did not use our modern system of harmony or our phrase structure or forms. So, at first, it may seem strange to us. But familiarity develops understanding; and anyone who sings Elizabethan madrigals learns to love them.

VOCAL MUSIC Music was mainly vocal, and instruments were not used for serious music such as that for the church. The mass and the motet were the chief forms of church music. (See Section 15, part 12.)

But by this period secular education had developed, and written secular music had therefore begun to flourish. The madrigal (see Section 15, part 12) was the secular counterpart of the motet; and cultured Elizabethans delighted in singing madrigals whenever the opportunity occurred in their homes.

INSTRUMENTAL MUSIC Musical instruments became very popular in the home. Chests of viols and recorders (see Section 13, parts 2 and 3) were kept in many homes, and contrapuntal music was written for ' consorts ' of them. The type of music was so similar to vocal music that sometimes it was marked as ' apt for voices or viols '. Towards the end of this period ' art ' songs began to be written with lute accompaniment. (See Section 13, part 7, for a description of the lute.)

Simple keyboard instruments such as the spinet and virginal (see Section 13, part 8) also became popular.

Fantasies (see Section 15, part 12) were often written for consorts of viols; and suites of dances (see Section 15, part 11(a)) and airs with variations (see Section 15, part 6) were popular for keyboard instruments.

Chief Composers

The most important composer in Italy in this period was Palestrina (1525-1594), who lived and worked in Rome, most of the time in the service of the church. He wrote 93 masses and 600 motets. His best known work is his mass dedicated to Pope Marcellus, which is full of sublime beauty.

England had so many composers in Tudor times that it is impossible to name them all. Tye, Tallis, Byrd and Gibbons wrote wonderful church music; Morley, Weelkes and Wilbye wrote some lovely madrigals; Giles Farnaby and John Bull wrote keyboard music; and Dowland wrote art songs with lute accompaniment.

4 *The seventeenth century*

The seventeenth century was an experimental century, as far as music was concerned, and many changes took place. By the end of the century the old modes had died out, and the major and minor mode had taken their place. Modern harmony had begun to develop; and the violin family had come to the fore.

BIRTH OF OPERA What provided the stimulus more than anything else was the birth of opera at the beginning of the century. A group of cultured people met together in Florence with the intention of reviving Greek drama. But what they inadvertently produced was a new art, ' opera in musica ', or ' opera ' for short.

The earliest operas were a mixture of recitative, coloratura and aria (see Section 15, part 12), and they sometimes included an occasional chorus like a madrigal. The harpsichordist played a continuo part throughout (see Section 13, part 8), and his part was written as a bass line with figures above it to show the chords intended to be used. (See Section 12, part 23.) He was free to arrange the chords as he liked.

There were a few simple instrumental interludes; but these grew in importance, and more instruments began to be used as the century progressed. Monterverdi was the first great operatic composer, and he experimented with harmonies and with different instrumental tone colours, in order to heighten the dramatic effects.

The earliest operas were produced in the houses of wealthy Italian nobles, but in 1637 the first public opera house was opened in Venice, and opera soon became immensely popular. A. Scarlatti was the popular Italian operatic composer at the end of the century. He wrote arias in aria da capo form (see Section 15, part 3) and was the first to write ' Italian ' overtures. (See Section 15, part 12.)

By then opera had also spread to France, where Lully wrote operas. They began with a ' French ' overture (see Section 15, part 12), and made much use of the ballet. (See Section 15, part 12.)

BIRTH OF ORATORIO Oratorio was born about the same time as opera. (See Section 15, part 12.) It took its name from St. Philip Neri's Oratory in Rome, where the first oratorios were produced, and where they had scenery, costumes and action. They were, in effect, operas on a sacred subject, and performed in a sacred building.

Gradually oratorios ceased to be acted, and they became musical entertainments, performed in theatres and concert halls, as well as in churches.

DEVELOPMENT OF INSTRUMENTS The growth of instruments was stimulated by their use in opera. The rather clumsy viol family gave way to the more versatile violin family, and it was in this century that the great violin makers, Amati, Guarneri and

Stradivari flourished. Performers on the violin improved too and the first great violin composer, Corelli, lived in this century.

Both Corelli and Purcell wrote sonatas for two violins and continuo. (See Section 15, part 11 (c).)

The instruments of the violin family gradually became the foundation of the orchestra. Corelli wrote concerti grossi for solo, concertante, instruments contrasted with a string orchestra, ripieno. (See Section 15, part 11 (b).)

The simpler spinets and virginals gradually gave way to the more elaborate harpsichord, and composers such as Couperin began to write suites of harpsichord pieces.

Chief Composers

MONTERVERDI (1567–1643) Italian. The first great operatic composer. Used exciting harmonies, experimented with new combinations of instruments to heighten the dramatic effect. After some years in Mantua he settled in Venice. Wrote many operas. ‘ Orpheus ’ and ‘ The Coronation of Poppea ’ are the best known. Also wrote some lovely madrigals and many church compositions, the best known being ‘ Vespers ’. Monteverdi was a revolutionary, and his works are of great historical importance, but they are only occasionally performed today.

SCHÜTZ (1585–1672) German. A church composer, coming midway between Palestrina and Bach. His settings of the Passion (see Section 15, part 12) are still occasionally performed today.

LULLY (1632–1687) An Italian who settled in France, at the court of Louis XIV. The first great French operatic composer. He established the form of the French overture, and developed recitative stromentato in place of recitativo secco. (See Section 15, part 12, for definitions of these forms.) Wrote many short ballets, in addition to ballets in operas. His best known operas are ‘ Thésée ’ and ‘ Armide ’

CORELLI (1653–1713) Italian. The first great violin performer, teacher and composer. Travelled in Europe before settling in Rome. Wrote 60 sonatas for two violins, cello and harpsichord continuo; and many concerti grossi. His Christmas concerto is well known.

PURCELL (1659–1695) English. Lived all his short life in London. Was a member of the Chapel Royal, both as a boy and as a man. Organist of Westminster Abbey and of the Chapel Royal. Wrote much church music for the Chapel Royal, mainly anthems; many festival odes (see Section 15, part 12) for royal occasions and for St. Cecilia's Day; incidental music to many plays; one opera, ‘ Dido and Aeneas ’; and plenty of instrumental music, including fantasies for strings, violin sonatas and suites (which he called ‘ lessons ’) for the harpsichord.

ALESSANDRO SCARLATTI (1660–1725). Italian opera composer, living alternately in Naples and Rome. Developed the da capo aria, and the Italian overture. His life coincided with the rapid growth of opera houses in Italy, and he wrote to please the people. Wrote over a hundred operas and many secular cantatas. But his works are rarely heard today.

COUPERIN (1668–1733) French. Lived in Paris. Organist at the court of Louis XIV. Mainly famous for his harpsichord suites, which he called ' ordres '. The separate movements were in a binary form or rondo form, and many of them were given fanciful titles, such as ' Butterflies ' and ' Little Windmills '. An early writer of programme music. (See Section 15, part 12.)

5 *The age of Bach and Handel*

The experiments of the seventeenth century led the way to the work of the two musical giants, Bach and Handel, who were both born in 1685. They were the greatest composers since Palestrina. Their music is regularly heard today, and is modern enough to appeal to most musical people. Music of this period is sometimes called ' baroque ', a term which was originally applied to the highly decorative architecture of the time. It is mainly contrapuntal, but is written in major and minor keys, and is based on our system of chords and tonality, with well-defined and firm, harmonic progressions. The harpsichord or organ is still used to play a continuo part in almost all vocal, chamber and orchestral music.

VOCAL MUSIC Opera continued to flourish in Italy and France, and Handel did his best to introduce it into England. But there was little opera in Germany, and Bach was uninterested in the form. Rameau continued to develop the French style of opera in France. Gluck was an operatic revolutionary who worked in Vienna and Paris.

Handel wrote many oratorios towards the end of his life. Bach wrote much vocal church music, including over 200 cantatas, a mass and several oratorios in the form of Passions. (See Section 15, part 12) Both also wrote secular cantatas, though they are not as famous as are their sacred works.

INSTRUMENTAL MUSIC In this field Bach is more important than Handel. He was particularly interested in keyboard instruments, for which he wrote many suites and the famous ' 48 ' preludes and fugues. Both Bach and Handel wrote concerti grossi, and many organ pieces. Domenico Scarlatti specialised on short pieces for the harpsichord.

Chief Composers

RAMEAU (1683–1714) French. Travelled much as a young man. Produced a theory of harmony which analysed and explained the new ideas about chords and their inversions, tonality and key relationships. Settled in Paris and began to write operas and ballets rather late in life. The best known operas are ' Hippolyte ', ' Castor and Pollux ' and ' Dardanus ', and the best known ballet is ' Les Indes Gallantes '.

BACH (1685–1750) A German who never left Germany. Was one of a very musical family, and several of his many sons became famous musicians. Held a series of posts in churches and small German Courts, ending with 27 years in Leipzig, in charge of the training of the choir boys at St Thomas's Choir School and being responsible for providing the music at the town's four churches every Sunday. Went blind at the end of his life.

A great church composer, who wrote over 200 church cantatas, the great Mass in B minor, four settings of the Passion, the Christmas Oratorio and six motets in German. Also wrote much fine organ music for the church. His music for the harpsichord (or clavichord) includes the ' 48 ' Preludes and fugues, and 18 suites; and his orchestral music includes six concerti grossi called the ' Brandenburg ' concertos, and many other concertos and orchestral suites.

DOMENICO SCARLATTI (1685–1757) An Italian, the son of Alessandro Scarlatti. Although he wrote other music he is chiefly remembered for his harpsichord sonatas in one movement, in binary form, which have great brilliance and delicacy. He was the first keyboard virtuoso, and he travelled in Italy and Spain, playing his own pieces.

HANDEL (1685–1759). A German who travelled extensively, until he finally settled in England. In his early years his chief interest was opera and he toured the Italian opera houses writing operas for them. When he reached England he tried to establish Italian opera in London, but his attempts twice brought him to bankruptcy. Then he turned to oratorio, which was more successful. Unlike Bach, he never married, but he, too, went blind in his old age.

His operas are rarely performed now, as the style seems too artificial to us today. But many arias from them are still sung. The oratorios ' Saul '; ' Israel in Egypt '; ' Messiah '; ' Samson ' and ' Judas Maccabeus ' are still performed today; and in England ' Messiah ' is the most popular of all oratorios. Also wrote anthems and secular choral works. His orchestral music includes ' The Water Music '; ' The Fireworks Music ' and a number of concerti grossi and organ concertos. Some harpsichord music, too.

GLUCK (1714–1787) Born in Bavaria. Much travelled. Wrote operas in Italy, Vienna and Paris. Influenced by Rameau. Decided that Italian opera was too conventional and too full of coloratura, and tried to make his operas more dramatic and more simple. (Monteverdi, Gluck and Wagner were the three great reformers of opera.) His chief opera, ' Orpheus ' is still performed today.

6 *The Viennese period*

Four of the five composers whose life and works are summarised below were connected with Vienna, so the period from about 1750 to 1830 in musical history is often called the Viennese period.

During this period sonata form and other kindred forms were evolved, the first piano sonatas were written, the string quartet was born, the modern orchestra was founded, and the symphony and the concerto as we know them today were established. Composers wrote less contrapuntally and very few fugues were written. Harpsichord continuo parts were no longer used and the concerto grosso died out. The modern art song was born, created by Schubert; and Weber wrote the first romantic German opera.

INSTRUMENTAL MUSIC Haydn experimented with musical forms and finally devised sonata form, as being the most satisfactory form for large, highly developed movements such as the first movements of sonatas and symphonies. (See Section 15, part 7.)

He wrote piano sonatas, usually in three movements, with the first movement in sonata form. They may sometimes have been played on the harpsichord, but the piano was rapidly taking its place. (See Section 15, part 11(c).)

Haydn was also the first great composer to write quartets for two violins, viola and 'cello. This combination sounded complete in itself without the need for a harpsichord continuo. (See Section 15, part 11(e).)

And it was Haydn, too, who established the general lay-out of the symphony orchestra. Its foundation was the strings (without a harpsichord continuo) and in his first symphonies he often used no more than two oboes and two bassoons for wood wind, and two horns and two trumpets for the brass. But he was soon adding one or two flutes, and two clarinets when players became available. (See Section 14, part 5, under ' the wood wind group '.)

Mozart wrote piano sonatas, string quartets, much music for other chamber combinations, and symphonies using the forms and the instruments that had become established by Haydn. But he was a gifted pianist, and he also wrote many piano concertos in which he played the piano part himself. So he established the modern virtuoso concerto. (See Section 15, part 11(h).)

Beethoven followed on, with piano sonatas, chamber music, symphonies and concertos in the ways that had, by now, become established. But his works tended to be rather longer, with more highly evolved development sections and codas, greater freedom of modulation and much more passionate expression. He also began to write scherzos in place of minuets. The sustaining pedal of the piano was invented in his lifetime and this enlarged the tone colour available for his piano sonatas and concertos. Also he began to write his own cadenzas in his concertos.

Schubert's chamber music and symphonies, while following on the same lines, have tuneful melodies and unexpected modulations. Weber was rather more conventional on the instrumental side, and few of his instrumental works have lived.

VOCAL MUSIC With the exception of the oratorio ' The Creation ' Haydn's vocal music is relatively unimportant. But Mozart wrote some wonderful operas, both in Italian and in German. Weber established German opera in Germany, particularly with his romantic opera ' Der Freischütz '. And Schubert, with his love of poetry and his gift of melody, wrote hundreds of German art songs, and was the first really great song composer.

Chief Composers

HAYDN (1732–1809) Austrian. A poor boy whose voice got him into the Vienna Choir School. After some years of struggle he eventually became the chief musician (Kapellmeister) to the wealthy and musical Prince Esterhazy. Here he was able to experiment with instruments and forms, as performers were always available to try out his works. As a result he established sonata form, the quartet and the modern symphony. Towards the end of his life he began to travel, and he came to England twice, writing 12 symphonies for London.

Wrote 83 string quartets, some with nicknames such as ' The Bird ', ' The Lark ' and ' The Emperor '; 104 symphonies including ' The Clock ', ' The Surprise ', ' The Drum Roll ' and ' The London ' symphony in D; the oratorio ' The Creation '; Piano sonatas; and many other works.

MOZART (1756–1791) Austrian. Born in Salzburg, where his father was a court musician. A musical prodigy, who travelled round the courts of Europe between the ages of 7 and 21, as a pianist, violinist and composer. Unsuccessfully tried to settle in Paris, then returned to Salzburg, where he found his patron, the Archbishop, uncongenial. So moved to Vienna, but was in almost continual poverty, as he had no regular appointment. Died there, aged 35.

A prolific writer, whose works include 39 symphonies, the last three, in E♭ major, G minor and C major (the Jupiter) being the greatest; 25 piano concertos and many other concertos; much chamber music; piano sonatas; a large number of operas, including ' The Marriage of Figaro ', and ' The Magic Flute '; and a good deal of church music, of which the unfinished requiem, written when he was dying, is the finest example.

BEETHOVEN (1770–1827) German. Born in Bonn, and had a hard childhood, with a drunkard for a father. Settled in Vienna, where he became famous, in spite of his uncouth ways. Had friends among the aristocracy, and earned his living by giving concerts, teaching and dedicating his compositions to wealthy patrons. Never married, and began to go deaf quite young. His deafness made him more and more lonely and he moved from lodging to lodging. Adopted a nephew who was continually in trouble.

His work is divided into three periods. In the first period he adopted and assimilated the styles of Haydn and Mozart. In his middle period his works became grander and more passionate and it was a period of mastery. In his last period, when deafness had made him withdraw into himself, his music was prophetic of the future and was not understood by his contemporaries.

Wrote nine symphonies including the ' Eroica ', the ' Pastoral ' and the Choral; five piano concertos including the ' Emperor ', and a violin concerto; 32 piano sonatas including the ' Pathetic ', the ' Moonlight ', the ' Waldstein ' and the ' Appassionata '; much chamber music of all kinds; one opera ' Fidelio ', for which he wrote four overtures, three of them now going under the name ' Leonora ', which are often played separately; and a mass in D major.

WEBER (1786–1826) A German, who held many appointments in German opera houses. His journey to London to produce his opera ' Oberon ' was the cause of his early death. He had little connection with Vienna, though his instrumental music inevitably owed much to Haydn and Mozart.

Although he wrote piano sonatas, ' The Invitation to the Dance ', and other piano pieces, and a fair amount of chamber and orchestral music including three concertos for the clarinet, it is relatively unimportant. It was his work for opera that gives him a place in musical history. He established German opera in Germany, and his opera ' Der Freischütz ', with its fantastic story full of superstitions and magic, is considered to be the first romantic opera.

SCHUBERT (1797–1828) Austrian. Lived in or near Vienna all his life. A poor boy who, like Haydn, got his musical education at the Vienna Choir School, owing to his good voice. Lived an irregular Bohemian life, among poets and other artistic friends. Not known by the aristocracy, as was Beethoven, so had little patronage. Died young, in poverty.

Composed easily and prolifically, with little attempt at revision. Wrote piano music including impromptus; piano trios, the ' Death and the Maiden ' quartet, the ' Trout ' quintet and an octet; and 11 symphonies including the ' Unfinished ' and the ' Great ' C major. It is all characterised by being full of melody, often with lovely unexpected changes of key. But sometimes his pieces are loosely constructed and contain too much repetition. His theatre music and church music is less good, but his incidental music to ' Rosamunde ' is popular.

His original contribution to the art of music is his development of the art song, of which he was the first great exponent. He used the piano accompaniment to enhance the poetry of the words, and his forms were very free and allowed to grow out of the words. Sometimes each verse of poetry had the same music (strophic form), but frequently the song was in one continuous whole (durchcomponirt). Wrote 600 songs, including three song cycles ' The Maid of the Mill ', ' Winter Journey ' and ' Swan Songs '. Famous separate songs include ' The Erl King ', ' Gretchen at the Spinning Wheel ', ' Hark, hark the Lark ', ' Hedge Rose ' and ' The Trout '.

7 *The early romantics* (1830–1860)

New movements in music were stirring in the first half of the nineteenth century, and it is customary to call the composers who reached maturity at that time 'the Early Romantics'.

Composers were more interested in the imaginative side than the formal side of music. They often wrote 'programme' music instead of 'absolute' music. (See Section 15, part 12, for a definition of these terms.) So they often gave their music fanciful titles instead of mere opus numbers.

INSTRUMENTAL MUSIC Although composers continued to write symphonies they exhibited greater freedom of form and key and they wrote for larger orchestras. Berlioz wrote a symphony for a very large orchestra, which was based on a story, 'Symphonie Fantastique'. Liszt began to write what he called 'symphonic poems' (see Section 15, part 12), and other composers followed suit. Mendelssohn wrote 'concert overtures', which had a programme and were not a prelude to a larger work.

During this period the piano really came into its own. Chopin and Schumann wrote much music for it, and Liszt wrote very difficult, showy piano pieces which he played himself on concert tours.

VOCAL MUSIC Schumann and Mendelssohn wrote art songs on the lines of those written by Schubert. Opera continued to be popular on the continent, and Rossini was the chief opera composer. But Russia was now coming into the picture, and Glinka wrote the first Russian operas. Mendelssohn wrote oratorios.

Chief Composers

ROSSINI (1792–1868) Popular Italian operatic composer. Director of opera house at Naples. Wrote 36 operas in 19 years; then, aged 37, refused to write any more, though he lived to be 76. Retired to Paris. Best known operas are 'The Barber of Seville' and 'William Tell'. Also wrote a Stabat Mater and a mass.

BERLIOZ (1803–1869) French. Led a dramatic, romantic life with frequent concert tours in Europe, including visits to Russia and England. Experimented with orchestral effects and wrote for large orchestras. Wrote requiem for large choir and orchestra and four brass bands; 'Symphonie Fantastique', a programme work in five movements; 'Harold in Italy', another programme work for viola and orchestra. Also wrote large-scale operas which were unsuccessful, though 'The Damnation of Faust' is sometimes given in a concert version. The overtures to the operas 'Benvenuto Cellini' and 'Beatrice and Benedict' are also heard today, as is 'Carnaval Romain', a concert overture based on 'Benvenuto Cellini'. Wrote musical criticism for 30 years. Published an important treatise on orchestration.

GLINKA (1804–1857) First important Russian composer. Travelled to Italy and heard Italian opera. Then studied in Berlin, with the aim of learning to write Russian opera. Returned to Russia and wrote operas 'A Life for the Czar' and 'Russlan and Ludmilla'.

MENDELSSOHN (1809–1847) German. Belonged to a wealthy Jewish family. Was very clever and well educated. A musical prodigy who wrote a concert overture based on ' The Midsummer Night's Dream ' when he was 17. Education completed by a grand tour of Europe, age 20–23. Wrote ' The Hebrides ' concert overture, the Scotch symphony and the Italian symphony as a result. Conductor in Leipzig and Berlin. Revived Bach's work, particularly the St. Matthew Passion, and gave the first performance of Schubert's ' Great ' C major symphony. Made concert tours, including several visits to England, where he was extremely popular. Wrote oratorio ' Elijah ' for Birmingham. Died young.

Although he belongs to the romantic period, and there was certainly a romantic strain in his music, he composed in classical forms, and had great contrapuntal skill. Wrote five symphonies and five concert overtures (some mentioned above); a popular violin concerto; chamber music; piano music; organ music; songs; and sacred music including the oratorios ' St. Paul ' and ' Elijah '.

CHOPIN (1810–1849) Polish. Concert pianist and piano composer. Settled in Paris. When Warsaw was captured by the Russians wrote his ' revolutionary ' study. Thenceforward an exile. Made concert tours in Germany and England. Enjoyed piano teaching and playing in Paris Salons. Went to Majorca with George Sand for his health, but became tubercular and, in spite of her continued care, died young.

Founded a new style of piano playing and composing. Strong sense of Polish nationality. Wrote little but piano music. Polish dances: mazurkas and polonaises; waltzes; studies; nocturnes; preludes; sonatas; scherzos; and ballades, all for the piano.

SCHUMANN (1810–1856) German. Well educated, with literary tastes. Started to study law, then changed to music, aged 20. Intended to be a pianist but damaged his finger, so changed to composition. Married Clara Wieck, a famous pianist and daughter of his piano teacher, after long parental opposition. Wrote 100 love songs in year of his marriage. Held posts as teacher and conductor, but ineffectual at both. Became increasingly morbid, and spent last two years of his life in a mental asylum.

Wrote four symphonies, a piano concerto and a 'cello concerto; some chamber music; much piano music, including ' Papillons ', ' Carnaval ' and three sonatas; many songs, of unequal merit, including song cycle ' Dichterliebe '. All the music is full of romantic warmth. Also wrote much valuable music criticism.

LISZT (1811–1886) Hungarian. Became Europe's most brilliant concert pianist, writing very difficult music, some of which only he could play, including many transcriptions of songs and operatic selections. Also became a great piano teacher and gave help to many young composers, championing Wagner, who became his son-in-law. Invented the symphonic poem. Lived to 75, so his life runs on into the period of the Late Romantics. Became an abbé later in life.

Famous for three things: his piano music, his symphonic poems and the help he gave to other musicians. Piano music includes studies; ' Années de Pélerinage ';

Hungarian rhapsodies; a sonata; and many transcriptions of songs and operatic fantasies, useful before the days of the gramophone record. His orchestral music includes two piano concertos; ' Faust ' and ' Dante ' symphonies; ' Mephisto Waltz '; ' Les Préludes '; and symphonic poems such as ' Hamlet ' and ' Mazeppa '. In these works he used short, recurring figures, linked with some mood, idea or person, called *idées fixes* or *leit motive*, which were first started by Berlioz, and which later became a feature of Wagner's operas. He also wrote a large number of songs and choral works, now rarely performed.

8 *The later romantics* (1850–1900)

INSTRUMENTAL MUSIC In the second half of the nineteenth century music grew in richness and complexity, without actually treading new paths. Most of the composers discovered the delights of writing for a larger orchestra. Those whose outlook was mainly classical, such as Brahms, Dvorak, Tchaikovsky and Bruckner, continued to write symphonies; while those in whom the romantic element was strong and who were influenced by Berlioz and Liszt, such as Smetana, Balakirev, Mussorgsky and Rimsky-Korsakov, wrote symphonic poems. But, looking back on their music today, it all seems to have a romantic element in it, even if written by a classicist such as Brahms.

Chamber music and piano music continued to flourish, and perhaps the greatest exponent of both was Brahms.

VOCAL MUSIC Wagner carried the strong romantic element into his operas, which he called music dramas. For a time most of the musical world took sides, being pro-Brahms and anti-Wagner or vice versa. Verdi was a popular operatic composer, who began in a conventional way, but was later influenced by Wagner.

Sacred choral music was represented by Verdi, Brahms and Dvorak, who each wrote a requiem mass; and by Franck, who wrote an oratorio ' Les Béatitudes '.

Brahms was the greatest song writer of the day.

DEVELOPMENT OF NATIONALISM Perhaps the chief new thing that happened in this period was the development of nationalism in music. Composers such as Borodin, Balakirev, Mussorgsky and Rimsky-Korsakov in Russia, Smetana and Dvorak in Czechslovakia, and Grieg in Norway, tried to express racial characteristics and to use national idioms and even national folk tunes in their music.

Chief Composers

As we approach nearer to the present day the canvas begins to get more crowded, and selection becomes more difficult. But the following is a brief summary of the chief composers and their works.

WAGNER (1813–1883) German operatic composer who led a stormy life, being a political exile from Germany at one stage, and always fighting to get his works recognised and performed. Eventually won the patronage of King Ludwig of Bavaria, and had a special opera house built for his music dramas in Bayreuth.

Wrote little of importance except music dramas, for which he wrote his own librettos. Demanded large-scale productions, and wrote for a very large orchestra, making much use of leit motive. His music dramas are ' Rienzi '; ' Flying Dutchman '; ' Tannhäuser '; ' Lohengrin '; ' The Ring ', a cycle consisting of ' The Rhinegold ', ' The Valkyrie ', ' Siegfried ' and ' The Twilight of the Gods '; ' Tristan and Isolde ', ' The Mastersingers '; and ' Parsifal '.

VERDI (1813–1883) Italian operatic composer, who began with conventional operas such as ' Rigoletto '; ' La Traviata' and ' Il Trovatore '. Later, affected by Wagner, he wrote on a larger scale, the chief operas being ' Aida '; ' Othello ' and ' Falstaff '. Also wrote sacred music, the best known work being his requiem.

FRANCK (1822–1890) A Belgian who settled in Paris. An organist and teacher who developed into a composer of importance only late in life. Wrote a fine symphony; Symphonic Variations for piano and orchestra; piano music; chamber music, including a violin sonata and a string quartet; organ pieces, and sacred music including the oratorio ' Les Béatitudes '.

SMETANA (1824–1884) The first famous Czech composer. Became conductor of the Prague opera house. Wrote the opera ' The Bartered Bride ' and six symphonic poems with the general title of ' My Fatherland '.

BRUCKNER (1824–1896) Austrian. A classic-romantic who wrote nine symphonies, which are much played in Germany and Austria, less elsewhere. Unlike Brahms's symphonies they were influenced by Wagner, and the movements were often linked by thematic connections. Also wrote organ music and a number of church works, including three masses and a Te Deum.

BORODIN (1833–1887) Russian. A chemist who later became a musician. Wrote an unfinished opera ' Prince Igor '; symphonic poem ' In the Steppes of Central Asia '; two symphonies; and some chamber music, including two string quartets.

BRAHMS (1833–1897) German. After a few years of travel he settled in Vienna, where he lived an uneventful life and never married. A devoted friend to Schumann's widow and children. Although his music has a romantic, nineteenth century flavour, he carried on in the classic traditions of Beethoven. Wrote four symphonies, a violin concerto and two piano concertos, several concert overtures, and ' Variations on a Theme of Haydn ' for orchestra; much lovely chamber music; piano music; and many songs. Also a German Requiem.

BALAKIREV (1837–1910) Russian nationalist composer, who helped to found Russian musical traditions. Wrote many Russian songs; a symphonic poem ' Thamar '; two symphonies; two piano concertos; and a quantity of piano music, some of it very difficult, such as ' Islamey '.

BIZET (1838–1875) French. Died young, before he had really become established. Wrote opera ' Carmen ', two ' L'Arlésienne ' suites and a symphony.

MUSSORGSKY (1839–1881) Russian nationalist composer, who died young. Inspired by folk music and wrote many Russian songs. Wrote operas ' Boris Godounov ' and ' Khovantchina '. Also wrote a piano suite ' Pictures from an Exhibition ' which was later orchestrated by Ravel.

TCHAIKOVSKY (1840–1893) The first Russian composer to achieve fame outside his own country, partly because his music was not distinctively Russian but owed much to German and Italian traditions. A shy, retiring man, who preferred to live alone in the Russian countryside, but who nevertheless undertook several tours to Europe and America.

His compositions include six symphonies; fantasie overture ' Romeo and Juliet '; two piano concertos and a violin concerto; ballets, including ' Swan Lake '; ' The Sleeping Beauty ' and ' The Nutcracker '; and operas, the best-known being ' Eugen Onegin '.

DVORAK (1841–1904) Czech. Helped by Smetana whose orchestra he joined in Prague, and later by Brahms who helped to get his music published. As his music became known he made concert tours to Russia, Germany, England and America.

Wrote nine symphonies, including ' The New World ', written for America; a violin concerto and a 'cello concerto; three concert overtures, including ' Carnival '; and Slavonic Rhapsodies for orchestra; some attractive and popular chamber music; and choral works including Stabat Mater and a requiem.

GRIEG (1843–1907) Norwegian. Educated in Leipzig. Married a singer, who helped to popularise his songs. A composer of slight but attractive songs and piano pieces. His best known larger works are his piano concerto, the two ' Peer Gynt ' suites, and the ' Holberg ' suite for strings.

RIMSKY-KORSAKOV (1844–1908) Russian. A naval officer who later became a musician. Influenced by Balakirev. Filled several musical posts in St. Petersburg (now Leningrad), and taught many younger Russian composers.

Wrote operas including ' Sadko ' and ' The Golden Cockerel '; three symphonies; a symphonic suite ' Scheherazade '; and many Russian songs.

9 *The early twentieth century*

Composers writing at the beginning of the twentieth century can very roughly be divided into two types: those who enlarged even further the romantic tendencies of their predecessors, often called ' neo-romantics '; and those who were influenced by impressionism.

NEO-ROMANTICISM Elgar, Mahler, Strauss, Sibelius, Vaughan Williams, Bax and Holst were all composers who, as we realise today, further enlarged the canvas of musical composition as it had been practised by Brahms and Wagner, without really revolutionising it. They wrote for an even larger orchestra, and they extended harmonies, modulations and chromaticisms as far as they could within the limits of the major and minor keys. Fundamentally their music was still emotional and romantic, though at times it was very discordant.

IMPRESSIONISM Impressionism began with painters such as Monet and Cézanne, who gave a general impression of what could be seen at a quick glance without recording every detail. They were much concerned with the play of light on objects, and they achieved shimmering, atmospheric effects. Their ideas soon spread to poets and musicians. The first musician to be affected was Debussy, who made various revolutionary experiments such as occasionally using the whole-tone scale; adding seconds and sixths to triads and still calling the result a concord; making use of overtones; and using parallel discords which produced a kind of linear harmony. The whole-tone experiments lead to a dead end; but other composers such as Delius, Ravel and Falla also wrote impressionistic music, while usually keeping within the bounds of major and minor tonality. But the music was still also fundamentally romantic.

Chief Composers

ELGAR (1857–1934) English. Born and died in the West Country, but spent brief periods in London. Wrote conventional choral works when young; then, about the turn of the century, produced ' Enigma ' variations for orchestra, and three great oratorios ' The Dream of Gerontius ', ' The Apostles ' and ' The Kingdom ', which established his fame. Became associated with Edwardian grandeur, and wrote the ' Pomp and Circumstance ' marches (one of which includes the tune ' Land of Hope and Glory '); the concert overture ' Cockaigne ', a description of London; and two symphonies, all for a very large orchestra. Was knighted, and later given the Order of Merit. Also wrote a violin and a 'cello concerto; a symphonic study ' Falstaff '; Introduction and Allegro for strings; and some chamber music. His work is valued more highly in England than elsewhere.

MAHLER (1869–1911) An Austrian, who lived and worked in Vienna and also visited America. A classic-romantic, who wrote nine symphonies which were influenced by Brahms, Wagner and Bruckner. ' The Song of the Earth ' is a symphony for orchestra and solo voices. Like the music of Bruckner, his work is valued more highly in Austria and Germany than elsewhere.

DEBUSSY (1862–1918) French. Joined the impressionist group of painters and poets. His first impressionist work was the orchestral prelude ' L'Après-midi d'un Faune ', based on a poem by Mallarmé, which contained entirely new harmony, orchestration and rhythm, and sometimes used the whole tone scale and parallel discords. His opera ' Pelléas et Mélisande ' was mainly recitative, and had the same dream-like atmosphere. Wrote other orchestral works with titles, such as ' La Mer ', but no symphonies; some chamber music; and many impressionistic piano pieces and songs.

DELIUS (1862–1934) English, but of German-dutch descent. After some years of travel and some study in Leipzig he settled in France. Was blind and paralysed in his later years. A romantic-impressionist, with his own peculiar harmonic idiom, which made comparatively little use of song-like melodies or varied rhythms. Wrote some songs and chamber music, and some rarely-performed operas. But his best known works are his orchestral pieces such as 'Brigg Fair'; 'In a Summer Garden'; 'On Hearing the First Cuckoo in Spring', and 'A Song Before Sunrise', which show a unique sense of orchestral tone-colour. Also wrote choral works with orchestra such as 'Sea Drift' and 'A Mass of Life'.

STRAUSS (1864–1949) German. A precocious composer who wrote the symphonic poem 'Don Juan' for a very large orchestra when he was 25. Was followed by other symphonic poems: 'Death and the Transfiguration'; 'Tyl Eulenspiegel's Merry Pranks'; 'Don Quixote' and 'Ein Heldenleben'. These were controversial but won him fame. Then switched to opera and wrote equally controversial 'Salome' and 'Elektra', both full of passionate excitement. Followed by the comic opera 'Der Rosenkavalier'. Refused to recognise a distinction between absolute and programme music, saying that all good music was expressive. A prolific composer, who also wrote many songs.

SIBELIUS (1865–1957) Finnish. Went to Vienna for study with disciples of Brahms; then returned to Finland. Was soon given a state pension so that he could be free to compose. Much revered in Finland. Wrote symphonic poems based on Finnish legends, such as 'En Saga'; 'The Swan of Tuonela'; 'Finlandia' and 'Tapiola'. But his most important works are his seven symphonies, very different from each other, yet all having a bold, stark quality, reminiscent of the frozen north. Also wrote a violin concerto. His music is more popular in England and America than in Europe.

VAUGHAN WILLIAMS (1872–1958) English, from the West Country. Had a cultured background and private means. Developed slowly as a composer. Began to collect English folk songs and to take an interest in early English music and in hymnology. First well-known works predominantly vocal, such as 'Towards the Unknown Region'; 'A Sea Symphony'; 'On Wenlock Edge', the opera 'Hugh the Drover' and much church music including a mass in G minor, 'Sancta Civitas' and 'Benedicite'. But the orchestral works 'Fantasia on a Theme of Tallis' and the overture to 'The Wasps' are also early works. Gradually orchestral work grew in importance. Wrote nine symphonies. In later years began to write incidental music for films. The music for 'Scott of the Antarctic' later became the basis of the seventh symphony.

HOLST (1874–1934) English—a friend and contemporary of Vaughan Williams, with similar interests, but with more need to earn his living, which he did at first by playing in orchestras and then by teaching in various schools and colleges near London. His varied output includes operas, the best known being 'At the Boar's Head'; 'Savitri' and 'The Perfect Fool'; orchestral works such as 'The Planets' (for a very large orchestra), 'A Somerset Rhapsody'; 'St. Paul's Suite for Strings', and 'Egdon Heath'; and choral works such as the choral symphony, the 'Rig Veda' hymns and 'The Hymn of Jesus'. Sometimes made use of folk song idioms, and was very fond of irregular rhythms.

RAVEL (1875–1937) French impressionist, but more classicly inclined than was Debussy. His music became more restrained and formal as he grew older. Preferred to write on a small scale. Wrote piano music such as the sonatina and 'Le Tombeau de Couperin', and many songs. Often made orchestral arrangements of his own piano works such as 'Le Tombeau de Couperin', and arranged Mussorgsky's 'Pictures from an exhibition' for orchestra. 'Bolero' is his only purely orchestral work originally conceived for an orchestra. Also wrote ballets 'Mother Goose' and 'Daphnis and Chloe', both now often played as concert works; and operas 'L'Heure Espagnole' and 'L'Enfant et les Sortilèges'.

FALLA (1876–1946) Spanish. Lived in Paris for a time, where he was friendly with Debussy and Ravel. Returned to Spain, but died in Argentina. Wrote ballet 'The Three Cornered Hat'; 'Nights in the Garden of Spain' for orchestra and piano; a harpsichord concerto; and some songs and piano pieces. All music strongly influenced by the dance.

10 *The anti-romantics of the mid twentieth century*

THE MOVEMENT AWAY FROM ROMANTICISM AND FROM TONALITY

If a comparison is made of the dates of composers under this heading with those under the last heading it will be realised that they partly overlap. But Schönberg comes into this group, in spite of being born at about the same time as the last four in the last group because, although he began as a neo-romantic, he soon set out on quite new paths. He became an anti-romantic who experimented with artificial combinations of notes that he called tone rows, and soon rejected all feeling of tonality and key-centre, saying that every note of the chromatic scale was equally important. Webern and Berg were his pupils, and they continued with experiments on the same lines. Their music is called atonal music, and the use of series of tone rows produced serial music.

Stravinsky and Honegger experimented with writing in two keys at once (polytonal music); and Hindemith invented a novel system of arbitrary key relationships based on the chromatic scale. Bartok tried returning to the old modes, basing his researches on Hungarian folk melody.

All these composers had three things in common. They were trying to escape from the tonality of the major and minor scales, were working out new theories, and were composing in a cerebral, anti-romantic way. Their music still sounds strange to most people. At times it is very harsh and discordant, and the lack of a key centre makes the music sometimes seem chaotic and formless. It is too soon yet to say whether their theories will have a lasting effect on the course of music.

Prokofiev is the one composer of this group who did not write music based on new theories. But he did write piquant, anti-romantic music, full of unexpected effects, until he was told by the Soviet authorities to write in a more popular lyrical style.

Chief Composers

SCHÖNBERG (1874–1951) Austrian Jew. He began by writing chamber music in a polyphonic, chromatic style. His early cantata the ' Gurrelieder ' was experimental, but owed much to Wagner. By 1908 he had abandoned tonality, and his ' Five Orchestral Pieces ' were one of the first results. In 1910 he wrote a treatise on harmony and in 1912 wrote ' Pierrot Lunaire ' for vocal declamation and five instrumentalists, which is quite atonal. Gradually he worked out his ' serial technique ' which was to take the place of tonality. He based each composition on a different arrangement of the 12 notes of the chromatic scale, which he called a ' tone row '. Wrote many works, including much chamber music and his difficult violin concerto, with this new technique. But aroused much opposition. Was dismissed from his post in Berlin, and settled in America.

BARTOK (1881–1945) Hungarian. Wrote in many different styles at different periods of his life, being influenced by Brahms, Wagner and Strauss. But gradually turned more and more to Hungarian folk tunes, written in the old modes. Arranged many of them. His later works are often very chromatic or even atonal. Emigrated to America. Wrote some stage works; many choral works; orchestral suites; several concertos; chamber music; and piano music including a graded collection of pieces called ' Mikrokosmos '.

STRAVINSKY (1882–   ) Russian, pupil of Rimsky-Korsakov. Went to Paris. Wrote ' The Fire Bird '; ' Petrouchka ' and ' The Rite of Spring ' for Diaghilev's ballet in Paris. These ballets had primitive, complex rhythms and astringent harmonies, and they shocked many people. Then began to write for smaller, unusual combinations in a very anti-romantic way. Wrote a symphony for 23 wind instruments, and an octet for wood wind and brass instruments. Settled in America in 1940, and wrote opera ' The Rake's Progress ' after this. Began to write serial music.

WEBERN (1883–1945) Austrian. Pupil of Schönberg and followed his methods. His music was banned during the 1939–45 war, as being ' cultural bolshevism '. Was accidentally shot by occupying troops after the war. Wrote many disjointed works for unusual combinations, such as a symphony for clarinet, bass clarinet, two horns, harp and strings; a quartet for saxophone, clarinet, violin and piano; and a concerto for nine solo instruments. Wrote two cantatas and a set of variations for orchestra during the war. Noted for his brevity.

BERG (1885–1935) Another Austrian pupil of Schönberg's, who adopted his serial technique. Wrote chamber music, including Lyric Suite for string quartet; operas,

'Wozzek' and 'Lulu'; and a violin concerto.

PROKOFIEV (1891–1953) Russian who travelled much but finally returned to Russia. Wrote anti-romantic, rhythmically exhilarating and often discordant music, though later, at the Soviet command, changed to a more lyrical style. Wrote six symphonies, including the 'Classical'; five concertos; 'Peter and the Wolf'; seven operas including 'The Love of Three Oranges'; six ballets; chamber music; piano music and songs.

HONEGGER (1895–1955) French. Wrote in polyphonic style, often in two or more keys at once. Anti-romantic. Wrote a number of operas, including the concert opera 'King David'; ballets; much incidental music and film music; and unusual orchestral pieces like 'Pacific 231'.

HINDEMITH (1895–1964) German. Played viola in quartet. Another anti-romantic who delighted in line drawing rather than in harmony, and in letting the lines clash. Invented a new system of tone relationships. Went to America during the war, then returned to Europe again. His works include a number of operas, the best known being 'Mathis der Maler'; ballets; a viola concerto; a symphony 'Harmonie der Welt'; much chamber music; and piano music including 'Ludus Tonalis'

11 *Composers born in the twentieth century*

Chief Composers

It is too early to assess or classify composers born in the twentieth century. Some of the chief ones are given here, with a brief list of their chief works.

COPLAND (1900–) American. Studied in Paris. Has done much to help other American composers. His early piano concerto and 'Dance Symphony' contained jazz elements. Has written three symphonies and some programme orchestral works; several ballets including 'Billy the Kid' and 'Appalachian Spring'; opera 'The Tender Land'; and music for films and radio.

RUBBRA (1901–) English. As a boy he used to browse in his uncle's music shop in Northampton. Later a pupil of Holst. Now music lecturer at Oxford. His music is mainly diatonic, but is full of modern melodic polyphony. Has written seven symphonies; several concertos; and works for chorus and orchestra including 'Song of the Soul'; 'The Morning Watch' and 'Te Deum'.

WALTON (1902–) English. Lancastrian. Educated at Oxford. Settled in Italy. 'Façade', a humorous early work, originally for speaking voice and six instruments, excited much comment. Has since been turned into a ballet and two suites. Other early works are 'Portsmouth Point', a gay overture; and the exciting oratorio 'Belshazzar's Feast'. Has written two symphonies; three concertos; opera 'Troilus and Cressida'; chamber music and film music. Diatonic music, growing out of the past, but virile and rhythmically alive.

RAWSTHORNE (1905–) English. Lancastrian. Educated in Manchester. Settled in

London. Has written mainly instrumental music: three symphonies; two piano, two violin, and several other concertos; three overtures, including ' Street Corner '; chamber music; and ballet ' Madame Chrysanthème '. Composer of absolute music which though based on tonal harmony, shifts so frequently that no key is established for long. Relatively consonant for present-day music, so not too difficult for the ordinary musical listener to enjoy.

TIPPETT (1905–) English. Cornish. Educated in Lincolnshire and in London. First well-known work was ' A Child of our Time ', an unusual oratorio which expressed his religious, humanitarian outlook on totalitarianism. Became known as a teacher and a conductor. Wrote operas ' Midsummer Marriage ' and ' King Priam '. Particularly interested in vocal music, but has also written two symphonies; a piano concerto; concerto for orchestra; and some chamber music. A mystical element runs through his music. Often complex in style.

SHOSTAKOVITCH (1906–) Russian. Works are of unequal musical value, partly due to Soviet pressure to conform. Is now secretary of the Soviet Union of Composers. Has composed eleven symphonies; three concertos; two operas; three ballets; much chamber music; piano music and film music.

BRITTEN (1913–) English. East Anglian. A prodigy, composing while still at school. Educated in London. Particularly interested in vocal music. Vocal works include ' Hymn to St. Cecilia '; ' A Ceremony of Carols ', and, more recently the War Requiem written for the re-opening of Coventry Cathedral. Also many songs. The first English opera composer to achieve international fame. Operas: ' Peter Grimes '; ' The Rape of Lucretia '; ' Albert Herring '; ' The Little Sweep '; ' Billy Budd '; ' The Turn of the Screw '; ' Noye's Fludde '; ' A Midsummer Night's Dream '. Ballet ' The Prince of the Pagodas '. Has written no symphonies except the ' Simple Symphony ' for strings, written when very young. But has written three concertos. His best-known orchestral work is ' Variations and Fugue on a Theme of Purcell '.

17 Study of Prescribed Composers and Works

1 *Background*

If any composer or any particular work by a composer is prescribed for study it is advisable always to start with sketching in the background.

(a) HISTORICAL PERIOD Relate the composer or the work to the general history known. For example, the Elizabethan composers can be linked up with Shakespeare and Drake; Lully and Couperin with Louis XIV; Purcell with the Restoration; Bach with Frederick the Great; Handel with the start of the Hanoverian dynasty; Haydn with the French revolution and the wars that followed it; Beethoven with Napoleon; Schubert with Goethe; Mendelssohn with Queen Victoria; Wagner with the 1848 revolution; Elgar with the Edwardian period and the 1914 war; and so on.

Exact dates are usually not of great importance, but a general sense of period certainly is. The student who confuses Queen Elizabeth with Queen Victoria, and to whom they are both equally far away, will have very little to help him with his appreciation of musical period.

The amount of general history known by the average music student varies very much, but an attempt should certainly be made to get it into historical perspective and to connect it with the chief composers in musical history.

A series of landmarks in musical history, combined with a very few 'key' dates, may help to give the perspective required. The following is a suggested outline, into which particular composers and works may be fitted:

1603 Death of Queen Elizabeth. Tudor composers writing at this time; Palestrina just died; opera just starting.

1643–1715 Reign of Louis XIV. Associate with Lully, Couperin and Rameau. Also with later Stuarts and Purcell in England. Corelli in same period.

1685 Bach, Handel and D. Scarlatti born. Therefore writing in first half of eighteenth century. Associate with George I and II and Frederick the Great.

1770–1827 Beethoven's birth and death. Haydn and Mozart alive when he was born; Schubert died about the same time; early romantics all born before he died.

1789 French revolution. Haydn, Mozart and Beethoven all alive.

1809–10 Mendelssohn, Chopin and Schumann born.

1883 Wagner and Verdi died. Brahms and Tchaikovsky still alive. Elgar, Debussy, Strauss and Sibelius all young men.

1939 Outbreak of World War II. Twentieth century composers listed in part 11 of last section were all young men.

(b) TYPES OF MUSIC BEING COMPOSED The next stage is to realise what kind of music to expect in the period which is being studied. The summary given in each part of Section 16, together with the cross references given there to Sections 13 and 15, should be sufficient in most cases. It is important to realise, for example, that a sonata in the days of Corelli does not mean the same thing as a sonata in the days of Beethoven; and that Bach and Handel wrote concerti grossi whereas Haydn wrote symphonies.

(c) CONTEMPORARY COMPOSERS Before starting the study of the particular composer or work required it is as well to complete the background picture with a brief consideration of the composer's greater musical contemporaries, as far as time allows. For example, Handel and his works will be much better understood if something is known about Bach and his music. Mozart can hardly be studied intelligently without a knowledge of Haydn; and Beethoven requires some knowledge of both. Again, the summaries given under each heading of Section 16 should be enough in most cases, supplemented, of course, by hearing as much actual music as possible.

2 *The composer*

(a) HIS LIFE Having sketched in as much background as possible the student is now ready to turn to the actual composer. The more that is known about his life the better will his music be understood and appreciated. For those who are very short of time or whose examination requirements are slight, the sketch given in this book of the life of the particular composer may be sufficient. But all who can do so are recommended to undertake further reading; and for some examinations this is essential. There are plenty of eminently readable books on the lives of the composers which can be found in public or school libraries. After such general reading many of the details may be forgotten, but the composer will probably have 'come alive', and the student will have greater sympathy with his ideas and his music.

(b) HIS HISTORICAL IMPORTANCE Some composers are of more importance historically than others, In the case of composers such as Corelli, Gluck, Haydn, Berlioz, Liszt and Wagner it is important to realise how they affected the course of musical history.

(c) HIS CHIEF WORKS If a particular composer is being studied as many as possible of his works should be heard; and any works that are within the capabilities of the student should also be performed.

But even if only one particular work is prescribed it is advisable to get to know as many of the composer's other works as possible. They are bound to shed light on the prescribed work. Students whose lesson time is limited can help themselves by listening to as many works as possible on the radio, or on their own record player.

(d) LIST OF WORKS HEARD Finally, every student is recommended to keep a list of all music by that particular composer heard by him. With a class there may be a common core of works heard by all the class. But if every student is encouraged to keep his own list, adding to it any works he has sung or played himself, anything that he, personally, has heard at a concert or on the radio or on records, he will be surprised to find how his list will grow. If he refreshes his memory by a reference to the list the night before an examination he will discover he has plenty of material to which he can refer in the examination.

3 *The prescribed work*

(a) ANY SPECIAL BACKGROUND Some works may require further background knowledge as a preliminary to the study of the actual work. The following are some instances:

1 A work in which musical form is important, such as a sonata or a symphony, will require a knowledge of the musical forms used in the particular work. (See Section 15.)

2 A work in which orchestration is important will require a knowledge of orchestral instruments, and of score reading if the work has to be studied with a score. (See Sections 13 and 14.)

3 Some works have been brought into existence by particular circumstances, which should be known. For example, there is a background history to the following works: Bach's 'Brandenburg' concertos; Handel's 'Water Music' and 'Fireworks Music'; Mendelssohn's 'Hebrides' overture; Schumann's 'Carnival'. It may be necessary to find this out by referring to a book on the life of the composer or to a reference book such as Scholes's 'Oxford Companion to Music' or Grove's Dictionary of Music. Sometimes this kind of information is given in the printed copy, particularly if it is a miniature score.

(b) STUDY OF THE ACTUAL WORK Different works require different kinds of study. But the following general hints may be helpful.

1 If it is possible at all for the students to perform the work they should do so. They can always make some kind of an attempt at a vocal work. They can sing Schubert songs, so as to get to know them, even though their voices are poor or the range is beyond them. They can sing the top part of a choral work, even if they cannot sing the complete harmony. But very often a school choir can learn a prescribed examination work even though it may not be fit for public performance.

A school class can usually attempt a Corelli sonata by dividing the work between them in some way. A pianist that cannot manage a Beethoven sonata can perhaps play one hand while the teacher plays the other. And all students can sing or play the main themes.

2 A great effort should be made to attend some kind of public performance of the work. It will provide something that the best type of record player will fail to do. But, of course, a record or a tape must also be available of the work, and should be heard as often as possible. The only exceptions are songs or piano pieces that can be adequately performed by the student or the teacher.

3 When time permits the work should be heard straight through first, before any

detailed study is made of it. The student should follow the score at the same time. (See Section 14.) Even when study of the work with the copy is not prescribed it is a great advantage to make use of copies. If necessary they can be shared, one between two.

4 Pencil marks made on the copy are more helpful than notes made in a separate book. If a copy free from markings is later to be taken into the examination room the pencil marks should be very light, and then can be rubbed out the night before.

5 If a work in sonata form is to be studied it is helpful to study the exposition and the recapitulation side by side. Students can look at the exposition while they are listening to the recapitulation, and then they will see and hear when and how the music changes.

6 Students should keep a manuscript music book in which they can copy all the main themes of the prescribed works. They can combine this with a brief analysis, if they wish. If they know that they may be required to quote or to recognise themes for their particular examination, they should learn these themes, preferably to sol-fa names.

Students should have practice in working questions on prescribed composers and their works. Such questions obviously cannot be given here, as they will vary with every work and also with every type of examination. But it is important that the student should see some previously set papers for his particular examination, and he should work similar questions, applied to his own prescribed composers and works.

It is not easy to write *about* music; and many students do not realise what are the essential facts the examiner is likely to require. Examiners do not want rambling anecdotes about composers' lives, or a string of adjectives about a work that could apply to almost any other work. Students should learn to express themselves clearly and tersely, and should realise that examiners primarily want proof that the candidates know and appreciate the music.

Quotations are one of the best means of showing actual knowledge of a work, and are acceptable to examiners even if they are not quite accurate. A quotation should always come to an end at the end of a phrase, which will not necessarily be the end of a bar.

Many examinations require candidates to recognise themes. This is rather easier, particularly if the quotations are played to the candidate, as now happens in some examinations. But if they have to be recognised by eye only, then the student requires practice in learning to hear what he sees. If he is at home with sol-fa names and rhythm names he will find this much easier.

Appendix

Suggestions for Miscellaneous Tests that can be given by the Teacher

1 *Detecting discrepancies between a copy of a melody and its performance*

This is an excellent way of testing if students can follow a melodic line, note by note, can hear what they see, and thus can recognise any changes from the printed copy. It is a useful form of ear test that need not present much difficulty in writing down the answer; and its value is obvious in helping the student to recognise his own mistakes when he is singing or playing a melody.

Material for this test can easily be found by taking a melody from any song book or sight singing book that the students possess. Melodies given in Sections 6–10 of this book can also be used.

The students should number the bars, if this has not already been done. The teacher should decide beforehand what changes he is going to make, and what instructions he is going to give the students. He may, for example, tell them to do any of the following, which are arranged in order of difficulty:

1 Put a x at every place where there is a change.

2 Mark, with an appropriate word, changes which he has been told will take place. (See example below.)

3 As 1, but state the nature of the change—change of rhythm, change of pitch, etc., giving the bar number.

4 As 1, but rewrite the bar which has changed in each case.

The melody should be played in its original form at least once, while the students follow the copy, note by note. It should then be played several times in the altered version. The test is useful at all stages of the student's development, and can be made very easy or quite difficult at the discretion of the teacher.

The following is an example of method 2, above. Tell the students that there are three changes: (a) of pitch, (b) of rhythm, (c) of a different number of notes in the bar, not necessarily, in this order. They are to mark these three changes with the words 'pitch', 'rhythm' and 'number' over the bar concerned in each case.

Original Version (placed in front of student)

Altered Version (not seen by student)

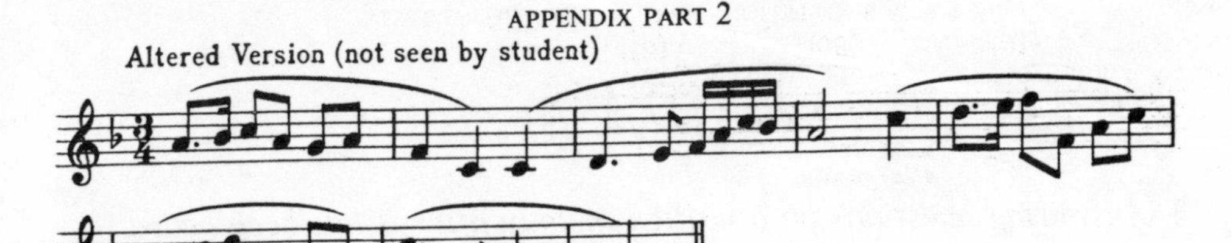

2 *Adding speed and expression marks to a melody as it is performed*

This is a practical way of testing that the chief Italian speed and expression marks have been learnt and understood, and also that students can hear changes of intensity and variety of interpretation.

But many Italian terms mean nearly the same thing. A student is obviously wrong if he labels a rather quick piece of music 'adagio'. But it could easily be moderato, allegretto, allegro or even vivace. Similarly, if the music slows down and works towards a climax on one note, all the following ways of showing it, or a combination of them, would be possible: rit; rall; ⟨crescendo hairpin⟩ ; cresc; allargando; sf; > ; and 𝄐.

So this is not a very exact kind of test, and it is difficult to give marks to the result.

Any book containing melodies free from expression marks, such as a book of sight singing exercises, can be used for this test. There are also quite a number of melodies in Section 6 of this book that have been left free from marks and are suitable for the purpose.

The teacher should add expression marks in his copy and then play it to the students with this interpretation. The students should add expression marks to their own copies and then the result should be compared.

Exercise 74(b) in Section 6 has no expression marks. Students can look at this while the teacher plays from the following version:

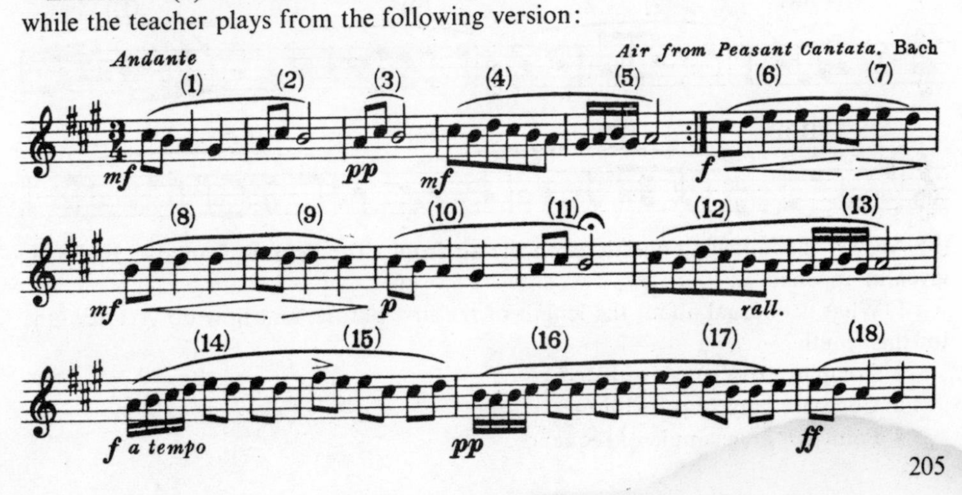

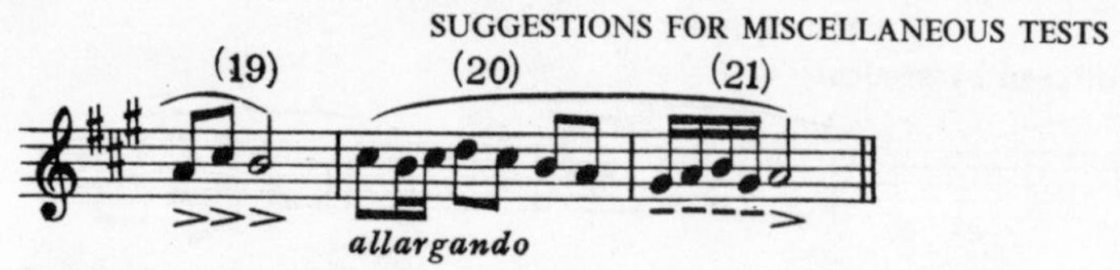

3 *Answering questions on a written melody after it has been heard*

This is a test which is valuable in that it not only involves realising what written notation sounds like, but also shows an appreciative recognition of the significance of what the composer has written. It is another test which can be made easy or difficult, according to the needs and the ability of the students.

Material can be found in any melodies of which the students possess a copy. Section 6 of this book may again be useful for this purpose.

The teacher must think out suitable questions for each melody, and dictate them to the students before he plays the melody, so that they know what they have to listen for.

Three examples of this kind of test are given below, graded in order of difficulty:

(a) 1 In what key is the following melody?

2 Is the melody in duple, triple or quadruple time?

3 The first two phrases of the melody are labelled A and B. Put A and B at any other places where either of them return, either exactly the same, or in a slightly modified form.

4 Write the word 'sequence' over the music at the place where one occurs.

5 Comment on the length of the last bar.

(b) Answer the following questions on the air from 'The Peasant Cantata' by Bach, given in appendix 2:

1 What is unusual about the length of the first phrase, and how do you account for this length?

2 Compare bars 10–13 with 1–5.

3 Compare bars 14–17 with 6–9.

4 Point out an example of sequence.

(c) 1 In what key does the following melody begin and end?

2 The melody modulates to three other keys. Put the name of the key over each phrase which is in a different key.

3 Compare bars 5–8 with 13–16.

4 Compare bars 1–4 with 9–12.

5 What term would you use to describe bars 16–18?

4 *Following a piano piece with a score and answering questions on it*

Like test No. 3 this can be made as easy or as difficult as the teacher wishes. It is an advantage for students to possess a volume of easy piano classics, for which many uses can be found, particularly with regard to score following and providing illustrations of elementary points about musical structure. It can also be used for the purpose of this kind of test. The teacher can frame suitable questions and dictate them to the class before playing the piece. Specimen questions on two pieces are given below.

(a) These questions relate to Schumann's ' Impressions of the Theatre ', quoted in Section 14, part 3, though they are limited by the fact that there is a fair amount of comment actually printed on the music.

1 In what key is this piece?

2 In what key is bars 9–16?

3 What kind of cadence occurs in bars 15–16?

4 Compare bars 18^2–20^1 with bars 16^2–18^1. Are they based on any previously heard material?

5 Point out one example of a masculine and one of a feminine ending.

(b) Answer the following questions on Handel's Courante given below:

1 In what form is this piece?

2 In what key is this piece?

3 In what key is the music at bars 8 and 16?

4 Comment upon the use made of the opening bar later in the movement.

5 Compare bars 5–8 with 23–26(a).

5 *Answering questions after hearing a record of chamber music*

If students listen to a record without having a copy in front of them they are much more likely to keep their attention focussed on the music if the teacher suggests certain things for which they should listen, before the record starts. These will vary, of course, with every piece of music. But the following are the kind of questions that might be asked about a piece of chamber music:

1 How many instruments play in this piece of music; and what instruments are they?

2 How often did you hear the first theme return? What instrument played the tune? Sing the tune.

3 Was there a second main theme? If so, sing it. What instrument played the tune?

4 In what form is this movement?

5 Was it in duple, triple or quadruple time?

6 Was it in a major or a minor key?

7 Did the highest instrument have the tune all the time? If not, what other instruments had the tune, and whereabouts in the movement.

6 *Answering questions after hearing a record of orchestral music*

In addition to questions of the type suggested for listening to chamber music additional questions can be asked about the orchestration of an orchestral piece. In some cases the student can be told to listen for a certain theme and to say what instrument plays it. Questions can also be asked about the way instruments are used, such as the use of pizzicato, mutes, glissando, etc.

Here is a list of questions that might be asked about the first part (bars 1–69) of Tchaikovsky's 'Dance of the Flowers' from the 'Nutcracker' suite. The students should be given the questions before the record starts; and if they are to answer as many questions as this, the music should be heard twice, with a space of time in between, for the student to write down some of the answers.

1 What family of instruments starts the music?
2 What instrument answers them and has a showy passage to itself?
3 What is this kind of showy passage called?
4 When the main tune starts, what family of instruments has the accompaniment?
5 The main tune is a duet between two kinds of instruments. What instruments are they?
6 This is a dance. What kind of a dance is it?
7 How do you know?

7 *Recognition of hidden tunes by ear*

It is important that the students should learn to hear a melody which is not at the top of the texture, as this so often happens in actual music.

The following example is the kind of thing that can be made up by the teacher, using eithe well-known tunes such as this, or melodies which are part of a prescribed work:

The teacher who wants more material of this kind is advised to purchase the two little booklets ' A Book of Hidden Tunes ' and ' A Second Book of Hidden Tunes ' by Geoffrey Shaw, published by Nelson.

8 *Recognition of themes which are heard*

The teacher should frequently play themes which the students ought to know, either because they are very well-known, have been used in previous singing or general music lessons, or come into prescribed works, and ask for their identification. Students should identify them as fully as possible. For example, in an orchestral work it may be possible to say ' Second subject of the first movement of the ——— symphony in —— major by —————, played by the 'cellos '. But if the details are forgotten he may be able to say little more than ' symphony by —————. If he does not recognise the theme at all he may still be able to make an inspired guess at the composer, judging by the type of music and its possible period.

9 *Recognition of themes which are written, and not heard*

This is more difficult than recognition of themes which are heard, because many students have difficulty in hearing what they see.

If they know that the theme must be one from a number of prescribed works they can often narrow down the possibilities by noticing such things as key, time signature and speed mark. For example, there may be only one movement from one work in D minor, in $\frac{6}{8}$ time.

But having done this when it is possible, the student must then do his best to hear the tune accurately in his head. It may be wise to start with the rhythm, as this is usually easier. He must notice the speed mark, and accurately reproduce the rhythm in his head, making use of rhythm names. If he hears a quick tune slowly, or vice versa, he may be completely misled. In some cases, where the example is easy and the rhythm is distinctive, reproducing the rhythm correctly may be enough to identify the tune.

In most cases, however, he must then go on to hear the pitch of the tune. He must notice the key signature, decide if the melody is major or minor, and then carefully start on the right note of the scale. If, for example, he hears the first note as doh when it is really soh he may get a completely false idea of the tune. It is worth while taking some time mentally singing the tune to sol-fa names. And, of course, he must eventually hear the pitch of the notes in the correct rhythm that he has already discovered.

As with the last test, the student should identify the theme as completely as possible. For example, if it is a second subject of a movement in sonata form, he should be able to state whether it occurs in the exposition or the recapitulation, by seeing what key it is in. Similarly a first subject theme may be in a form and a key in which it occurs in a development section.

The teacher should frequently give themes for recognition in this way, as most students require practice in being able to identify themes from a copy.

ndex